A Journey Toward Christian Maturity

Parables
of the

by Carl Schmuland

PHOTO CREDITS: Chapter 13 photo by my wife, Mary Schmuland; Appendix A, photo by my mother, Inez Schmuland; all other photos by the author. To purchase prints of any picture in this book, go to www.parablesofthedeer.com

FIRST EDITION

ISBN: 978-1-936989-64-5

Library of Congress Control Number: 2012915419

Published by
NewBookPublishing.com, a division of Reliance Media, Inc.
2395 Apopka Blvd., #200, Apopka, FL 32703
NewBookPublishing.com

Printed in the United States of America

Reliance
Media

Acknowledgements

Many people have been of invaluable assistance in writing this book; chief among them my wife Mary who has been a constant encourager, lovingly sharing me with my blinds for the hundreds of hours needed to take the photos and additional hundreds of hours spent writing this book. She also was invaluable in reviewing the contents of the book, offering many helpful suggestions.

I thank my father for taking me hunting with him for the first time when I was four years old, and for teaching me how to not get lost by leading lead me deep into the woods and then requiring me to lead him home.

My good friend Bill Hintz and his son Chris allowed me to photograph their bucks for the chapters requiring dead deer. Bill also posed as the hunter dragging the buck in chapter 46. My neighbor, friend and avid deer hunter Donald Kluck provided insightful opinions on selecting the pictures for this book. My friend, Chuck Morris, thoughtfully reviewed this book and offered many helpful suggestions as well as much encouragement.

Carol Steinbach's, Gary Steward's and Matt Crutchmer's careful, professional reviews were invaluable in assuring the theological and grammatical correctness of the book.

The many years of sitting under the preaching of my pastor Dr. John Piper and the teaching ministry of Dr. R.C. Sproul have shaped my understanding of the Bible. Their ministry has not only been helpful theologically in writing this book, but invaluable to me in living the Christian life.

Finally, I thank God who called me out of darkness into His marvelous light on June 19, 1986. I also thank Him for providing me with so many incredible opportunities to take the pictures in this book. My only hope of being able to take these pictures and write this book rested upon Him being sovereign over all things, including the activities of deer. To God alone be all the glory!

Table of Contents

Appendix

Index of Non–biblical Names

Preface: The Book's Humble Beginnings

"Those who have never been told of him will see, and those who have never heard will understand." Romans 15:21

I cannot remember a time that I was not interested in deer. I grew up in northern Wisconsin on an east-west road from which one could walk six miles north or south before coming to another road. Deer were always available to watch and when I reached the age of twelve, they could be hunted for nine glorious days every year. I thought about deer daily, studying them and reading everything I could about them. One day I read a magazine article that pointed out that there was no closed season on deer photography. This sounded good to me, so armed with a simple box camera I began my quest for deer photos. We had a salt block in the pasture directly behind the north window of my bedroom. Deer would often come to the salt and I made many unsuccessful attempts, slithering through the tall grass, to get close enough for a decent picture with my simple equipment. The picture above, from the early 1960s, was one of my better photos.

I got really serious about deer photography in 1993, spending much time photographing the large deer herd that lives within the greater Minneapolis–St. Paul, Minnesota metro area. While these deer live in an urban area, they are wild deer subjected to bow hunting. Upon first seeing my pictures, people often remark that I must have a really good camera. Of course my equipment has improved considerably from my first camera. However, the real breakthrough occurred when I discovered the effectiveness of lying on the ground under a blow-down. Subsequent observations of deer travel patterns resulted in the need to set up blinds constructed out of sticks from the immediate vicinity of the blind when no convenient blow-down existed. Careful clearing of "shooting" lanes about a month before I start taking pictures, camouflage clothing, the various products available to limit the emission of human scent, and especially, the sovereignty of God over all things have enabled me to take the pictures in this book.

At first my only objective was to take good photos. I imagined that I might someday produce a calendar, but my plans were vague at best. All this changed in a most surprising way in September 2004 at a conference sponsored by Desiring God Ministries called "Sex and the Supremacy of Christ." C.J. Mahaney was speaking on the male sex drive and referenced Song of Solomon 1:9: "*I compare you, my love to a mare among pharaoh's chariots.*" (Pharaoh's chariots were drawn by stallions!) My mind jumped to the reckless pursuit of does by normally secretive and cautious bucks, often at the cost of their lives. Suddenly, I saw a purpose for my deer photography. I would, with God's help, write a book drawing parallels between my deer pictures and Scripture passages to explain and defend Christianity*.

Using my first digital camera, 2004 turned out to be a watershed year (only six pictures in this book were taken before 2004), as God paraded 14 different bucks past my blind constructed in a new area. The book you are presently reading is the result of eight years of effort. The degree to which I have succeeded is entirely due to God's grace enabling me to take the necessary pictures and write effective interpretations of them. In the final analysis I wrote this book to empower Christians to be more effective witnessing to unbelievers and making disciples for Christ so that *those who have never been told of him will see, and those who have never heard will understand.*

*Each Bible verse has one correct meaning but many applications. Therefore, this book could have been based upon parables ranging from agriculture to zebras, including hundreds of occupations, hobbies, sports, and animals.

An Explanation of the Book's Name

Then the disciples came and said to him, "Why do you speak to them in parables?" And he answered them, "To you it has been given to know the secrets of the kingdom of heaven, but to them it has not been given. For to the one who has, more will be given, and he will have an abundance, but from the one who has not, even what he has will be taken away. This is why I speak to them in parables, because seeing they do not see, and hearing they do not hear, nor do they understand." Matthew 13:10–13

Jesus taught primarily through the use of parables. The word parable, is from the Greek word *parabole*, literally meaning "to throw along side of." Thus a parable refers to an illustration, story or, comparison. Everybody loves a good story, but Jesus' reason for using parables is startling. Jesus says that some people (His disciples), *"have been given* (by God) *to know the secrets of the kingdom of heaven"* and some have not. By using parables, people who *"know the secrets of the kingdom of heaven"* grow in faith and understanding, while those to whom this gift has not been given become even more confused. Why this is true and not unjust will unfold as you read this book.

The Gospels of Matthew, Mark and Luke contain forty different parables (some are reported in more than one gospel). Jesus' parables used subjects familiar to the people of first century Israel like an agricultural practice or a social custom. His parables always make one spiritual point using non-technical everyday language. For example, Jesus says the mustard seed is the smallest of all seeds (Matthew 13:21–32). The Southeast Asian poppy is actually the smallest known seed, but to Jesus' audience, the mustard seed was the smallest seed they usually encountered. So, if an unbeliever took the parable to literally say the absolute smallest seed is the mustard seed they could miss the main point and conclude the Bible is inaccurate. *"seeing they do not see, and hearing they do not hear, nor do they understand."* On the other hand, those to whom *"it has been given to know the secrets of the kingdom of heaven"* will correctly see the parable's main point is that the largest, common garden plant grows from the smallest common seed just as Jesus and the twelve Apostles will grow into a great, uncountable multitude of Christians from every people group in the world (Revelation 7:9).

According to David Crystal (author of *The Story of English in 100 Words*) the oldest known written English word is *roe* and was found in England inscribed on a roe deer femur dated to the fifth century. Eighteen times words appear in the Bible that are translated as deer, doe, fawns and the like. But none of these are the reason for using deer parables. Instead, the reason is that deer are not only fascinating creatures, but they are also the most widely distributed large, wild mammal within the continental United States. From urban back yards (back cover) to the National Parks (front cover), deer are a familiar reality for most Americans, few of whom do not delight in seeing these beautiful, graceful creatures. Admittedly, the photographs in this book are intended to attract readers, but I hope most readers will get beyond the pictures and deer stories to seriously ponder the theological points associated with each parable. For example, in this chapter the parable is that some people are gifted by God to see deer and will see there is a large buck in the background. The rest will see the doe but dismiss the second deer as part of the unfocused background, failing to see the buck's antlers among the confusion of the branches (*"seeing they do not see"*). My parables are not in the same league as Jesus' parables, but I pray that through *Parables of the Deer* many readers will increase their faith in the gospel and understanding of it to become more effective witnesses for Jesus.

A Word to the Reader

... you need someone to teach you again the basic principles of the oracles of God. You need milk, not solid food, for everyone who lives on milk is unskilled in the word of righteousness, since he is a child. But solid food is for the mature, ... Hebrews 5:12–14

For a week after giving birth, a doe's milk contains 12% butterfat (twice that of a cow) and then drops to about 8%. Fawns thrive on this diet, increasing their weight from six to seven pounds at birth to 25–30 pounds at one month of age. Two months after giving birth, a doe's milk production starts to decrease to force fawns to switch to solid food. By ten weeks of age, fawns are chewing cud and by five months of age, they weigh 50–60 pounds and are weaned. Over the next three or four years, whitetail does will gain another 90–100 pounds and bucks twice that amount. Fawns will not survive the first three months of life without milk, but to continue to grow, they must switch to solid food to produce the majority of their total weight gain.

Similarly, the basic tenets of Christianity (milk) are mandatory for the new, "born again" believer. But without serious study of the Bible (solid food), a new believer will not mature in faith and effectiveness. Obviously, the massive mule deer buck in this photo, munching on a bouquet of flowers, will not run back into the woods and begin nursing, despite the impediment of his antlers, to obtain the lion's share of its nourishment. Yet, this is what many professing Christians try to do by relying on a "skim milk" superficial understanding of the Bible. To be sure, a Christian's faith must be child-like, trusting implicitly in Christ alone for salvation as a child trusts its parents. But a Christian's faith must not be childish and without substance.

There is a second ironic parable, for even though the vast majority of Americans live within ten miles of significant numbers of wild deer, they have little knowledge of deer and their behavior. Similarly, many 21st century Christians, though surrounded by incredibly able teachers armed with learning resources unimaginable a century ago, lack a deep, mature understanding of their faith. The modern world exalts tolerance and education, but it is increasingly hostile (both verbally and physically) toward and very ignorant of Christianity. Against this backdrop, Christianity cannot thrive in the pluralistic market place of 21st century ideas if it is grounded on milk rather than solid food. To positively influence their culture, Christians must be able to respond with well reasoned arguments to the challenges of liberal Christianity, cults (Mormons, Jehovah Witnesses and the like), other religions (such as Islam, Judaism, and Hinduism), atheists and agnostics.

Parables of the Deer is a layman's attempt to at least partially remedy the prevailing illiteracy regarding Christianity, both in secular society and regrettably among many Christians. Christianity has stood the test of time and intellectual scrutiny. It is grounded in fact and reason not merely emotions or feelings. But as R.C. Sproul has said, "Burning hearts are not nourished by empty minds." My objective is primarily to empower professing Christians to confidently present, defend, and contend for the truth claims of Christianity. While the book has some milk for the new believer, it quickly moves to solid food, addressing many topics that Christians should understand. Drawing on history, logic, philosophy, science, and theology to make my points, the book is intended to be read sequentially and slowly to allow time for reflection and further investigation. *Parables of the Deer* will not answer every question about Christianity or silence every unbeliever's objections, but I hope many will find it to be a useful first step on the journey to Christian maturity and effectiveness.

Part I: A Brief Survey of the Bible

All Scripture is breathed out by God and profitable for teaching, for reproof, for correction, and for training in righteous, that the man of God may be competent, equipped for every good work. 2 Timothy 3:16–17

God's genius in creating the genetic code causes deer, and all other creatures, to faithfully reproduce themselves from generation to generation. At Monticello, there is a magnificent set of trophy elk antlers that Lewis and Clark sent back to Thomas Jefferson in 1805. After about 200 years (100 generations for an elk or deer) they appear identical to today's elk antlers. If the Pilgrims had preserved some deer when they landed at Plymouth Rock in 1620, they would also look just like the pictured deer above after nearly 200 generations. Similarly, the Bible has been faithfully reproduced for about 175 human generations (20 years each) from the earliest writings.

The Bible is the best selling book in the world every year. In the last 2,000 years no book has been more thoroughly reviewed, studied or survived more criticism. Reasonably, no person can claim to be well educated without having seriously studied it. Unfortunately, few people (including many professing Christians) have ever read the entire Bible despite 2 Timothy 3:16–17's claim that the Bible (Scripture) is the very word of God. Written originally in Hebrew, Greek and Aramaic, the Bible is divided into two major sections. The Old Testament was completed about 450 B.C. and contains 39 books written over approximately 1,000 years. It comprises about 75% of the total Bible. The New Testament has 27 books and was written in less than 50 years in the first century A.D. Essentially the Bible is God's authoritative revelation to humans. The Old Testament looks forward to a coming Messiah while the New Testament declares the Messiah is Jesus of Nazareth.

Each book in the Bible is divided into numbered chapters and verses. Chapters and verses were not part of the original writings. They were added to facilitate referencing a particular passage in the Geneva Bible published in 1560, and are used in all current translations. The Geneva Bible was the first study Bible with commentary by various Protestant reformers. When James I ascended to the English throne in 1603, the Church of England was Protestant in doctrine but appeared Roman Catholic in ceremony and clerical dress. The Puritans ardently promoted more austere worship as practiced in Scotland and continental Europe and the removal of any semblance of Catholicism. James I thought the notes in the Geneva Bible were too critical of kings so he commissioned a new translation without commentary that would be a compromise between the Church of England and the Puritans while retaining the Geneva Bible's numbering system. The result was the famous King James Bible published in 1611 that in many ways defined the English language as we know it today. But the Puritans rejected it and brought the Geneva Bible with them to America, and both Shakespeare (1564–1616) and John Milton (1608–1674) quoted extensively from the Geneva Bible.

The King James Bible is still popular with many Christians. Today several other excellent literal English translations exist that faithfully translate the original Hebrew, Aramaic, and Greek texts into today's vernacular English. Translated from earlier original manuscripts than the King James Version, these include the New American Standard Version (1960), the New Revised Standard Version (1989) and the English Standard Version (2000) quoted throughout this book.

1. Introduction to the Old Testament

On May 28, 585 B.C. a solar eclipse occurred that had been predicted by Thales of Miletus. Thales was a very good scientist and is considered the father of Western philosophy and science. He claimed that water, not God, was ultimate reality (everything arose from it). About 250 years later Aristotle came to the conclusion that what he called an *unmoved mover* (God) must logically exist. The Old Testament stands in stark contrast to Greek philosophy. Genesis, the first book of the Old Testament, written in the 15th century B.C. (850–900 years before Thales) opens by declaring God is the creator of everything there is. While Western philosophy (Greeks) wondered if there was a God, the Jews were trying to understand what God was like. Copies of Thales' writings no longer exist. We know of him only through other people's writings. But the Old Testament, comprised of 39 books written over a span of approximately 1,000 years, has been faithfully preserved to this date. Roman Catholic and Orthodox churches also recognize certain so called "Apocrypha texts," written during the roughly 400 year period between the restoration of Israel following the Babylonian exile and the birth of Jesus. However, Protestants do not included the Apocrypha texts because they were not included in the Hebrew Bible used during Jesus' ministry.

The Old Testament is made up of five sections.

1. The *Pentateuch*, also called the "Law," is made up of the first five books in the Old Testament. Written by Moses, they are a mixture of history and God's laws governing the Jews, God's chosen people.

2. The *Historical Books* are made up of twelve books (*Joshua* through *Esther*). They give the history of Israel prior to the Babylonian exile and the subsequent restoration of Israel. The Babylonian exile is a watershed Old Testament historical event in which God delivered the Jews into the hands of Assyria and Babylon (modern Iraq) to punish them for falling away from faith in God and turning to the gods of the surrounding nations. Jerusalem fell to the Babylonians in 586 B.C., just before Thales instituted Western philosophy.

3. The *Psalms* are 150 poems used as Jewish worship songs, and among the most beautiful writings in the Old Testament.

4. *Wisdom Literature* refers primarily to the books of *Job*, *Proverbs*, and *Ecclesiastes*. Generally, the wisdom writings are concerned with sage observations of human behavior and suffering. *Song of Songs* is a poetic, sometimes erotic, description of the love between a man and a woman and is considered part of the wisdom literature.

5. The *Prophets* comprise the last 17 books of the Old Testament (Isaiah through Malachi). Primarily, these books focus on God's pending judgment of the Jewish people. Included in the writings are references to judgments on other nations as well as God's faithfulness as expressed in the promise of the coming *Messiah* (Jesus) who will rescue Israel.

The massive, venerable buck in this picture is like the Old Testament, large and having stood the test of time. I think he suffered from heart failure since he breathed heavily as he walked along. But, despite his age, he was actively seeking does as a relevant participant, in the rut (mating season) just as the Old Testament, despite its antiquity, remains a relevant guide to the reality and nature of God. As the buck has two very different antlers (one superior to the other), so the Old Testament proclaims two different covenants of God with his chosen people. The first was a covenant of law-keeping for only the nation of Israel that was impossible for fallen humans to keep perfectly. However, there is also a promise of a superior new covenant of grace that would be for all nations through the coming Messiah whom the New Testament declares to be Jesus the Christ.

2. Creation

Reference Texts: Genesis, Chapters 1 and 2

This beautiful doe, staring intently at her hopeful suitor, reminds me that God is the creator of everything. From the intricacies of her coat to the glorious light of sunrise bathing the forest background, the conclusion is inescapable: the reason that there are deer, and woods for them to live in, and people to enjoy them, and light so we can see them, and billions upon billions of other things is because God created them. Why would God (a spiritual being in three persons, in perfect harmony, and lacking nothing) create a physical universe? The answer is the universe was created for the pleasure and glory of God. God is the supreme being of ultimate value. He is the only being for which it is mandatory that He always acts to bring Himself maximum praise and adoration so that His ultimate value is supremely honored. By creating the universe and populating earth with people who can know him, and love him and praise him for his creation, he increases his glory compared to remaining just a totally sufficient, happy, triune God. (See *The Pleasures of God,* chapter 3, and *Desiring God* by

John Piper for further study of these ideas.)

Many books have great opening sentences, but the Bible eclipses all other books as it opens with the declaration: *In the beginning, God created the heavens and the earth* (Genesis 1:1). In one sentence the Bible tells us that the universe is not eternal, it has a beginning, and that there is a God who created it. Christians accept this statement as absolute truth, but there is substantial disagreement between Christians as to when the creation took place. Irish Archbishop James Ussher (1581–1656) literally added up the lifetimes listed in the genealogies and concluded the universe was created Sunday, October 23, 4004 B.C. The traditional Hebrew calendar begins with creation and adds 3,760 years to our modern calendar. Modern Christians date the world to be between 6,000 years of age to the "scientific" age of billions of years. With six orders of magnitude separating the extremes, the critical point of agreement is that God is the creator!

Genesis 1–2 says that God created the universe, and populated the earth, with all forms of plants and animals. He spoke all of this into existence by his command, making, it out of nothing.* God created Adam and out of Adam's rib God created Eve as Adam's helper. God placed them in the perfect Garden of Eden where they could have lived eternally, since they were uniquely created in the image of God having: 1) a body and a soul; 2) ability to know and worship God; 3) morality; 4) dominion over the earth; 5) eternal life; 6) ability to communicate with God thru prayer; and 7) comprehension of God's glory by observing the creation and reading the Bible.

As a new Christian, I believed in evolution and tried to reconcile science and Genesis 1–2 with some kind of theistic evolution (God created evolution as a "natural law"). But I soon realized that if the outcome of creation was open (a product of chance, unknown and uncontrolled by God), then God was not omniscient or sovereign, since he did not know or control how creation would turn out. Such an unbiblical view could not reconcile the Bible and science. But if evolution was a natural law that could turn out only one way, then it was an unbiblical way to state the biblical truth that God sovereignly created the universe. As I matured in my understanding of the Bible I saw that reconciling Scripture and science on this point was a fool's errand. The only rational explanation for the universe is that God created it out of nothing for His glory (chapters 57–70).

*This does not violate the foundational truth of logic "out of nothing, nothing comes," because out of God (who is not nothing!), everything comes!

3. The Fall

Reference Text: Genesis 3

This slightly guilty looking doe eating an apple is emblematic of the Fall (entrance of sin into the world). My neighbor had given me a pail of blown down apples, so I put them at a trail junction in the marsh behind my house where I had set up a blind. When Eve ate the forbidden fruit (an apple is traditional, but biblically the fruit is unnamed) it was not only Adam, Eve and the rest of humanity that fell into a state of imperfection, but the creation as a whole was also corrupted (Genesis 3:18). The effects of the Fall are far reaching, resulting in the sin that surrounds us and the inherent fallibility in all that we do. Indeed, almost everything we do is necessitated by the disease, decay and evil that originated with the Fall.

God told Adam and Eve they could eat of every tree in the Garden of Eden, except the "tree of the knowledge of good and evil" (Genesis 2:16–17). They were told that if they ate of it, they would be barred from the "tree of life" (Genesis 3:22) and they would die. Into this perfect setting came the serpent (Satan) who persuaded Eve to eat of the "tree of the knowledge of good and evil" and give some to Adam who also ate. This is called the "Fall". The first consequence of the Fall was that Adam and Eve realized they were naked and were ashamed, covering themselves with fig leaves. God came to Adam, showing his responsibility for and headship of Eve (even though it was Eve who first sinned). Because of these sins, Adam and Eve were cast out of the Garden. God pronounced judgments on them. Adam would be subjected to hard work to get his food, Eve would have great pain in childbirth, and the serpent would be cursed, eventually being defeated by Eve's offspring (Jesus). The Bible does not tell us a great deal about Satan. Jesus identifies him as a "liar and the father of lies" (John 8:44). People are often deceived into thinking Satan does not exist, or he is just a metaphor for evil, or an absurd cartoon character in a red suit with a long tail, horns and a pitchfork! In reality Satan is a formidable foe, but he is not God's equal and is constrained by God as to his sphere of influence (Job 1:12; 2:6).

God was not at all caught by surprise by this turn of events, forcing Him to implement a "plan B" after the Fall. On the contrary, the Fall was part of God's plan, since without the Fall, all of God's attributes could not be fully known. In particular, without the Fall, the outpouring of His wrath in regard to sin would not be displayed. This wrath comes as a consequence of His holiness which makes it impossible for God to sin, and at the same time does not allow anyone without perfect holiness to be in His presence. In addition, without the Fall, God's grace (unmerited favor) and mercy (not punishing us according to our sin) would not be understood.

Sin entered into the world through Adam and Eve and it was passed on to all their offspring including you and me. When we are born, we are born with a heart inclined to sin before we actually have committed any sins. This is called the doctrine of original sin. Original sin persists in us in different forms, but in essence, it is that we think we will be happier by not following God's commandments. Hence, we do not first and foremost love God and show that love by obeying His commandments. Christians take the account of the Fall as historical fact. All this, of course, seems foolish to the contemporary secular mind which thinks people are intrinsically good. However, as Blaise Pascal (1623–1662) noted, "The doctrine of original sin seems an offense to reason, but once accepted it makes total sense of the human condition."

4. Sin/Mercy: Cain and Abel, Noah and the Ark

Reference Text: Genesis Chapters 4-8

Territorial battles to establish breeding rights are usually quickly resolved by the inferior buck wisely withdrawing. However, twice I have been entertained for nearly an hour by the sound of antlers crashing against each other as I lay in my blind waiting for sunrise. The two young bucks in this photo might be brothers like Cain and Abel, but they did not engage in a real fight to the death.

Adam and Eve had two sons, Cain and Abel. Cain raised crops and Abel raised sheep. Both brought an offering to the LORD. The LORD was pleased with Abel's first-born lamb, but not pleased with Cain's offering which was neither his best nor first produce. Cain became angry and murdered his brother. But nothing escapes God's sight, so He inquired where Abel was. Cain said he didn't know, sarcastically adding the famous line, *"Am I my brother's keeper?"* (Genesis 4:9), hence showing no remorse, repentance or fear of God who made him.

As the human population of the earth grew and sin proliferated, God saw the wickedness of man was great and decided to blot out mankind in a great flood. God had mercy on Noah and his family commanding him to build an ark (a ship 450 feet long, 75 feet wide and 45 feet deep; a very stable, seaworthy design according to modern experts) and take on board his family, seven pairs of clean animals and birds and a pair of every other land-living creature. Then God caused it to rain for 40 days and 40 nights such that every living thing on earth was drowned except for those on the ark. (Of course all water creatures could survive without the ark.) Eventually, the flood abated and Noah and his family left the ark along with the creatures that had survived the flood. From the time the rain began until Noah left the ark, a little more than one year elapsed. Upon leaving the ark, Noah worshiped God by sacrificing the additional clean animals (six pairs). God made a covenant* with Noah to never again strike down every living creature on earth as long as the earth remains (Genesis 8:21–22). God established the rainbow following rain as a sign reminding us of God's covenant promise. Notice, however, that there is a proviso that it only holds as long as the earth remains. This points to the final judgment, after which a new heaven and a new earth will be established (Revelation 21). Numerous other cultures have a flood story. For this reason critics often shed doubt on the story, but it is more likely that there really was a global flood, the story having been passed down through the ages. Christians take the flood story as a literal historic fact because Jesus confirmed the flood really happened (Matthew 24:37–39).

*A covenant is a solemn binding agreement between two parties, establishing promises and penalties for breaking the agreement. But when God makes a covenant, He alone establishes its terms. God has made three basic covenants:

1. The *covenant of redemption* was made before creation within the Trinity: The Father gave the Son a people he would redeem (John 17:2, 6); The Son agreed to become a man and live under the Law, dying for the sins of all that believed in Jesus (Hebrews 2:14–18); The Holy Spirit agreed to fill and empower Jesus while on earth and regenerate God's chosen people (Luke 4:1, 14, 18; 2 Thessalonians 2:14).
2. The *covenant of works* (Genesis 2:16–17) was made with Adam and Eve who immediately broke it in the "Fall".
3. The Noahic covenant is part of what is called the *covenant of grace*. This was not a plan B because God was taken by surprise by the Fall. Instead, it was part of His plan to demonstrate that He would give justice to some and grace and mercy to others (Genesis 6:5–8). Beginning with Adam and Eve (Genesis 3:15) the covenant of grace is progressively revealed through specific individual covenants culminating with the New Covenant ("to write the Law on their heart" Jeremiah 31:31–34) which was ultimately fulfilled by Jesus.

5. Abraham, Isaac and Jacob

Reference Text: Genesis Chapters 9–50

This old doe was obviously being courted by a very large buck early in the rut. About ten days later, I saw her, again, in the company of another large buck. Perhaps she was too old to become pregnant, explaining the apparent second attempt at mating. Nevertheless, with God all things are possible, and it is through the birth of a baby to a 90-year-old woman that the 12 tribes of Israel arose.

Following the flood, God blessed Noah and his family and told them to be fruitful and multiply and fill the earth (Genesis 9:1). From this family arose all the people groups we find on the earth to this day. Roughly 4,000 years ago God spoke to Abram in present day Iraq and told him to go to Canaan (modern Israel) where he would make him into a great nation more numerous than the stars. Now Abram had no offspring. When he was 85, his wife Sarai arranged for him to father a child with her servant Hagar. The child was named Ishmael, from whom the Arabs have descended. When Abram was 99, God made a covenant with him that he would be the father of a multitude of nations and gave him circumcision as the sign of the covenant. God changed his name to Abraham and his wife's name to Sarah, promising that within the year, Sarah would bear a son. Both Sarah and Abraham laughed for Sarah was 90 years old.

God was faithful to his promise and Isaac (Isaac means laughter in Hebrew!) was born a year later. When Isaac was about 13, God tested Abraham telling him to take Isaac, his only son, and sacrifice him on Mount Moriah (eventually, the temple site in Jerusalem) as a burnt offering. Abraham made plans to obey, and as he and Isaac walked toward the mountain with Isaac carrying the wood on his back for the fire, Isaac asked, "where is the lamb for the sacrifice?" Abraham prophetically replied that God would provide the lamb. When they reached the mountain and Abraham was about to plunge his knife into Isaac to fulfill the sacrifice, God intervened, satisfied that Abraham trusted Him. Abraham saw a ram caught in a thicket which he sacrificed in place of Isaac (Genesis 22). This passage is pregnant with imagery of the ultimate, substitutionary sacrifice of Jesus in the same place.

Isaac grew up and fathered twins, Esau and Jacob. Esau's descendents became the Edomites, who would later war with Israel when they reentered the Promised Land following 430 years of slavery in Egypt. Jacob was the favored son who in turn fathered 12 sons from whom the 12 tribes of Israel arose. The youngest of these 12 sons, Joseph, was sold into slavery by his brothers because they were jealous that he was his father's favorite son. Joseph, through divine intervention, rose to be second in command in Egypt. When a famine struck, Jacob and his sons were reunited in Egypt with Joseph, who had stored up vast food reserves under the direction of God. The book of Genesis reaches its grand climax with Joseph's observation to his brothers that they meant evil against him, but God meant it for good (50:20). This is a common theme in Scripture: we humans often fail to see the big picture and are consumed by present pain and suffering, unable to see God's wise plan in our affliction. *And we know that for those who love God, all things work together for good, for those who are called according to his purpose* (Romans 8:28).

6. Moses

Scripture reference: Exodus chapters 1–15

The woods literally exploded with the sound of breaking branches, shattering the near perfect 8:00 AM silence of a crisp morning in early November. Fleeing in desperate haste from a human enemy this regal buck conveniently stopped as abruptly as his mad dash for safety had begun in one of my "shooting lanes" about thirty yards away. Turning to intently watch his back trail, great clouds of breath erupted from his nostrils due to the intensity of his flight. This picture reminds me of how the regal prince of Egypt, Moses, had to flee for his life once his true identity was known as the son of Israelite slaves. Yet, it pleased God to raise him up as his chosen instrument to lead the nation of Israel out of bondage in Egypt. Listen to how the first martyr of the Christian faith, Stephen (a Jewish convert to Christianity), summarizes the story from Exodus just prior to his execution by an angry mob of fellow Jews:

"But as the time of the promise drew near, which God had granted to Abraham, the people increased and multiplied in Egypt until there arose

over Egypt another king who did not know Joseph. He dealt shrewdly with our race and forced our fathers to expose their infants, so that they not be kept alive. At this time Moses was born; and he was beautiful in God's sight. And he was brought up for three months in his father's house, and when he was exposed, Pharaoh's daughter adopted him and brought him up as her own son. And Moses was instructed in all the wisdom of the Egyptians, and he was mighty in his words and deeds.

When he was forty years old, it came into his heart to visit his brothers, the children of Israel. And seeing one of them being wronged, he defended the oppressed man and avenged him by striking down the Egyptian. He supposed that his brothers would understand that God was giving them salvation by his hand, but they did not understand. And on the following day he appeared to them as they were quarreling and tried to reconcile them, saying, 'Men, you are brothers. Why do you wrong each other?' But the man who was wronging his neighbor thrust him aside saying, 'Who made you a ruler and a judge over us? Do you want to kill me as you killed the Egyptian yesterday?' At this retort Moses fled and became an exile in the land of Midian where he became the father of two sons.

Now when forty years had passed, an angel appeared to him in the wilderness of Mount Sinai, in a flame of fire in a bush. When Moses saw it, he was amazed at the sight, and as he drew near to look, there came the voice of the Lord: 'I am the God of your fathers, the God of Abraham and of Isaac and of Jacob.' And Moses trembled and did not dare to look. Then the Lord said to him, 'Take off the sandals from your feet, for the place where you are standing is holy ground. I have surely seen the affliction of my people who are in Egypt, and have heard their groaning, and I have come down to deliver them. And now come, I will send you to Egypt.'

This Moses, whom they rejected, saying, 'Who made you a ruler and a judge?' – This man God sent as both ruler and redeemer by the hand of the angel who appeared to him in the bush. This man led them out, performing wonders and signs in Egypt and at the Red Sea and in the wilderness for forty years." (Acts 7:17–36)

Hence, Moses became one of the three great patriarchs of Israel along with Abraham and David. Though he saw God and received the Ten Commandments he was not perfect. Ultimately, he never entered the promised land because he failed to believe God once, showing how seriously God takes sin and demands perfection.

7. The Ten Commandments

Scripture Reference: Exodus 20:3–17

We have ten fingers, ten toes, our number system is based upon ten, and Ten Commandments, so naturally, I selected a picture of a ten pointer for the chapter on the Ten Commandments.

Five comments may be helpful to the reader: 1) The concept of one God ruling the entire universe was a radical idea at the time the Ten Commandments were given to Moses on Mount Sinai. In that era nations either practiced polytheism (multiple gods each assigned specific responsibilities and often represented by statues or idols) or henotheism (one god for each nation) 2) The purpose of the Ten Commandments was to maintain order in the life of God's chosen people (Israel). 3) While we commonly speak of Ten Commandments, the Bible does not actually number them as one through ten. 4) By now some readers may be wondering why capital letters are used sometimes in the word "LORD." Most translations use this spelling to refer to the Hebrew word *"Yahweh"*, the most intimate word for God literally meaning *I am* to emphasize the eternal nature of God. Jews would usually not speak it aloud for fear of violating the third commandment, to not take the name of God in vain. 5) The Ten Commandments in Exodus 20:3–17 (quoted below) are repeated in Deuteronomy 5:6–21.

"You shall have no other gods before me.

You shall not make for yourself a carved image, or any likeness of anything that is in heaven above, or that is in the earth beneath, or that is in the water under the earth. You shall not bow down to them or serve them for I the LORD your God am a jealous God, visiting the iniquity of the fathers on the children to the third and the fourth generation of those who hate me, but showing steadfast love to thousands of those who love me and keep my commandments.

You shall not take the name of the LORD your God in vain, for the LORD will not hold him guiltless who takes his name in vain.

Remember the Sabbath day, to keep it holy. Six days you shall labor, and do all your work, but the seventh day is a Sabbath to the LORD your God. On it you shall not do any work, you, or your son, or your daughter, your male servant, or your female servant, or your livestock, or the sojourner who is within your gates. For in six days the LORD made heaven and earth, the sea, and all that is in them, and rested the seventh day. Therefore the LORD blessed the Sabbath day and made it holy.

Honor your father and your mother, that your days may be long in the land that the LORD your God is giving you.

You shall not murder.

You shall not commit adultery.

You shall not steal.

You shall not bear false witness against your neighbor.

You shall not covet your neighbor's house; you shall not covet your neighbor's wife, or his male servant, or his female servant, or his ox, or his donkey, or anything that is your neighbor's."

Today we have untold numbers of laws, but in God's wisdom he singled out these ten for special consideration. Notice that the first four regulate how the people are to relate to God and the last six how they are to relate to one another. Of course, no one ever has or ever will keep them all perfectly except for Jesus. In fact, we will see later that Jesus elevates keeping them to the point that we must not just refrain from, literally, breaking them, but must also refrain from even thinking about breaking them (Matthew 5–7).

8. The Old Testament Sacrificial System

Scripture Reference: The Pentateuch (Genesis, Exodus, Leviticus, Numbers, and Deuteronomy)

Under the Old Testament sacrificial system, young, blemish free animals, like this perfect specimen of a young buck, were killed to cover the sins of people. But this sacrificial system only hinted at Jesus' perfect sacrifice that would give eternal life to Christians, just as this bold, little eight pointer is only a hint of the powerful bucks that will give life to next year's fawns.

Following the Fall in Genesis 3, the remainder of the Bible is devoted to explaining how a person can get right with God once they have sinned. The Pentateuch (written by Moses) provides 613 laws (not just the Ten Commandments) that cover all aspects of life, with the clear requirement that a person must perfectly obey every one of them to have eternal life. The law had three purposes: 1) to show human sinfulness and God's perfect righteousness; 2) to restrain evil by requiring physical punishment for offenses; and 3) to guide believers to the good works that please God.

There were three categories of laws: 1) moral law commanded what pleased God and forbid what offended him; 2) political law applied the moral law to Israel's theocracy; and 3) ceremonial laws on diet, purity and sacrifice that enacted symbolically what the Messiah would fulfill. (Today only the moral law applies to Christians.) But because of the Fall, no one (except Jesus) could perfectly obey all of these laws. Thus the Pentateuch laid out an elaborate sacrificial system in which sins (breaking the law) could be atoned for (i.e., reconciling sinners with God) by offering sacrifices of grain, wine and animals. This system culminated with the annual Day of Atonement. It is still celebrated by Jews as *Yom Kippur*, but without animal sacrifices.

The Tabernacle was originally a tent, but, later a permanent building in Jerusalem called the temple. In both cases it contained a square room called the Most Holy Place in which the Ark of the Covenant (a box about 27 x 27 x 45 inches made of acacia wood and covered inside and out with gold) was kept. The stone tablets with the Ten Commandments written on them were stored within the Ark of the Covenant. The High Priest was the only person who could enter the Most Holy Place, and he could only enter one day each year, the Day of Atonement, and only with blood from animals.

On the Day of Atonement (Leviticus 16), the High Priest washed himself and put on special garments. After slaughtering a bull to atone for his sins and the sins of the other priests, he would sprinkle some of the bull's blood in the Most Holy Place. Then, the High Priest went outside the tabernacle and chose two young, blemish free male goats. One goat, chosen by casting lots, was killed. The High Priest re-entered the Most Holy Place, and sprinkled the goat's blood to atone for the people's sins. Next, the High Priest laid his hands on the head of the other goat, called the scapegoat, to transfer the sins and guilt of the Israelites to it. The scapegoat was then released in the wilderness, symbolizing the removal of sin and guilt from the people. Finally, the body of the slain goat was taken outside the camp and burned. Since the people and the High Priest continued to sin, this sacrifice had to be repeated every year. Of course these ceremonies could not really satisfy God's wrath against sin thus preserving his holiness nor could they remove the sin and guilt from the people (Hebrews 10:4). They were only a symbolic foreshadowing of Jesus who would actually full fill both the role of the sacrificed goat and the scapegoat.

9. A Brief History of Israel Part 1:
The Exodus to the Babylonian Captivity

Scripture Reference: Exodus 21–2 Chronicles; Isaiah –Ezekiel

After 430 years of slavery in Egypt, the Nation of Israel was poised to enter the Promised Land flowing with milk and honey. But instead of following the Ten Commandments that would have assured their happiness, they entered into a repetitive cycle of falling into sin, experiencing God's judgment, repenting and receiving his mercy, only to fall into sin again. The first cycle began during the forty days Moses was on Mount Sinai receiving the Ten Commandments. The people disobeyed and began worshiping a golden calf despite having crossed the Red Sea on dry land while pharaoh's pursuing army drowned. Yet, God was gracious and did not destroy Israel for this idolatry. As they neared Canaan (the Promised Land), God commanded Moses to send spies into Canaan. When the spies returned they reported the land did indeed flow with milk and honey. But, except for Caleb and Joshua, all the spies said the military might was too great for them to take the land. This was the last straw. God decreed that this rebellious generation would never enter Canaan. So for 40 years they wandered in the Sinai Wilderness until the entire generation died except for Caleb and Joshua. Even Moses and Aaron died because once they didn't trust God to provide water in the desert.

Joshua succeeded Moses and led the Israelites into the Promised Land, miraculously crossing the Jordon River in flood stage on dry land (like Moses had crossed the Red Sea). God commanded Joshua to kill all the inhabitants of the Promised Land, because they were very wicked, and God did not want Israel to intermarry with them. However, Israel did not obey God and destroy the inhabitants. Rather, Israel intermarried with them and worshiped their foreign gods.

After Joshua died, a series of 12 political and military leaders called Judges led Israel. The last Judge was Samuel the prophet, who ruled Israel according to God's desires. However, the people demanded a king so that they could be like the other nations. God warned the people through Samuel that a king would take the people into his service and tax them, but they persisted. So God gave them Saul, the most handsome man in the land as their first king. Saul began his reign about 1050 B.C. He was replaced by David and David by his son Solomon, the wealthiest and wisest man of all time. Solomon built the first temple in Jerusalem using Jewish forced labor. In about 940 B.C., Rehoboam replaced his father Solomon. Rehoboam treated the people even more harshly than Solomon. For this reason God enabled Jeroboam (Solomon's official in charge of the forced labor) to split off the ten northern tribes (Israel) of the kingdom with Rehoboam retaining control of Judah. The succeeding kings were usually wicked, leading the people into detestable idol worship, including child sacrifice. In Israel nine different families vied for the kingship while David's lineage was preserved in Judah. God sent Prophets (Isaiah, Jeremiah and others) to tell the people of the coming judgment, but they did not listen. Assyria conquered Israel in 722 B.C. and Babylon (modern Iraq) captured Judah in 586 B.C.

So how is this picture a parable of Israel's history? The green buckthorn leaves in the background are a fleeting promise of summer (the Promised Land). The cocky buck (the 12 tribes of Israel) struts along literally licking his chops intent on fulfilling his carnal desires. But, he is unaware of the trials of winter (God's judgment through the Assyrian and Babylonian captivity) that await him as foretold by the fallen leaves and bare saplings (the Prophets) in the foreground.

10. David

***And your house and your kingdom shall be made sure forever
before me. Your throne shall be established forever.*** 2 Samuel 7:16

This yearling buck is a parable of David. Awash in hormones, he
laid back his ears to signal his foolish challenge to the large buck. This
David and Goliath confrontation ended quickly, with one good shove from
the large buck forcing the yearling to prudently withdraw. But when the
youthful David faced the Philistine giant Goliath, God's hand was upon
David. Armed with only his shepherd's sling, against all human expectation,
he mortally wounded the giant with a single stone, and dispatched him with
Goliath's own sword.

Few stories in all of literature are more captivating than 1 Samuel
16–1 Kings 2 account of the real life adventures of David. He is, perhaps,
the best known, but most enigmatic character in the Old Testament. Born
the youngest of eight brothers in Bethlehem, he spent his boyhood as a
shepherd, courageously defending his father's flocks against wild animals.
In his youth the prophet Samuel anointed him to be the disobedient King

Saul's eventual successor.

David was a gifted musician and his simple shepherd's life was interrupted occasionally to play soothing music for Saul when an evil spirit fell upon King Saul. His valor against Goliath as Saul's cowardly army watched catapulted David into national prominence as a great warrior. On one occasion the women of Israel greeted the returning army by singing, "Saul has slain his thousands and David his ten thousands." This ignited Saul's rage and jealousy. For several years David lived as a fugitive as Saul made numerous attempts to take David's life. During this time Saul's son Jonathan remained David's confidant and friend. Twice David had the opportunity to kill Saul, but did not out of respect for Saul's office as King. Eventually, Saul and Jonathan were killed by the Philistines on Mount Gilboa.

David was crowned King, but years of civil war ensued until David united all the tribes of Israel into a world power. David's great military prowess often overshadows his many administrative skills as he brought order to the government and worship, established Jerusalem as Israel's religious center and capital, and was the most prolific of all the Psalm writers.

Despite all David's triumphs, his adultery with Bathsheba led to his downfall. Subsequently, he murdered her husband, Uriah, by placing him in battle under circumstances that would virtually guarantee his death. David repented deeply for this transgression (Psalm 51), but the child of this union died in infancy. Later, Bathsheba would bear Solomon, David's successor, but David's glory years were over and his life was one of continual angst from that time forward. His daughter Tamar was raped by her brother Amnon, who was in turn murdered by servants of David's son Absalom. Absalom rebelled against David, seeking to gain the throne militarily. Absalom was killed by David's troops only to have David's son Adonijah attempt to wrest kingship from God's chosen successor, Solomon.

So why is David such a central player in redemptive history? It is the Davidic covenant of 2 Samuel 7:16 that has in view David's earthly descendants who would comprise the ancestry of the long awaited Messiah (Matthew 1, Luke 3). Despite David's moral failures, he repented from his sins. Though the Judean kings who would follow in the Davidic line were mostly a rogues' gallery, David was a man after God's own heart (1 Samuel 13:14), under the power of the Holy Spirit (1 Samuel 16:13) and wholly true to the LORD (1 Kings 15:3).

11. The Psalms

The LORD is my shepherd; I shall not want. He makes me lie down in green pastures. He leads me beside still waters. He restores my soul. He leads me in paths of righteousness for his name's sake. Even though I walk through the valley of the shadow of death, I will fear no evil, for you are with me; your rod and your staff, they comfort me. You prepare a table before me in the presence of my enemies; you anoint my head with oil; my cup overflows. Surely goodness and mercy shall follow me all the days of my life, and I shall dwell in the house of the LORD forever. Psalm 23

I had positioned myself along a golf course frequented by does and fawns as they browsed their way to a water hazard they used for their evening drink. A doe with two fawns was passing by when one of the fawns conveniently plunked itself down on the "green pastures" of the fairway. The image of this contented fawn beautifully captures for me the believer's peace and trust in God depicted in Psalm 23, perhaps the best known and most loved of all the Psalms.

The word *Psalms* means "songs" and comes from the Septuagint (early Greek translation of the Old Testament). They are really Hebrew poems used as the hymn book and prayer book throughout the history of Israel. The 150 Psalms were written over a period of at least 1,000 years spanning the time from Moses to beyond the Babylonian captivity. Moses, Solomon, the sons of Korah, Asaph, and Ethan the Ezrahite are all named as the authors of various psalms. But the most frequent author is King David. The Psalms contain both the shortest chapter in the Bible (Psalm 117) and the longest chapter (Psalm 119). Interestingly, Psalm 118 is the exact midpoint of the Bible. The Psalms range in subject matter from praise, thanksgiving, and trust in God, to laments expressing fear, sadness, and anger, sometimes to the point of calling on God to destroy the author's enemies.

Psalm 23, penned by King David, uses the rich imagery of a shepherd caring for believers in life, and the certainty of a great banquet for all eternity in God's presence after death. The shepherd tends his flock by finding them green pastures and still waters, valuable commodities in an arid land like Israel. The LORD refreshes the souls of downcast believers and leads them in paths of righteousness (being right with God or pleasing to God). Why does God do this? For the same reason He does everything: for His namesake and glory. Since God's reputation is at stake, believers can be confident He will always do what is best for them. Even in mortal danger the believer takes comfort in God as protector and leader just as the shepherd fought off wild animals with the rod and guided the sheep with the staff.

The imagery then shifts to the great, eternal banquet celebrating victory over the believer's enemies. In the context of Jewish culture, guests were anointed with oil at feasts, but at this feast the cup of oil is not just full, it overflows, so great is God's goodness. This leads to the grand conclusion that goodness and mercy follow the believer throughout life, culminating in an eternal celebration with God after death.

Traditionally, translations say goodness and mercy *follow* but the original text is much stronger. The Hebrew word *radaph*, translated as "follow," has a primary meaning of pursue. Old Testament translations usually render *radaph* about 5 times conveying the idea of following, and about 121 times with the idea of pursuing. Therefore, a better translation would be goodness and mercy *pursue* us all the days of our lives. So God is really chasing after believers, looking for ways to heap His lavish love upon them.

12. Job

Reference Text: Job

For seven weekends in 1994, I tried to photograph this buck. One morning, just before Christmas I carefully worked my way along the edge of a large marsh. Suddenly he exploded out of heavy cover accompanied by a doe. Deer normally run a short distance directly away from danger and then walk into the wind. In these cases, I sometimes try to beat them to an intercept point. Employing this strategy, I arrived before a doe passed by. Minutes later, no buck had appeared. Stepping from my hiding place behind a tree, I heard loud crashing as the buck furiously sought refuge in a wooded peninsula extending into the marsh. Figuring that he would spend the day in this impregnable sanctuary, I waited until late afternoon before returning. As I entered the peninsula, I saw a flash of brown enter the cattails ahead. Sprinting hard to my intended intercept point, I hunkered down behind a tree moments ahead of a doe and spike buck. Disappointed, but not about to be fooled again, I waited. Suddenly there he was, having abandoned the trail in an attempt to outflank me. He spotted me and froze as his image was captured. I walked to my car worshiping and thanking God for this marvelous experience. People often comment that I have remarkable patience pursuing deer, but my patience is nothing compared to the legendary patience of Job.

As the book of Job opens we learn Job was "blameless and upright, one who feared God and turned away from evil" (1:1). He had seven sons and three daughters and was very wealthy. The scene turns to a meeting between Satan and the LORD. The subject of Job comes up and Satan agrees Job is blameless and upright, but claims this is only because God's favor rests on him. God replies that Satan can do whatever he wishes, except he may not touch Job. Satan responds by killing Job's children and plundering his property. Job did not turn from trusting God, declaring, *The LORD gave and the* LORD *has taken away; blessed be the name of the LORD* (1:21). Satan then ups the ante, alleging Job would turn from God if his body were afflicted. The LORD allows Satan to afflict Job, but not kill him. So Satan struck Job with "loathsome sores" (2:7). In great agony, Job is visited by three friends. Their basic message is that Job is guilty of some great sin and that is why he is suffering. Job remains steadfast in his claim that he has not sinned. Much of the discussion centers on the age-old question of 'why do bad things happen to good people?' Job protests the treatment he is receiving from God, but he does not turn from God. In the end, God meets with Job. Job repents of his careless words, his health is restored, his wife has more children and his new wealth exceeds what he had previously.

The book of Job shows God is totally sovereign. Satan is a powerful enemy, but he must get God's permission to work his evil. Job knows that God is ultimately sovereign, because he holds God responsible for his suffering. If Job thought God was not totally sovereign, he would not have held God responsible, supposing instead that God was impotent to prevent these calamities. Ultimately, the story shows that God's purposes and our understanding of suffering do not necessarily align. As humans, we tend to not see the big picture, and want instantaneous relief from our suffering. Sometimes, God afflicts Christians and enables them to remain faithful in order to glorify God through their suffering (1 Peter 4:16), but God ultimately works all things for good for Christians (Romans 8:28). This is a hard teaching. One of the most common arguments launched against Christianity is why a good and all powerful God allows evil and suffering? These questions will be addressed in chapters 81 and 82.

13. A Brief History of Israel Part II:
The Babylonian Captivity to the destruction of the temple

Scripture Reference: Ezra, Nehemiah, and Daniel–Malachi

Most of the pictures in this book were taken from a blind in a narrow strip of woods where four large deer trails converge. Deer seeking to travel between several choice bedding areas, food sources and water must pass within 20 yards of me. This picture shows how I appear to a deer at the convergence of the trails. This location is a parable of the narrow strip of land called Palestine, where the ancient trade routes linking Europe, the Far East, and Egypt converged. God ordained that Jesus would be born here so the gospel could radiate rapidly along established trade routes to the far corners of the earth.

In 609 B.C. Egypt captured Judah. Four years later, Nebuchadnezzar led the Babylonian army into Palestine, wresting Judah from Egyptian control and beginning the Babylonian captivity. Among the first captives taken to Babylon was the prophet Daniel. Between 605 B.C. and the destruction of the temple in 586 B.C., a complicated political drama unfolded in which

Judah's kings walked a tightrope between being a Babylonian vassal, while trying to forge an alliance with Egypt to gain autonomy from Babylon. In 538 B.C. God enabled Persia under the leadership of Cyrus to capture Babylon. As prophesized by Jeremiah in about 605 B.C. (Jeremiah 25:1–14), Cyrus decreed in 537 B.C. that the captives could return to Jerusalem (Ezra 1:1). Once the Jews returned to Jerusalem, Zerubbabel's temple was built on the site of the original temple (536–516 B.C.), Scripture based worship was restored, and by about 450 B.C. the last book in the Old Testament was completed by the prophet Malachi.

The period from Malachi to the birth of Jesus is called the intertestamental period and was characterized by the absence of any prophets*. It was a defining time for Judaism: there was a rampant hope that God would send a messiah to rescue Israel from foreign rule; the synagogue emerged as the place of worship; the Hebrew Scriptures were translated into Greek (the Septuagint); and Judaism was divided into three main sects, the Sadducees, Essenes, and Pharisees. The intertestamental period was also the golden age of Greek philosophy including Socrates (470?–399 B.C.), Plato (427?–347 B.C.), and Aristotle (384–322 B.C.). The Persians ruled Palestine until 330 B.C. when they were defeated by the Greeks under Aristotle's greatest student, 24 year old Alexander the Great. Initially, the Greeks allowed the practice of Judaism. But eventually, Antiochus Epiphanes (ruled 175–164 B.C.) attempted to destroy Judaism. He erected a statue of the Greek God, Zeus, in the temple and sacrificed a pig there! The Maccabean revolt, begun in 167 B.C. (still celebrated as Hanukkah), successfully restored the practice of Judaism.

In 63 B.C., the Romans led by Pompey, captured Jerusalem. To placate the Jews, Herod the Great in 19 B.C. began revamping Zerubbabel's temple into a magnificent new temple, 172 feet high, wide and long. Most scholars believe Jesus was born between 6 and 4 B.C. However, Judaism did not recognize him as the long awaited Messiah, and God's judgment descended on Israel in A.D. 70 when the Romans destroyed the temple and surrounding structures, as they brutally crushed a Jewish revolt. Without a temple for sacrifices to atone for sins, Judaism would be supplanted by Christianity as the dominate religion in the Mediterranean area.

* During this era the *Apocrypha* were written and are included in the Bible used by Roman Catholics and Eastern Orthodox Christians. Protestants do not use the *Apocrypha*, because neither the Jews nor Jesus viewed them as authoritative.

14. Introduction to the New Testament

Scripture Reference: The New Testament

As a gentle snow drifted down, a harbinger of winter, the fawn watched its back trail, while the doe looked ahead. Similarly, the Old Testament looks at the past from the beginning of time (creation) to the intertestamental winter of prophetic silence, while the New Testament looks ahead from Jesus' birth to the restored perfection of the new heaven and earth when Jesus returns at the end of time.

The New Testament is about one third the size of the Old Testament. It contains 27 books divided into four parts: 1) the Gospels (Matthew, Mark, Luke and John) document Jesus' birth, ministry, death and resurrection; 2) the book of Acts describes the history of the early church; 3) the 21 Epistles (Romans through Jude) are letters addressed either to individual churches, groups of churches or persons. They deal with specific theological issues and interpret the gospels. 4) the book of Revelation describes future events that will happen before Jesus returns to earth.

Approximately half of the New Testament was written by two authors: Paul (13 epistles, Romans through Philemon) and Paul's associate Luke (Gospel of Luke and Acts). There were seven other authors: Matthew, John and Peter (members of the original 12 apostles); James and Jude (Jesus' half brothers); Mark (Peter's associate); and the unknown author of the epistle to the Hebrews.

Both Testaments deal with a relatively undisputed historical time period and an undetermined longer period of time. The Old Testament undetermined time runs from the creation to the call of Abraham. It could be as short as 2,000 years or a much longer time.* From Abraham to the intertestamental period, about 1,500 years of detailed history is covered. In contrast, the New Testament covers, at most, 75 years of history (Beginning with the birth of Jesus and ending prior to the destruction of the temple in A.D. 70 since this watershed event in Jewish history is not mentioned in the New Testament). The New Testament undefined period of time begins with the death of Jesus in, approximately, A.D. 30 and extends to the unknowable end of time when Jesus returns (Matthew 24:36). While the Old Testament was written over a period of about a thousand years, the New Testament was written over a much shorter period of time, beginning no earlier than 50 A.D. to at most 95–96 A.D. Liberal scholars claim the New Testament writing extended well into the second century A.D. However, the consensus among conservative scholars and validated by the early church fathers is that the entire New Testament was completed in the first century A.D.

There is some confusion about the selection of the New Testament books. Liberal theologians claim that hundreds of viable books were excluded. But only a handful of these were ever seriously considered, because most of them date to the second century and promote various heresies. Of the 27 books included in the New Testament, only Philemon, Hebrews, James, 2 Peter, 2 and 3 John, and Jude (less than 10% of the New Testament) were ever seriously challenged at any point in church history. In August A.D. 397, the Council of Carthage was convened and officially certified the 27 books as authoritative using three criteria: 1) they were written by an apostle or someone under an apostle's authority; 2) they were accepted as authoritative by the early church; 3) they are consistent with the rest of Scripture.

*God created Adam and Eve as adults not embryos. They immediately appeared to be adults an instant after their creation. Similarly God could have created the universe to appear to be billions of years old even though it may actually have been created as recently as six thousand years ago as "young earth" Christians believe.

15. The Gospels

Scripture Reference: Matthew, Mark, Luke and John

I captured this unusual perspective of a buck walking past me as I lay on the ground in my blind. Nose to the ground, he earnestly sought the sweet aroma of a receptive doe that might have passed this way. Such a scent would indeed be good news to him. In our common usage we often use "gospel" to mean truth, but while the gospels are true, "gospel" literally means "good news." What is this good news that we should seek with greater fervor than a buck seeks a doe? It is that God has revealed himself in the person of Jesus who died to satisfy the wrath of God against every person who has ever sinned (from the most heinous to the seemingly most trivial sin) if and, only if, they confess Jesus as their Lord, and believe God raised Jesus from the dead (Romans 10:9). To those who believe, God grants them to live eternally with Jesus in *incomprehensible* joy. But those who do not truly profess faith in Jesus God condemns to unending and *incomprehensible* conscious torment in hell.

The gospels (Matthew, Mark, Luke and John) are essentially

biographies of Jesus. Scholars generally agree that Mark (called "Peter's interpreter" by the one of the church fathers, Papias, A.D. 140) was written first as a succinct apostolic witness of the life, death, and resurrection of Jesus. Matthew expanded on Mark for a Jewish audience, and Luke expanded on Mark for a Gentile (non-Jewish) audience. Matthew, Mark and Luke are called the synoptic (literally meaning "to see the same") gospels, since they repeat much of the same material from different ethnic or cultural perspectives. John, on the other hand, fills in some theological details missing from the synoptic gospels with lengthy discussions of individual topics. Biographies usually span the person's life from birth to death. Two of the Gospels (Matthew and Luke) begin with the birth of Jesus. All of the Gospels cover his death, but none end there. Instead, all four Gospels end with the resurrection of Jesus. Thus, the Gospels are book-ended with two outrageous claims that separate Jesus from every other person in history: 1) he was born of a virgin; and, 2) he rose from the grave to everlasting life following his death. The virgin birth and resurrection are God's authenticating stamps that Jesus is who he says he is.

History pivots about the birth of Jesus, being divided by our reckoning of time into what happened before his birth (B.C.) and what has happened since his birth. All of Christianity hangs on the resurrection. If the resurrection is not true, then Christianity is the greatest hoax ever perpetrated. But if the resurrection is true, then it poses the most important question ever asked, a question that cannot ultimately be avoided, according to the New Testament. Jesus asked this question himself of his disciples. Listen to the question, the answer and the explanation in Mathew 16:15–17: *"But who do you say that I am?" Simon Peter replied, "You are the Christ, the Son of the living God." And Jesus answered him, "Blessed are you Simon Bar-Jonah! For flesh and blood has not revealed this to you, but my Father who is in heaven."* Notice that Jesus asks who do **YOU** say Jesus is? Peter answers correctly that Jesus is the Christ, the Savior, the Son of God, and Jesus explains that apart from God, no one can know that Jesus is who he says he is. In the Gospel of John, Jesus says he is: the bread of life; the light of the world; the door; the good shepherd; the resurrection and the life; the way, the truth, and the life; and the true vine. Each of these claims are addressed in chapters 23–29 so that you might be able to answer as Peter did and have eternal life.

16. The Birth of Jesus Christ

Scripture Reference: Matthew 1:18–2:23; Luke 1:26–2:52

I watched the buck in this picture for about half an hour as he relentlessly pursued an unwilling doe in the intense drama of procreation. We instinctively know that every person has a physical mother and father. Yet, the New Testament tells us there is one instance in which a person was born without a physical human father, the birth of Jesus. There are at least four important points that should be understood concerning the birth of Jesus.

First, the birth of Jesus fulfilled several important Old Testament prophecies recounted in the referenced texts: Genesis 3:15 (the "seed" of the woman will ultimately triumph over the serpent), Isaiah 7:14 (the Christ will be born of a virgin), and Micah 5:2 (the Christ will be born in Bethlehem). Notice that Isaiah and Micah made their predictions about 700 years before the birth of Jesus as the Old Testament looked forward to the promised Messiah. In the New Testament, written in Greek, the Hebrew word messiah is rendered *christos* from which we derive the title Christ.

The New Testament almost always uses "Christ" not "Messiah" in referring to Jesus.

Second, the virgin birth sets Jesus apart from every other human being, since he was conceived by the power of the Holy Spirit (Luke 1:35). This is to signal that the birth of Jesus is God's sovereign work, and that he is the promised Christ.

Third, Jesus is fully God and fully man without inheriting the sinful nature of Adam. Luke 1:35 says the child to be born would be holy. This means that somehow the Holy Spirit not only fulfills the role of the father of Jesus, but also prevents the sin nature of Mary to be passed on to Jesus. All other humans inherit the sin nature from both their father and mother.

Fourth, since Jesus was born without sin, he could become the once for all time, perfect sacrifice to atone for the sins of all who believe in him for the forgiveness of their sins. Jesus was born to die to pay the price of all believers' sins.

The well-known story of the birth of Jesus comes from the referenced passages. Jesus was born of a virgin (Mary) betrothed but not married to Joseph. They had traveled to Bethlehem to be counted in a census of the Roman Empire. Mary gave birth in a stable, because there was no room in the inn. The stable might have been a cave outside Bethlehem or the home of a poor family in which the animals lived under the same roof as the people. In this second case the "inn" would refer to guest quarters of the home, usually the flat roof. Jesus was visited by shepherds, and wise men (Magi) following a star. Three wise men have been inferred from the gifts they brought of gold, frankincense and myrrh. They did not visit Jesus at the manger, as is commonly depicted, but arrived later, visiting him in a house (Matthew 2:11). Herod, fearing Jesus was a rival to his authority, killed all the boys around Bethlehem (prophesized in Jeremiah 31:15) two years old, or under, based upon his conversation with the Magi about the "King of the Jews" that the Magi were seeking (Matthew 2:16). God protected Jesus by sending an angel to warn Joseph of Herod's plot to kill the "King of the Jews." Joseph moved the family to Egypt (prophesized in Hosea 11:1) and, then, after Herod died he moved the family to Nazareth in Galilee. Looking forward, the title "King of the Jews," is the very charge the Jews brought against Jesus (i.e. a rival of Roman authority), that ultimately resulted in his crucifixion according to God's perfect plan.

17. Jesus, Light in the Darkness

In the Beginning was the Word, and the Word was with God, and the Word was God. He was in the beginning with God. All things were made through him, and without him was not anything made that was made. In him was life, and the life was the light of men. The light shines in the darkness, and the darkness has not overcome it.

There was a man sent from God, whose name was John. He came as a witness, to bear witness about the light, that all might believe through him. He was not the light, but came to bear witness about the light.

The true light, which enlightens everyone, was coming into the world. He was in the world, and the world was made through him, yet the world did not know him. He came to his own, and his own people did not receive him. But to all who did receive him, who believed in his name, he gave the right to become children of God, who were born, not of blood nor the will of the flesh nor of the will of man, but of God. And the Word became flesh and dwelt among us, and we have seen his glory, glory as of the only Son from the Father, full of grace and truth. (John bore witness about him, and cried out, "This was he of whom I said, He who comes after me ranks before me, because he was before me.") And from his fullness we have all received, grace upon grace. For the law was given through Moses; grace and truth came through Jesus Christ. No one has ever seen God; the only God, who is at the Father's side, he has made him known. John 1:1–18

This young buck seems to shine from the darkness of the two trees just as the coming of Jesus is like a light shining in the darkness of evil and sin. The Gospel of John speaks of light 23 times in reference to Jesus. Elsewhere in Scripture, light is often contrasted with darkness as an example of the contrast between good and evil.

The Apostle John refers to "the Word," translated from the Greek word *logos*. (Don't confuse the Apostle John with John the Baptist referenced in the above passage and who came only to point to Jesus as the true light.) Who or what is the *logos*? In Greek philosophy *logos* is the force that brings order to the creation. In the Gospel of John *logos* is not some Star Wars-like concept of the "force" which is both good and evil. It is true that Jesus holds all things together and is always upholding the universe (Colossians 1:17, Hebrews 1:3). So, in a sense He does maintain order in the creation like the Greek idea of *logos.* But in the Gospel of John "the Word" refers to Jesus, since the Apostle John declares "the Word was God."

The magnificent opening of the Gospel of John is reminiscent of the opening line of Genesis. Here we learn that Jesus was with God (the Father) in the beginning, meaning that Jesus is part of the creator Godhead. Jesus shines in the darkness and the darkness (sin/evil) has not, will not and cannot overcome Jesus. Yet, the world did not recognize him. The Jews did not recognize him. But to everyone who does believe in him, he makes them children of God, born of God not by the will of flesh or man. Jesus as part of the Trinity became flesh so that we could see what God is like. Jesus is greater than Moses since he is the embodiment of grace and truth. These 18 verses raise three important questions that consume much of the New Testament. 1) How can you become a child of God? 2) What are the characteristics of a child of God? 3) What happens if you don't become a child of God? By the time you have finished this book, you should know the answers to these questions.

18. The Book of Acts

Scripture Reference: The Book of Acts (or Acts of the Apostles)

I had seen this orphaned fawn several times, wondering how, without its mother, it would ever survive the perils of winter. But its plight was not so much different from the fledgling church following Jesus' ascension. Without its leader, and numbering only about 120 timid believers (1:15), it would increase 25 fold immediately following Peter's first sermon at Pentecost (2:14–36), survive numerous bloody persecutions throughout its history, and go on to shape the course of western civilization, eventually spreading throughout the entire world. How could such an impossible thing happen? It could happen only through the direction of the sovereign God of the universe!

Acts is a sequel to the Gospel of Luke. Both books were written by Luke (a gentile physician who traveled with the Apostle Paul) to an otherwise unknown official named Theophilus. Carefully researched and documented, Acts tells the beginnings of the Christian church in the compelling style of a great adventure story. Archeology has consistently shown that Luke's attention to detail is extraordinarily accurate, and he is generally regarded as the most reliable historian of the era. The book might be better titled Acts of the Holy Spirit because it recounts how the Holy Spirit empowered the conversion of Jews (chapters 2–6), the despised Samaritans (chapter 8), uncircumcised gentile converts to Judaism, (chapter 10) and pagan gentiles (chapters 13–20). Here is the story that unfolds in Acts.

Jesus commanded the Apostles to wait in Jerusalem for the Holy Spirit and promised that he would return one day. Peter was immediately established as the leader of the Apostles. At the feast of Pentecost (50 days after Passover) the Holy Spirit descended on the Apostles with the appearance of tongues of fire and the apostles began speaking in other languages, so that people from all the nations assembled for the feast could hear in their own language. Peter stood up and delivered the first sermon. 3,000 people believed and were baptized (2:41) signaling that Christianity is about changing the hearts of unbelievers through preaching the gospel. As the church grew, persecution arose mainly from the Sanhedrin (Jewish ruling body) culminating in the stoning of Stephen, the first martyr. Following the stoning, a great persecution broke out driving the Christians out of Jerusalem into Samaria and Judea.

Saul was at the forefront of the persecution*. But on his way to Damascus to continue the persecution, Jesus appeared to him and he was converted from the chief persecutor of Christianity to its chief spokesman (chapter 9). This shows the power of God and that his ways are not our ways. As a trained rabbi, Saul (Paul) was the ideal person to prove that Jesus was indeed the long awaited Messiah as foretold in the Old Testament. The majority of the book of Acts (chapters12–28) authenticates that Paul has true apostolic authority and summarizes Paul's ministry of traveling from city to city (primarily in modern day Turkey and Greece). He usually began in the synagogue, resulting in, literally, being thrown out before going to the Gentiles. Along the way he was often beaten and imprisoned by the ruling authorities, because he caused such a commotion among the Jews. The book of Acts culminates with Paul's ministry in Rome that became the epicenter for the shock wave that Christianized Europe and shaped its history to the present time.

*Saul, a Pharisee from Tarsus in Asia Minor, is better known as the Apostle Paul (Acts 13:9). Historically Christianity is spread by persecution (Acts 11:19). As Tertullian observed, "The blood of Christians is the seed of the church."

19. The Epistles and the Reformation

Scripture Reference: The Epistles (Romans through Jude)

Rutting bucks declare their presence at strategic points within their territory by making "scrapes". The buck begins by rubbing scent glands on their head on a branch (pictured above). Using their front hooves they scrape away the leaves and grass under the branch, and then urinate on glands on their back legs so that the urine lands on the cleared soil. Inevitably bucks make scrapes that encroach on rivals' territory, but the ensuing battles rarely result in serious injury. However, when Martin Luther started making the equivalent of new "doctrinal scrapes" in Roman Catholic territory based upon his study of the Epistles, things got nasty in a hurry. From 1522 until 1660 religious violence almost always plagued at least a part of Europe.

It all began innocently enough. Martin Luther was an Augustinian monk. While studying Romans, he realized that the phrase the "righteousness of God" did not refer to some absolute standards God expected humans to live up to as he had always thought, but rather, it referred to the righteousness God credits to those who by faith trust in Jesus alone for salvation. This insight defined Protestant theology and made Luther a well known professor at the University of Wittenburg as he taught and wrote on his new understanding of righteousness.

Meanwhile in Rome, Pope Leo X was building St. Peter's Basilica. To raise money he decided to sell indulgences and authorized the Dominicans to carry out the sales. The idea was that by giving money to build St. Peter's Basilica, a person could reduce their time in purgatory. Abuses were inevitable, most notably by Johan Tetzel, who aggressively sold the idea that an indulgence was a surefire ticket to heaven for the living and the dead. Luther was upset about the indulgences on theological grounds so he challenged the Dominicans to a debate. Following the standard academic debate protocol, he nailed his famous 95 theses, covering a wide range of theological issues besides indulgences, to the Wittenburg University church door on October 31, 1517. Thanks to the relatively recent invention of the printing press, within two weeks, copies of Luther's 95 theses were being read everywhere in Europe. At first Pope Leo X thought that the controversy could be handled as an issue between Augustinians and Dominicans. In 1519 the Pope asked Luther to recant all of his writings. Luther refused, and the Pope excommunicated him, declaring Luther to be, "a wild boar ravaging his (the Pope's) vineyard." The issue was no longer just indulgences or the 95 theses but had expanded to all of Luther's writings. Between 1519 and 1520, Luther fanned the flames by publishing six major works attacking a wide range of Catholic doctrines. By 1521 the religious chaos was so disruptive that the Holy Roman Emperor, Charles V, summoned Luther and gave him one last chance to recant his writings. Luther refused and went into hiding at Wartburg castle where he translated the New Testament into German, continued writing and directed the Reformation. In frustration Charles V called Luther, "a demon in the habit of a monk," but could do little else.

Luther was at odds with Rome in three significant ways by maintaining that: 1) the Bible is the only infallible and final Christian authority; 2) salvation is by faith alone, in Christ alone, by grace alone; 3) Christ commanded two sacraments, baptism and the Lord's Supper, not the seven Catholic sacraments. Chapters 32–35 will explore the Roman Catholic rationale for their positions on authority, salvation and sacraments and the Protestant reasons for change.

20. The Book of Revelation

Scripture Reference: **The Book of Revelation**

Seeking a receptive doe, this old buck obliviously twice crossed the path a doe had taken minutes before as she eluded an unwanted suitor. Eventually, he passed by me before eagerly heading down a trail unused in the last three hours. Details in the book of Revelation are often difficult to interpret much as this buck failed to interpret the deer sign he encountered. Deer live only in the moment. They do not know that there is a future nor do they worry about it. Unlike deer, we humans ineptly try to predict what the future holds. The Book of Revelation brings the Bible to its grand climax as it unpacks the end of history, not as a human prediction, but as a divine disclosure.

The Greek title for Revelation is *apokálupsis* ("apocalypse" in English) meaning a revelation or disclosure and is similar to parts of Ezekiel, Daniel, and Zechariah. It contains visions, symbolism, allusions, promises and warnings woven together into the themes that embrace all of scripture. Much ink has been wasted throughout history trying to position

Revelation as a treasure chest of mysteries waiting for a clever interpreter to unveil, but it is best to read it as a comfort to Christians that God will ultimately triumph over evil.

Revelation describes a vision of the Apostle John during his imprisonment on the island of Patmos, a Roman penal colony. After a brief prologue (1:1–3) to explain the purpose of the book, Revelation is in the form of a letter similar to Paul's letters. It has a greeting (1:4–5) and a farewell (22:21). In between is the main body of the book. Much of Revelation is organized in sevens, the biblical number of completion: exhortations to seven churches (chapter 2–3); seven heavenly visions and the scroll with seven seals (4:1-8:1); seven angels with seven trumpets (8:2–11:19); seven symbolic histories (chapters 12–14); and seven bowls of God's wrath (chapters 15–16). The rest of the book covers: the judgment of Babylon and vindication of the Church (17:1-19:10; the final battle of Armageddon (19:11–21); the millennium, the reign of the saints and the final judgment (20:1–21:8); the new heaven and earth and the New Jerusalem (21:9–22:5); and some final exhortations (22:6–20).

It is safest to say Revelation declares that a time is coming when Jesus will return to earth to usher in the end of time. Before Jesus returns, the present restraints on Satan will be removed resulting in a time of unparalleled persecution of the church called the Tribulation. Christ will ultimately triumph over the forces of evil in a great battle called Armageddon. Following Armageddon, Christ will preside in judgment* over every person who has ever lived. Those whose names are in the "Book of Life" will go to their eternal reward in the new heaven and the new earth (a restoration of the original creation). The rest will be thrown into the "Lake of Fire" for eternal punishment.

Revelation appeals to our desire to know the future, but Christians should be content that the new heaven and the new earth will be wonderful beyond our imagination. Symbolic and figurative wording, arising because words are inadequate to describe what John saw, makes Revelation a very difficult book to interpret. It is wisest for Christians to avoid divisions over nuances of what is presently unknowable with certainty, and simply long for Christ's return and spending eternity with Him in the new heaven and the new earth.

*This judgment is based upon works to decide the degree of reward or punishment (2 Corinthians 5:10), not one's eternal destiny in heaven or hell.

Part II:
Christian Doctrine

If anyone teaches a different doctrine and does not agree with the sound words of our Lord Jesus Christ and the teaching that accords with godliness, he is puffed up with conceit and understands nothing. 1 Timothy 6: 3–4a

This young buck had a lot to learn about being a mature, dominant buck. His puffed up, blood engorged neck made him look like he was physically ready for the rut. He had a cocky swagger as he strutted along, but he didn't understand that he would not be a significant participant in the rut. In fact he was likely in for some sound thrashings from dominant bucks if he tried to mate with a doe. Professing Christians who have never progressed beyond spiritual milk are similar to this buck. They may appear to understand Christianity but do not know exactly what the whole Bible says about a wide variety of topics. As a result, their understanding of Scripture and doctrine is not robust enough to enable them to be significant participants in propagating the truth of Christianity.

Part II of this book addresses key Christian doctrines. Differing positions are assessed to help Christians biblically determine and defend their doctrinal positions. Some Christians believe doctrine divides the church and hence should be avoided like the plague. But this view often leads to diluted doctrinal understanding that may compromise truth for the sake of unity. In the end, truth must trump unity because only a "solid food" mature understanding of doctrine will enable the church to be an effective voice against mankind's oldest and most pervasive problem: separation from God due to sin.

Theology literally means the study of God. There are many different specialties in theology, but in Part II of this book we will be looking at systematic theology, defined by Wayne Grudem as any study that answers the question of what the whole Bible teaches us today about any given topic. Doctrine is the result of doing systematic theology and is what the whole Bible teaches us today about a given topic.

Over the course of Christian history many false doctrines have arisen. These false doctrines have been invaluable in helping theologians to draw clear distinctions to clarify Christian understanding of key issues. What seem like new ideas in opposition to historic Christian doctrine inevitably boil down to old heresies previously refuted. For unlike science which always seems to expand knowledge and discover new laws, there are no new doctrines or heresies. Therefore, each generation of theologians is called to defend historic Christian doctrine against the temptation to define new doctrines or understandings that are nothing more than old heresies.

There is a broad spectrum of biblical interpretation among professing Christians. My theology is definitely Reformed, having been shaped by past teachers like Saint Augustine, Martin Luther, John Calvin, and Jonathan Edwards, and contemporary teachers like R.C. Sproul, and John Piper whose preaching I am privileged to sit under. Though all of these men have influenced my doctrinal positions, no one should suppose that Part II of this book espouses their exact positions on any given topic. Since my chosen format limits me to about 600 words on a given topic, I encourage reader's to investigate the websites of Ligonier Ministries (R.C. Sproul) and Desiring God Ministries (John Piper) as well as Wayne Grudem's *Systematic Theology* to delve deeper into the topics addressed in Part II of this book.

21. Who is God?

This motley buck is like many of us, not very powerful and aware that there could be something much greater than us and possibly dangerous "up there." Of course the buck was not looking for God, and was relieved to discover a squirrel and not a hunter in the tree.

A careful reading of the Bible reveals that God exists in three persons (Trinity): the Father, the Son (Jesus), and the Holy Spirit. Each of these persons is fully God, but there is only one God. Each of the three persons is perfectly united in purpose, thought, and essence. God is multidimensional, being wholly comprised of each of His attributes, but not simply a collection of parts. In the final analysis God is humanly incomprehensible and we often describe his attributes as the antithesis of what we humanly do understand. For example, we have finite lifetimes but God is eternal, or we change continuously but God is immutable. The attributes of God are as follows:

- God is independent. He does not need us or the rest of creation for any reason. (Acts 17:24–25)
- God is immutable. He never changes. (Psalm 102:25–27)

- God is omnipresent. He is spiritually present at every point in the universe with his whole being. (Psalm 139:7–10)
- God is spirit. He is not made of matter like we are. (John 4:24)
- God is invisible. His total essence cannot be seen by us but he can reveal himself to us. (1 Timothy 6:16)
- God is omniscient. He knows everything from the past, present and future. (1 John 3:20; Matthew 6:8; Isaiah 46:9–10)
- God is wise. He always chooses what will bring the best results from his perspective. (Romans 11:33)
- God is truthful. He is the true God and standard of truth. (John 17:3)
- God is faithful. He always does what he says. (Numbers 23:19)
- God is good. He is the standard of goodness. (Luke 18:19)
- God is love. He eternally gives of himself to others. (1 John 4:8)
- God is merciful, gracious, and patient. (Psalm 103:8)
- God is holy. He is separated from sin, always seeking what brings him greatest glory. (Psalm 77:13)
- God is characterized by peace, not disorder. (Romans 15:33)
- God is righteous. He always acts in accordance with what is right and is the final standard of what is right. (Isaiah 45:19)
- God is jealous. He always acts to protect his honor. (Exodus 34:14)
- God is wrathful. He hates sin. (Romans 1:18)
- God is free to do whatever he wants. He is not constrained except by his other attributes, i.e. he cannot sin. (Psalm 115:3)
- God is omnipotent (sovereign). He has infinite power to do whatever he desires in conformance with his will. (Ephesians 3:20)
- God is in possession of a will which is the ultimate reason for everything that happens. (Ephesians 1:9–11)
- God is perfect. He has all the qualities he needs and lacks nothing. (Matthew 5:48)
- God is blessed. He is completely happy in himself. (1 Timothy 6:15)
- God is beautiful. He is the sum of all desirable qualities. (Psalm 27:4)
- God is glorious. He is worthy of everyone's highest praise and honor. (John 17:5)

22. Who is Jesus?

Jesus said to them, "Truly, truly, I say to you, before Abraham was, I am." John 8:58

Sometimes a doe's fawns from the previous year (yearlings) accompany a doe and her fawns from the current year. In this case the two pictured deer are probably brothers. Obviously, the yearly buck is older than the buck fawn so the yearling buck could say to the fawn, "Before you were, I was." But what Jesus says in John 8:58 is analogous to the fawn saying to the buck, "Before you were, I was. In fact I created deer and the entire universe because I am God!"

Our only reliable source of information about Jesus is revealed in the Bible. One of the best ways to learn about Jesus is to study what He says about himself, and in the Gospel of John Jesus makes seven "I am" statements about who He is. John 8:58 is not traditionally included in the list of "I am" sayings. In the traditional "I am" statements Jesus speaks metaphorically that he is the Messiah. But John 8:58 is as emphatic a statement as Jesus could have made to the Jews that he is the Messiah. He uses the repetitive "truly, truly" preface to his declaration which in Jewish literature is like the captain of a ship saying, "Now hear this." To get the full impact of John 8:58 we need to step back to understand the context in which the statement is made. The referenced text follows Jesus' proclamation that he is the light of the world. But the Jews did not put their trust in Jesus. Rather, they put their trust in being Abraham's descendants (8:33). Jesus retorts that if they were truly Abraham's children, they would not be trying to kill him (8:40). They respond that Jesus is an illegitimate child (8:41) to which Jesus replies that their father is not Abraham, but the devil (8:44). Despite Jesus' continual attempts to explain he is the long awaited Messiah, they do not understand and try insulting Jesus, suggesting he is a Samaritan (a despised offshoot of Judaism) and has a demon (8:48). Finally, they come to understand that Jesus claims to have seen Abraham who had died about 2,000 years before the conversation took place! Noting that Jesus cannot even be 50 (actually he is about 30!), they sarcastically say: "you have seen Abraham?" (8:57) Without batting an eye, Jesus replies, "Truly, truly, I say to you, before Abraham was, I am."

In the original Greek of John 8:58 "I am" is rendered *ego eimi*. The same phrase occurs in the Greek translation of the Old Testament (in use during Jesus' life on earth) in several messianic texts in Isaiah (41:4; 43:10, 13, 25; 46:4 and 48:12) and is translated as "I am he." *Ego eimi* is also used in the Greek translation of Exodus 3:13–14 where God tells Moses that God's name is "I am who I am" (*ego eimi ho on*). But this cannot be what John refers to or he would have used *ego eimi ho on*. It is more likely that he is quoting Isaiah in which "I am he" (*ego eimi*) must mean I am the same as God due to the context. In any event, the meaning is not missed by the Jews because they pick up stones to kill him since Jesus has committed blasphemy as reckoned by their unbelief. By saying he is the same as God he has committed a capital offense according to the Judaism of that era.

Things are not so different today since in some societies, you may be killed for saying Jesus is God. Yet, that is what all Christians are called to do regardless of the consequences, in some cases literally uniting Christians with Jesus' death and resurrection (Romans 6:5). To see who Jesus truly is, the following seven chapters will unpack each of the traditional "I am" (*ego eimi*) sayings: the bread of life; the light of the world; the door; the good shepherd; the resurrection and the life; the way, the truth, and the life; and the vine.

23. I am the Bread of Life

Scripture Reference: John 6:1–35

In John 6:1–14, Jesus fed 5,000 people with five barley loaves and two fish. Afterwards, the 12 apostles each picked up a basket of leftovers. The people recognized that a great miracle had taken place, so the next day they sought out Jesus hoping to be fed again. Jesus saw through their motivation. They were not seeking Jesus because they saw in the miracle the authenticating sign that he was the Son of God. Rather, they sought him as a source of free physical food. So Jesus said to them,

> *"Do not labor for the food that perishes, but for the food that endures to eternal life, which the Son of Man will give to you. For on him God the Father has set his seal." Then they said to him, "What must we do, to be doing the works of God?" Jesus answered them, "This is the work of God, that you believe in him whom he has sent." (John 6:27–29)*

In their unbelief they asked for a sign, being blind to the fact that they had already seen the sign in the miracle of feeding the five thousand. They reasoned that the miracle on the previous day was not such a big deal, since Moses had fed a nation with manna for 40 years in the wilderness (Exodus 16). Before they believed in Jesus they wanted some more evidence. So Jesus said to them,

> " Truly, truly, I say to you, it was not Moses who gave you the bread from heaven, but my Father gives you the true bread from heaven. For the bread of God is he who comes down from Heaven and gives life to the world." They said to him, "Sir, give us this bread always." Jesus said to them, "I am the bread of life; whoever comes to me shall not hunger, and whoever believes in me shall never thirst." (John 6:32–35)

What does Jesus mean when he says that he is the bread of life? The people did not understand that Jesus was speaking spiritually to them and they were thinking physically. They asked him to give them this bread always since they physically needed to be fed every day. But, Jesus says, whoever comes to him will never hunger and whoever believes in him will never thirst. Coming to Jesus (i.e. believing in Him) satiates the soul once and for all. That does not mean that the believer in Jesus does not continue to depend upon Jesus and have fellowship with him. What it does mean is that the essential emptiness in the unbelieving soul has had its hunger and thirst satisfied by the initial encounter of believing in Jesus. The ultimate consummation of the promise has to wait for heaven where *they shall hunger no more, neither thirst anymore* (Revelation 7:16). Many have taken this passage to be speaking of the Lord's Supper, but that is not the main point of the passage. Without getting into a detailed study of the different ways Christians understand the Lord's Supper (chapter 41), notice that it is those who **come** to Christ that do not hunger, not those who eat. Similarly, those who **believe** in him do not thirst, not those who drink!

The above picture is a parable for John 6:35. By early November the woods are a dead, dreary, brown place almost entirely void of green leaves. Before we believe in Jesus our souls are dead like the November woods. The green leaves of the buckthorn are highly desirable nourishment for the doe, just as Jesus is the bread of life for our dead souls. As the doe must come to the green leaves to live, so we must come to Jesus to have eternal life. May you come to Jesus and believe in him now!

24. I am the Light of the World

I am the light of the world. Whoever follows me will not walk in darkness, but will have the light of life. John 8:12b
As long as I am in the world, I am the light of the world. John 9:5

Twice Jesus says he is the light of the world. In John 8, the context is that the Pharisees (a conservative Jewish group) do not believe Jesus is who he says he is, the long awaited Messiah. Apart from the light of Jesus, the world is in spiritual darkness. One cannot see what is spiritually true except through the illumination Jesus provides. So everyone needs this light if they are to escape the darkness of this present fallen world and the "outer darkness" of hell (Matthew 8:12–30). But for the one who believes in Jesus there also awaits the glorious promise that in the new heaven and earth the light of Jesus will totally eliminate all darkness forever (Revelation 21:23). So Jesus is the light of the world now and forever.

In John 9, the statement is made just before he heals a man who was born blind. No sooner has the healing taken place then the Pharisees are incensed, because he healed the man on the Sabbath when Jews were not supposed to work, and the discussion quickly degenerated into justification for why they didn't believe Jesus was the Messiah.

In the first century, light was a highly prized commodity. Without electric lights to illuminate darkness, people struggled to safely find their way at night. When Jesus says he is the light of the world, he is addressing two fundamental issues: 1) his light leads and guides those who believe in him, so that they are not in peril stumbling around in the darkness of a sin-filled world; and 2) his light exposes the sin of unbelievers that is often shrouded under the cover of darkness, and at the same time blinds them to the truth of who Jesus really is. The episode in John 9 is particularly poignant. Jesus heals the blind man, so he can see physically, and despite his lack of education he believes (sees spiritually) that Jesus healed him. The highly educated Pharisees with good physical eyesight are, ironically, spiritually blind to who Jesus is by their repeated attempts to disprove the healing. Evil (metaphorical darkness) does not appreciate the illumination of "the light of the world" any more than the thief working under the cover of darkness appreciates the bright light of the policeman's flashlight.

A deer's retina is composed almost entirely of rods which enable it to see well at night. The downside is that a deer is easily blinded by looking into bright light. The buck in the picture is a parable of the Pharisees. My encounter with him is described in chapter 111. For now, it is sufficient to know the buck must look into the sun to see me. Closing his blinded eye on the sunlit side of his face, he used his shaded eye to discern if I was a serious threat. Since the wind was blowing from him to me, he could not pick up my scent and wetted his nostril with his tongue to improve his sense of smell. He was the proverbial deer in the headlights, blinded by the bright light of the sun and unable to comprehend the peril he would have faced had I been armed with a weapon, not a camera. The Pharisees were like deer in the headlights. Their eyes were adjusted to spiritual darkness and were blinded by the light of the Son. As a result they closed their spiritual eyes and could not see who Jesus was. As a deer blinded by the headlights of an oncoming truck is in danger of physical death, so the blinded Pharisees were in danger of eternal spiritual death. On the other hand, Jesus is a guiding light through the perils of this dark, sin-filled world for those who do believe in him. Do not close your eyes to the *"light of the world."* Believe in Him so that you are not overcome by the darkness (John 1:5).

25. I am the Door

"Truly, truly, I say to you, I am the door of the sheep. All who came before me are thieves and robbers, but the sheep did not listen to them. I am the door. If anyone enters by me, he will be saved and will go in and out and find pasture. The thief comes only to steal and kill and destroy. I came that they may have life and have it abundantly." John 10:7–10

Doors do two things: they control authorized access and egress and they provide protection for those behind them. In ancient Israel sheep were placed in a secure enclosure at night to protect them from marauding predators and thieves. There was only one door and the shepherd stood guard by it. Sometimes several shepherds used the same enclosure but their sheep only followed the voice of their shepherd as he led them through the door into the enclosure at night and out of the enclosure in the morning. Only authorized sheep could enter and exit the enclosure and once in they were protected from harm. But all physical doors are imperfect and do not necessarily provide access only to those who are lawfully allowed entry.

Similarly, physical doors do not necessarily keep the "bad guys" at bay. No matter how impregnable a structure may appear, thieves will eventually figure out how to open the bank vault to steal, criminals will escape from jail and terrorists will eventually break down the door and kill the vulnerable, innocent "sheep" behind it. By analogy, Jesus is the door because he is the only way out of this sinful world into heaven for those authorized entry, i.e. Christians. Jesus is also the Christian's protector against the forces of evil that try to lead them astray from saving faith in Christ alone. Thus, Jesus fulfills both functions of doors just like the door to the sheep enclosure.

At a second and perhaps more profound level, the statement, "I am the door" harkens back to Exodus 12. This passage describes the first Passover, in which the LORD killed all the first-born in Egypt *except* that he "*passed over*" the houses of those protected by the blood of the Passover lambs. God had instructed the Jewish people through Moses to have each family kill a lamb at twilight outside their door and place blood from the lamb on the lintel and door posts, and then go into their house and close their door until morning. When the LORD saw the blood around a door, the LORD passed over that house. The blood on the door foreshadows where Jesus would bleed on the cross: from the crown of thorns on his head (lintel), his nail pierced hands (door posts) and the nails through his feet (blood at the foot of the door where the Passover lamb was killed). As a result, Jesus is the access to safety and protection for those who trust in His blood, keeping them safe from the wrath of God, just as the Passover lamb's blood on Jewish doors saved the nation of Israel from God's wrath against sin on the first Passover.

The trees in this picture remind me of the homemade barn door my father had constructed. It was made of individual vertical boards and framed by two door posts and two horizontal rails. A diagonal board held the assembly square. This magnificent buck peers out from behind a parable of my childhood memory of our barn door, suggested by the two mostly vertical trees and the third diagonal tree. But with leaning door posts and without horizontal rails or solid vertical boards, this "door" does not restrict the buck's access to the doe he is watching, since he could easily leap over the diagonal tree. Similarly, this dilapidated "door" would offer the buck pathetically inadequate protection from a hunter. Only Jesus and his shed blood on the cross is the perfect door that absolutely provides both access to heaven and infinite protection from God's holy wrath against sin for all who by faith alone trust in Christ alone for their eternal salvation.

26. I am the Good Shepherd

"I am the good shepherd. The good shepherd lays down his life for the sheep. He who is the hired hand and not a shepherd, who does not own the sheep, sees the wolf coming and leaves the sheep and flees, and the wolf snatches them and scatters them. He flees because he is a hired hand and cares nothing for the sheep. I am the good shepherd. I know my own and my own know me, just as the Father knows me and I know the Father; and I lay down my life for the sheep. And I have other sheep that are not of this fold. I must bring them also, and they will listen to my voice. So there will be one flock, one shepherd. For this reason the Father loves me, because I lay down my life that I may take it up again. No one takes it from me, but I lay it down of my own accord. I have authority to lay it down, and I have authority to take it up again. This charge I have received from my Father." John 10:11–18

In the world of deer, the doe is the good shepherd, tenderly leading her fawns, often calling to them with soft grunts. The fawns will only follow their doe and the doe will only accept her fawns. Newborn fawns have little scent and a doe may try to lead a predator away from her hidden fawns (apparently intending to sacrifice her life for theirs).

Jesus says he is the good shepherd who lays down his life for the sheep, contrasting himself with a shepherd who is hired to watch over the sheep. It would seem that a good shepherd wouldn't flee when the wolf comes. Without a doubt there were instances in real life shepherding when a man was killed defending the sheep from a wild animal or a thief. One might suppose this would be a good shepherd who defended the sheep to the death. But, what "good" would that be? Such a shepherd performed his duty honorably, but maybe not wisely. Is a literal sheep worth a human life? Can a dead shepherd protect his sheep? The net result is the shepherd is dead and the wolf has his pick of the sheep for dinner. But this cannot be what Jesus means by "good." Jesus does not merely die defending his sheep, but is saying something very different. He is good in a noble, altruistic sense. He does not lose his life in a vain attempt at defending the sheep, rather he gives his life in place of the lives of the sheep and his death satisfies the wrath rightfully due the sheep.

A literal shepherd who does not own the sheep may flee, because he does not really care about the sheep. But Jesus not only cares for his sheep, he knows them, and they know Jesus with the same intimacy as the Father knows Jesus and Jesus knows the Father. The sheep belong to Jesus. Jesus owns the sheep. He does not own every sheep, but only certain sheep for which he lays down his life. While Jesus' death is of sufficient worth to satisfy the Father's wrath for every sin of every person who ever lived, it is only effective for a select group of the sheep (Jesus' "own," called the "elect" or the children of God in the Bible). People often see this as unfair, that all are not saved from the wrath of the Father, but it is very fair. God gives mercy to the elect (using the infinite worth of the death of Christ to pay for their sins) and justice to everyone else (allowing them to suffer the consequences of their own sins in hell). All of the elect from every people group on the earth hear his voice making up one great flock of sheep with Jesus as their shepherd. Not only does he lay his life down, but he takes it up (resurrection) as proof that he is in complete control. He is not killed against his or the Father's will but in fulfillment of their combined will. I know this is a difficult concept but much more will be said about it as we proceed through the rest of the book.

27. I am the Resurrection and the Life

Where the tree falls, there it will lie Ecclesiastes 11:3 *Jesus said to her, "I am the resurrection and the life. Whoever believes in me, though he die, yet shall he live, and everyone who lives and believes in me shall never die. Do you believe this?" She said to him, "Yes, Lord; I believe that you are the Christ, the Son of God, who is coming into the world."* John 11:25–27

A week after this picture was taken an arrow rendered this buck as dead as the fallen trees behind him. In our experience, he could not live again any more than the rotting, fallen trees could stand erect with green leaves! But the Bible says a person can die and live again, not metaphorically living in people's memories, genes, or recycled elements from their body, but literally living physically forever.

In John 11 we read the story of Lazarus, the brother of Mary and Martha. Jesus, knew Lazarus was seriously ill, but did not immediately go to him despite the fact that he loved Lazarus and his sisters (John 11:5). Instead Jesus waited until Lazarus had died and had been buried four days.

Once Jesus arrived on the scene, he engaged Martha in conversation and she expressed her faith in the resurrection of the dead, a common Jewish belief. In this context Jesus proclaims, *"I am the resurrection and the life."* Then Jesus asks the ultimate question, "Do you believe this?" Martha says yes, but her belief is limited to the Jewish understanding of a resurrection that will occur at the end of time. She does not grasp that Jesus will restore Lazarus to life immediately. However, despite not understanding what Jesus is about to do, Martha proclaims that Jesus is the long awaited Messiah who will save his people. He is the Son of God (John 11:27).

Against this backdrop looms an obvious thought that both Martha and Mary expressed before Lazarus is restored to life. *"Lord if you had been here, my brother would not have died."* (John 11:21, 32) Their faith in Jesus is great, but why did he not come right away and heal Lazarus so that he did not die? The answer was given previously in John 11:4, *"It is for the glory of God, so that the Son of God may be glorified through it."* Healing Lazarus would not have been spectacular enough. There was a rabbinic belief that the soul of a deceased person hovered over the body for three days intending to reenter it. But after three days decomposition had begun and death was irreversible. Therefore, Jesus waited four days to make it clear when he said, *"Lazarus come out."* and Lazarus came out of the tomb alive (John 11:43–44) that Jesus had performed a great miracle, attesting to his deity and the truth of his claims. (Note: Jesus did not technically resurrect Lazarus since Lazarus was only restored to life in a fallen state from which he would die, physically, a second time.)

So what exactly does it mean that Jesus is the resurrection and the life? Resurrection in this verse refers to the resurrection of the bodies of dead believers following the second coming. Life refers to God's eternal life, wrought by God within the souls of Christians. This passage does not mean that Christians will not die physically, but rather when they die physically, their souls continue to live with Jesus. Furthermore, though believers die physically, they do not remain physically dead forever. At the end of history they will be physically resurrected with perfectly functioning bodies and united with their souls to live, eternally, with Jesus.

What about you? Do you believe like Martha that Jesus truly is the Messiah, the Son of God?

28. I am the Way, the Truth, and the Life

Jesus said to him, "I am the way, and the truth, and the life. No one comes to the Father except through me." John 14:6

Nose to the snow, this eager buck persistently tracked a doe, who only moments earlier had dashed by my blind. Deer do not have eternal life. The only way to maintain a population of wild deer is through reproduction. Every fall a ritual is played out thousands of times as bucks patiently follow does waiting for just the right time for fertilization to result from mating. There are no other viable alternatives such as artificial insemination or cloning for fawns to be born. No knowledgeable person seriously doubts that the only way to life for a deer is exclusively through sexual reproduction. By analogy, the Bible says there is only one way to be "born again" to eternal life with God. It is exclusively through faith in Jesus Christ. At this the world chafes, desperately seeking other ways such as good deeds, painstaking adherence to man-made rules, hocus-pocus rituals or hoping that God doesn't exist at all. But the Bible says God does exist and Jesus is the only way to God.

The context of John 14:6 is that Jesus is going away and the disciples cannot come with him. To comfort them, Jesus declares, "In my Father's house are many rooms." (John 14:2) Jesus will go and prepare a place for them and then come back for them. When he tells them they know the way to where he is going, Thomas confesses they do not know the way. Jesus responds with John 14:6. The way to God is not by imitating Jesus, or following him as a leader as the buck follows the doe. Jesus is the only way to God because he is the truth of God, clothed in flesh, not merely spirit, so physical humans can see what God is like (John 1:14). God is self existent while humans are created beings dependent upon God for their temporal lives. However, Jesus is part of the triune God having life in himself, i.e., Jesus is eternal like the father (John 5:26). Since Jesus is the truth and the life he is "*the way*" for others to come to God.

Then Jesus drops a bombshell that is perhaps the most offensive statement possible to the 21st century secular mind. *"No one comes to the Father except through me."* If Jesus had said he is a way to God that would be fine with most people in our modern pluralistic world. Then, Christianity would be a way to God just as Judaism, Islam, Buddhism, Hinduism, Jehovah's Witness, Mormonism, or a host of other "isms" that claim to be the way to God. But Jesus doesn't say that he is a way to God, rather he is *the* way to God. There is no other way. This exclusive statement is the hallmark of Christianity. You cannot get to God by accomplishing more good deeds than your sins, religiously following man-made rules, appeasing God with sacrifices, or participating in perfectly performed religious rituals. You can only get to God, and, hence, have the eternal life that Jesus gives, by faith in Jesus alone as the one who satisfied the wrath of God against your sins. God placed the sins of all who would ever believe in Jesus upon Him on the cross to pay the penalty for their sins. At the same time, God credited to their account Jesus' sinless life. The great rediscovery of the Reformation was that salvation is by faith alone, in Christ alone, by grace alone. We are not saved by faith in Christ plus works, but only by faith in Christ, and that is purely the result of God's grace. We cannot come to faith ourselves. Good works are only the result of being a Christian, not the cause of becoming a Christian (Ephesians 2:8–10). The Bible says this is truth. It is neither arrogance nor ignorance to believe it, though it is arrogance and ignorance to think that humans know other or better ways to God. Our only response to such good news must be worship!

29. I am the Vine

"I am the true vine, and my Father is the vine dresser. Every branch of mine that does not bear fruit he takes away, and every branch that does bear fruit he prunes, that it may bear more fruit… I am the vine; you are the branches. Whoever abides in me and I in him, he it is that bears much fruit, for apart from me you can do nothing."
John 15:1–2, 5

The "I am" statements of Jesus culminate with John 15:1 and 5. Vineyards are used as analogies throughout the Bible, usually as an image for the nation of Israel in the context of not being as fruitful as God's chosen people should be. Like all of the "I am" statements, Jesus says he is *"I AM,"* the true vine, God clothed in human flesh. He is the fulfillment of what Israel pointed toward, not what it was. The Father is the vine dresser pruning the vines so that they may produce more fruit. This pruning is two fold: 1) branches that produce no fruit are cut away; 2) those that bear fruit are pruned to stimulate more growth and fruit production. This horticultural metaphor is easily understood in the context of first or twenty-first century agriculture. By analogy, anyone who claims to be a Christian, but does not produce fruit is not a true believer and ultimately will be cut off by the Father. Jesus' true followers will always produce fruit, but the Father still prunes them to stimulate even more fruit production. Just as too much branching on a grape vine saps the vines energy and reduces the vine's fruit production, so Christians who are overly involved in many activities may need to be pruned to focus on only a few ministries to be really fruitful. Notice that pruning is a painful process, but it is out of adversity that strength of faith arises. Hence, Jesus does not promise the health-wealth gospel of certain TV evangelists, but rather a life not spared from adversity. It is this adversity that causes the Christian to produce "fruit of the Spirit": love, joy, peace patience, kindness, goodness, faithfulness, gentleness, self-control (Galatians 5:22).

In John 15:1–5, Jesus repeats that he is the vine and his followers (Christians) are the branches. The branches derive their life from the vine (it is the shed blood of Christ that enables their eternal life) and the vine (Jesus) produces its fruit through the branches (good works of believers). If the vine is cut off, the branches will die. True believers abide in Jesus, because Jesus (via the Holy Spirit) is the believer's "life blood" that enables them to be fruitful. All their good works (fruit) are a result of the life of Jesus' Spirit within them.

The fuzzy antlers on this mule deer buck are covered by skin, called "velvet" that looks and feels exactly like velvet cloth. The velvet contains a network of blood vessels that deposit bone salts to form the antlers. Antlers are one of the fastest known forms of tissue growth. During the process calcium from the buck's diet and skeleton are utilized to produce the antlers. Biologists reckon that the nutrient drain on a buck to produce a large set of antlers is as great as the drain on a doe to produce twin fawns. By late summer the growth is complete and the buck rubs off the velvet in a day or less to expose his bone-hard rack. The parable is that a buck's antlers (branches) derive their growth from the buck (the vine) through his blood. If the buck's diet is inadequate, the rack will not grow and be useless for the fall skirmishes that determine which buck will sire the next generation (fruit). Each winter the rack is shed (pruned) so that a larger rack can grow the next year to enable the buck to be more competitive in determining breeding rights so that he can produce even more fruit (offspring). So, the same principle applies to antlers and the Christian life: increased fruit results from pruning and the "blood of the vine."

30. The Trinity

Go therefore and make disciples of all nations, baptizing them in the name of the Father and of the Son and of the Holy Spirit. Matthew 28:19

   The doctrine of the Trinity (the word is not included in the Bible) is progressively revealed in Scripture. Genesis 1:26 says *Then God said, Let us make man in our image.* This shows that God is somehow plural (our). Specific statements in Matthew 28:19 and other New Testament passages state that there is a Father, a Son and a Holy Spirit. People sometimes say that the Trinity is a logical contradiction. But this is untrue though it is a mystery, in that we do not fully understand it. By definition, a logical contradiction requires something to be A and not A at the same time and in the same relationship. In its simplest definition the Trinity can be summarized as there is one God existing in three co-equal and co-eternal persons (Father, Son and Holy Spirit) with each person being fully God. Since this is not an "A" not "A" statement, the Trinity is not a contradiction.
   Our finite minds cannot fully comprehend the Trinity so theologians

have tried to place boundaries on the doctrine to avoid misunderstanding among Christians. The three biggest errors surrounding the Trinity have been: *Tritheism* (there are three Gods); *Modalism* (there is one person who appears to us in three different forms or modes); and *Arianism* (only the Father is eternal having created the Son before the Holy Spirit or anything existed). The Council of Nicaea in A.D. 325 refuted all of these heresies in the Nicene Creed. Another major class of errors about the Trinity arose as to the nature of Jesus. These misunderstandings were clarified at the Council of Chalcedon in A.D. 451: namely that Jesus is one person with two natures, being fully man and fully God without any mixture, confusion, separation or division of the two natures. This also is not a contradiction since Jesus is fully God and fully man. If he were God and not God, that would be a contradiction.

Each person in the Trinity has different primary functions. In Creation, God the Father spoke the Creation into being with the *"and God said, 'Let there be"* statements (Genesis 1:3, 6, 9, 11, 14, 20, 24). God the Son carried out the decrees: *All things were made through him, and without him was not anything made that was made* (John 1:3). God the Holy Spirit was present at Creation. *And the Spirit of God was hovering over face of the waters* (Genesis 1:2b). In redemption God the Father designed the plan and sent his Son (Ephesians 1:9–10; John 3:16). God the Son obeyed the Father (John 6:38–40), dying in place of all who trust in Him for salvation (Romans 5:6–10). God the Holy Spirit was sent by the Father and the Son after Jesus returned to heaven (John 14:26; 16:7). God the Holy Spirit completed the work planned by the Father and begun by the Son, causing the elect to be born again (John 3:5–8), sanctified (Romans 15:16), and empowered for service (Acts1:18).

Despite all the parables in Scripture to show us what God is like, there are no parables about the Trinity nor has anyone, to my knowledge, ever put forth a usable parable for the Trinity. The picture hints at some Trinitarian aspects in that the doe and her two fawns are three individuals with the same nature, each enjoying intimate fellowship with one another, and fulfilling different roles as they look for danger in all directions. Do not think that in any way this is an image of the triune Godhead in violation of the Second Commandment, and do not read any more meaning into this picture (like God is she not He) than a feeble attempt to at least have a picture for this chapter.

31. Prayer

Pray then like this: "Our Father in Heaven, hallowed be your name. Your Kingdom come, your will be done, on earth as it is in heaven. Give us this day our daily bread, and forgive us our debts, as we also have forgiven our debtors. And lead us not into temptation, but deliver us from evil." Matthew 6:9–13

Perhaps the most common and beloved Christian prayer is the Lord's Prayer from the Sermon on the Mount (Matthew 6:9-13). The Lord's Prayer is a model for our prayers. It begins by addressing God the Father using the normal word for the father in a family thus, making the prayer very intimate. It is a petition for God and us to keep God's name holy. *Your kingdom come*...asks for the sovereign reign of God to be consummated on earth (Kingdom of God) just as it is in heaven. *Give us this day*...asks for our physical needs this day. Notice it does not ask for windfall provision, but assumes that we trust God to provide each day what we need. *Forgive us our debts*...means help us to forgive others as we have been forgiven by God. *And lead us not into temptation...* Christians pray this way because they do not trust in themselves but in God. God may test us, but he will not allow us to be tempted beyond our ability to resist (1 Corinthians 10:13). Finally, Jesus teaches in John 14:13–14 that we are to ask of the Father in Jesus' name. Jesus is the intercessor to the Father on our behalf. Hence, Protestants usually end each prayer with the phrase, "in Jesus' name."

Prayer is a two way communication between God and believers: God speaks to believers through the Bible, and believers speak with God through prayer. ACTS is a popular acronym for Adoration, Contrition, Thanksgiving and Supplication which are the components that should be included in our prayers. Adoration includes praise, and contrition includes confession of sin and a request for forgiveness. Supplications are either petitions (person praying makes their requests to God) or intercession (person praying presents the needs of others to God). Prayers may be standardized and recited from memory (more common among Roman Catholics), or composed, aided by the Holy Spirit, as the person prays (more common among Protestants). God answers every prayer yes, no, or maybe later, so we may have to persevere in our prayers for extended periods of time. But God always acts in our best interest (Romans 8:28). When we do not get what we ask for, it is because it is not the best thing for us.

In 2008, I glimpsed a huge, heavy beamed buck with an urn shaped rack, but wasn't able to photograph him. The following prayer shows how I often used ACTS in 2009 to pray before entering the woods.

Father, I praise you that you know the location of every deer that ever was, is, or will be, at every moment in time past, present or future. It seems good to me that you would bring to me the heavy beamed buck I saw last year. I can do nothing to cause this deer to come to me and apart from you it is impossible to photograph this buck, but for you to bring him to me is easy if it be your will. Forgive me of my sins of thinking yesterday's or today's success has anything to do with me. Give me the skill I need to capitalize on every opportunity you give me. Grant that my camera would work flawlessly. I pray it would please you to allow me to take excellent photographs of this buck. But whether I photograph no deer or ten trophy bucks, to you be all the glory. In Jesus' name I pray. Amen.

ACTS is not a magic formula, but I believe God answered this prayer, enabling me to photograph this magnificent buck four times in 2009.

32. Roman Catholicism Part 1: Authority

All Scripture is breathed out by God and profitable for teaching, for reproof, for correction, and for training in righteousness, that the man of God may be competent, equipped for every good work. 2 Timothy 3:16

So far our study of doctrine has not uncovered any major disagreements between Roman Catholics and Protestants, but before proceeding further it will be useful to explore the Catholic doctrinal distinctions on authority, salvation, and sacraments that were the flash points for the Reformation. We will begin with authority, meaning: *where does one find the answers to religious questions?*

Deer have two authority sources for their safety questions. 1) A doe teaches her fawns a basic understanding of what is harmful and what is not. Her example of being ever vigilant, like the pictured doe, will keep them safe in the hostile world they inhabit. 2) As adults, this experiential learning coupled with a God-given, innate instinct, leads them through the trials and tribulations of their life. Christians find their answers to their eternal safety in the Scriptures according to 2 Timothy 3:16. But is this the only source? Is there also a second, human-based source under the guidance of the Holy Spirit? This question was perhaps the biggest point of contention between Protestants and Catholics that lead to the Reformation.

For centuries, Catholicism taught there were two sources of authority, the Bible and tradition. Tradition had been elevated to a position of authority because not everything Jesus said and did was included in the New Testament. The Apostles had told other stories about Jesus' ministry, and these stories had been passed on from generation to generation of church leaders with a pseudo-authority. In addition, Jesus promised the Holy Spirit would guide the church (John 16:13), so Catholics reasoned that decisions of church counsels, writings of prominent theologians and papal decrees were also authoritative.

Luther agreed some traditions were accurate summaries of biblical teaching, but they were not an independent authority. He argued that since the Bible was written under the guidance of the Holy Spirit by the Apostles, who were eyewitnesses of Jesus' ministry, it was a superior authority to traditions. Therefore, truth was simply a matter of biblical interpretation. In Luther's opinion every text had only one true meaning (but many applications), and the interpretation of difficult texts had to square with the meaning of the clearest, most unambiguous texts. To Luther, the clearest biblical message was that salvation was by grace alone, through faith alone, in Christ alone. Through this interpretive lens, he defined basic Protestant theology. When the Holy Roman Emperor, Charles V asked him to recant all of his writings, Luther's famous answer, before the Diet of Worms* in 1521, became the Protestant manifesto that Scripture, interpreted by reason and conscience, was the only legitimate authority.

"Unless I am convinced by the testimony of the Scriptures or by clear reason (for I do not trust either in the Pope or councils, alone since it is well known that they have erred and contradicted themselves), I am bound by the Scriptures I have quoted and my conscience is captive to the Word of God. I cannot and will not retract anything, since it is neither safe nor right to go against conscience. Here I stand. I cannot do otherwise. May God help me. Amen."

*The Holy Roman Empire's legislative body was called the Diet and rotated its meeting place between several cities. In 1521 it met in the German city of Worms.

33. Roman Catholicism Part 2: Salvation

For by grace you have been saved through faith. And this is not your own doing; it is the gift of God, not a result of works, so that no one may boast. Ephesians 2:8–9

Deer have no souls to save spiritually, but a deer is regularly saved from physical danger by either avoiding it, escaping detection by the threatening creature, and as a last resort, fleeing to safety. The greatest danger humans face is eternity in hell as a consequence of their sin. Except for Jesus, no human can perfectly avoid sin, and given God's omniscience, no human can escape God's detection of their sin. Protestants believe we can flee to everlasting safety from God's wrath against sin by grace enabled faith in the perfect protection of Jesus' shed blood on the cross. Is it really this simple?

Prior to the Reformation, there were three competing Roman Catholic views of salvation (how one gets to heaven): 1) Each person has a divine spark that the individual has to fan into flames of love to obtain salvation; 2) A person receives grace at baptism. By cooperating with this grace, more grace is earned. This repetitive cycle of cooperating with grace which earns more grace to be cooperated with eventually earns the person salvation; 3) The process of salvation begins with a person's own, self-generated, moral effort. The moral effort earns grace that allows more moral effort leading to more grace, and so on until eventually salvation is earned.

All of these views had two things in common: 1) they all required human effort or works that eventually earned salvation; 2) the human effort had to initiate the salvation either through baptism or the moral effort of the person receiving the eventual salvation.

Luther had a much simpler idea. Using texts like Ephesians 2:8–9 he said salvation was a free gift of God, who by grace enabled faith in the person *receiving* (not earning) salvation. The saved individual contributed nothing of their own effort (works) to earn the salvation. The result is that there is no room for boasting and pride but only gratitude that God saved them. In chapters 45–56 we will delve much more deeply into the intricacies of how this works. For now notice only that the most straight forward reading of Ephesians 2:8–9 torpedoes all three Catholic positions because it says unequivocally that "it is not your own doing." No works are involved.

The reformers position on salvation is often referred to as the five *solas* (meaning alone in Latin).

1. *sola scriptura* (Scripture alone) Scripture is the only basis for authority. Catholics disagree by adding traditions.
2. *sola gratia*: (grace alone) Catholics disagree since they see grace arising through baptism and works (i.e. human merit).
3. *sola fide* (faith alone) Catholics cannot agree since sacraments and works are eliminated.
4. *Solo Christo* (Christ alone). Catholics include works and the mediation of Mary, other Saints, and the Church.
5. *Soli Deo gloria* (Glory to God alone)

So the Protestant position on salvation can be summed up as follows: The Bible provides the only source of information that is completely reliable on religious questions. With respect to salvation, the Bible teaches that we are saved by grace alone through faith alone in Christ alone. To God alone be all the glory.

34. Roman Catholicism Part 3: Sacraments

Go therefore and make disciples of all nations, baptizing them in the name of the Father and of the Son and of the Holy Spirit. Matthew 28:19 *Do this in remembrance of me.* Luke 22:19b

      Deer tracks in the mud are a visible sign of an invisible deer. Muddy tracks do give us some understanding of the deer that made them (a doe and a fawn in this case) but they do not give us the pleasure we get from actually seeing the deer. Similarly, a sacrament is a visible sign of an invisible grace. Augustine described a sacrament as a visible promise. The idea is that God is far beyond our ability to understand. So God has established physical signs to illustrate his promises and hence comfort us and strengthen our faith in those promises. For example, in baptism the washing of the body reminds us of God forgiving our sin by washing away our guilt. The Lord's Supper reminds us that just as food and drink nourish us physically, Christ also nourishes us spiritually. But in all cases the sacrament is only a foretaste of experiencing the actual promises of being free of sin and fellowshipping in heaven with Jesus.

Protestants believe Jesus commanded only two sacraments: baptism in Matthew 28:18; and the Lord's Supper in Luke 22:19. Catholics also recognize both baptism and the Eucharist as sacraments, but they do not agree with the Protestant understanding of either. In the 13th century Catholics decided on seven sacraments, one for each of the seven deadly sins. Protestants have historically rejected the other five Catholic sacraments for the following reasons.

1. *Penance* or confession was initially accepted by Luther. But he soon realized that while James 5 says we should confess sins to one another, it does not require an enumeration of every sin (impossible because of the pervasiveness of sin), or require that the confession be made to a priest. Most importantly, Roman Catholicism elevates penance to a necessary work for salvation which means that Christ's work on the cross is somehow inadequate for salvation to be *sola gratia* and *sola fide*. To Protestants this is tantamount to blasphemy. Without a clear command from Christ penance was rejected.

2. *Confirmation* was a good idea according to Luther, but it was not commanded by Christ so he rejected it as a sacrament

3. *Marriage* is a model of Christ's relationship with the church (Ephesians 5), but it is not commanded by Jesus. 1 Corinthians 7 says it's better to not be married, and Jesus was not married. Marriage is common in all cultures and not uniquely Christian, so there are several reasons it was rejected as a sacrament

4. *Holy Orders* or ordination has been considered by nearly all Protestants to be a good idea but not a sacrament. Again the reason is that there is no command in Scripture to do it or any example of how to do it. A second reason is that the reformers didn't want anything like a priest to appear to stand between believers and God, citing 1 Peter 2:9 that all believers are priests and do not need any intermediary except for Jesus.

5. *Extreme unction* or last rites was never commanded by Christ. James 5:14–15 does say we should call for the elders to pray for us when we are sick and anoint us with oil, but there is no implication in James that it is reserved for the deathbed but rather that it is the normal thing to do when we are sick. In actual practice extreme unction is used by Catholics as a final work of salvation prior to death and therefore must be rejected as a sacrament for the same reasons as penance.

35. Roman Catholic Reforms

If possible, so far as it depends on you, live peaceably with all. Romans 12:18 *But as for you, teach what accords with sound doctrine.* Titus 2:1

Generally, bucks can peacefully coexist with one another. But the important implications of the rut cause frequent sparring matches with one another to establish dominance. Similarly, a tension exists within Christianity to be tolerant and promote harmony regarding minor differences and yet vigorously defend major doctrinal positions. The reform of Roman Catholicism continued the struggle for dominance between the Pope and Protestants, the Pope and the Holy Roman Emperor, and added the conflict between Catholics over post-Reformation Roman Catholic doctrine.

In 1534 the reform minded Paul III became Pope and established a commission to investigate abuses within the church. The commission's report was finished in 1537. It summarized widespread abuses within the church and laid the blame squarely on the papacy. Amazingly, Paul III took no action on the report's findings. By 1538 the supposedly confidential report had been printed in German with a preface by Luther! Undaunted, Paul III tried to negotiate a settlement with a series of meetings between Protestant and Catholic leaders in 1540–41. This made it clear to everyone that negotiation could not resolve the issues. So in 1542 Paul III took two decisive actions by beginning the Roman Inquisition to eliminate Protestantism in Rome, and calling for a church council to reform Catholicism. Paul III wanted to meet in Rome but Charles V wanted to meet in Germany. They settled on Trent in northern Italy. The resulting Council of Trent, met on and off from 1545–1563. Paul III wanted to focus on condemning Protestantism, but Charles V wanted to focus on abuses. They compromised, alternately addressing doctrine and abuse issues.

The Council of Trent was a watershed for Roman Catholicism. Bishops were made responsible for the souls in their diocese. They had to preach, establish seminaries, ordain priests, and assure priests preached in their churches. Every three years they had to call synods to deal with disciplinary action. This significantly reduced abuses and guaranteed consistency in doctrine and teaching. Catholic doctrine was more clearly defined to eliminate alternate views, and the Council of Trent officially separated Catholicism from Protestantism by declaring: tradition and Scripture were equal sources of authority; original sin no longer affected a person following baptism; justification was by faith and works; and there are seven sacraments.

Following Trent there have been two additional Roman Catholic Church councils. Vatican I (1868–1870) reaffirmed the doctrines of Trent and officially declared the infallibility of the Pope when he speaks *ex cathedra* i.e. as the shepherd and teacher of all Christians or defines a doctrine concerning faith or morals to be held by the whole church. Vatican II (1962–1965) initiated several significant changes including lay participation in the liturgy and encouragement for Catholics to read and study the Bible. Following Vatican II, mass was allowed to be said in the vernacular. Finally, Vatican II expressed a desire to reconcile with Protestants in ecumenical worship. Though conservative Protestants and Catholics have much in common, their significant doctrinal differences make it unlikely that these efforts will be more successful than Paul III. However, liberal Protestants have shown some openness to unite with Catholics. These unions have been essentially limited to social action since liberal Protestants reject much of true Christian doctrine that Roman Catholicism affirms.

36. Faith and Works

For by grace you have been saved through faith. And this is not your own doing; it is the gift of God, not a result of works, so that no one may boast. For we are his workmanship, created in Christ Jesus for good works, which God prepared beforehand, that we should walk in them." Ephesians 2:8–10

Before auto-focus and image stabilized lenses, I used a manual-focused film camera. The camera was mounted on a tripod making it very hard to escape detection as I operated it. On a cold, snow-dusted, November morning this buck and doe "froze" almost perfectly for this two-second exposure. If you look closely you can see the top line of the doe's face through the buck's blurred, right ear as the buck flipped his ear back and forth in an attempt to discern if I was a threat. Ephesians 2:8–10 teaches I did not earn any part of my salvation by doing good works like taking technically difficult pictures of deer and turning them into a book glorifying God. Rather, God ordained that I be saved by grace through faith, sovereignly enabling me to take the pictures and write this book as a good work for His glory. To see this, two key questions must be addressed.

Are Christians saved by faith alone, works alone, or faith and works? It is surprising that this should even be a question, given the clear answer in the referenced passage. Nevertheless, Judaism has understood that salvation is by works through the perfect keeping of the Law (moral and ceremonial) and Roman Catholics believe salvation is a combination of faith and works. The great rediscovery of Martin Luther and the other reformers is that the New Testament teaches that salvation is by faith alone, through grace alone, in Christ alone. The relationship of faith and works is that our good works *result* from saving faith, not that our good works and faith are *required* for salvation. An important distinction is that a particular work of charity, such as feeding the hungry, can be done by believers or unbelievers. The difference is that when the work is done out of a desire to be obedient to the teachings of Christ and for the glory of God it is a good work, but when it is done by an unbeliever for any other reason, it is not reckoned by God as a good work (Matthew 6:1–4). However, salvation always has been by perfect adherence to the moral law. But no human except for Jesus has ever perfectly kept the moral law. So, Christians are saved by their grace-enabled faith in Jesus who perfectly kept God's moral law. God counts Jesus' sinless life as their righteousness and punishes Jesus on the cross for their sin.

Is salvation by works in the Old Testament and by faith in the New Testament? In Romans 4 Paul argues that Abram (later Abraham) was saved by faith: *And he believed the LORD, and he counted it to him as righteousness."* (Genesis 15:6) This was before the covenant of circumcision (Genesis 17) and before the aborted sacrifice of Isaac (Genesis 22) when God tested Abraham to see if his faith was true. Sometimes Christians are confused by James 2:14: *What good is it, my brothers, if someone says he has faith but does not have works? Can that faith save him?* James is not arguing that good works bring about salvation. Rather, he says they are evidence of salvation. James appeals to Genesis 22 to show that Abraham's works demonstrated his faith, while Paul appeals to Genesis 15 to show Abraham's salvation arose from believing God. Paul shows that salvation has always been by faith. But we cannot know another person's heart to see if their faith is true, so James says if someone claims to have faith and doesn't have good works, they are not saved. Ephesians 2:8–10 concisely summarizes the teaching that salvation is by faith alone, in Christ alone, by grace alone, and that the believer's good works are also God's gracious doing.

37. Regeneration and Conversion

But when the goodness and loving kindness of God our Savior appeared, he saved us, not because of works done by us in righteousness, but according to his own mercy by the washing of regeneration and renewal of the Holy Spirit, whom he poured out richly through Jesus Christ our Savior, Titus 3:4-6

The two does approached each other with laid back ears, indicating their anger towards each other as enemies. The left doe put her ears forward and stretched out her neck to touch noses with the right doe (ears still laid back representing an unbeliever, hostile to God). Somehow the right doe's attitude was changed by this gesture for suddenly the right doe's ears came forward indicating the does were reconciled and no longer enemies. In this story the left doe represents God reaching out to an unbeliever and changing their disposition toward God through regeneration of the unbeliever's heart while the response of the right doe represents conversion (ears forward).

Most people do not realize their greatest need is to be reconciled to God. Regeneration* ("born again" in John 3) is a work of God in which he *imparts* spiritual life to an unbeliever by removing their spiritually dead heart and replacing it with a new heart of faith, love and obedience as prophesized in Ezekiel 36:26-27. Scripture is clear that regeneration is totally a work of God the Holy Spirit (John 3:8) and God the Father (Ephesians 2:5). None of us chose to be born physically, and no one independently chooses to be "born again" spiritually because prior to regeneration everyone is spiritually dead and therefore unable to do anything spiritually (Ephesians 2:1).

Conversion is the willing response to the call of God of a person formerly spiritually dead and hostile to God. Regeneration must logically precede conversion. For, if we are spiritually dead before conversion, we must first be regenerated or made spiritually alive before we can respond to God by conversion. Conversion is expressed in two ways, faith and repentance. Faith includes basic knowledge of the gospel of Christ, intellectual agreement that the gospel is true, and a personal decision to trust in Jesus Christ alone for the forgiveness of sins and eternal life with God. This faith results in a love for God that replaces the unbeliever's former hostility toward God. Similarly, repentance requires knowledge of what is sin and that it is wrong, an intellectual agreement with Scripture's depiction of sin and a personal decision to renounce sin and lead a life of obedience to Christ's teachings. As a new Christian matures and grows in understanding, their faith increases (Romans 10:17). Faith is not increased by ignorance or believing something contrary to evidence, but rather the more one knows the true character of God as revealed in the Bible, the more one can put their confidence in Him. Repentance is also an ongoing process because as the Christian matures and becomes more aware of their sinful nature, they increase their hatred of sin and desire to be increasingly Christ-like (chapter 39).

Much more will be said about regeneration and conversion. For now it is simply useful to distinguish between regeneration (the Divine cause) and conversion (resulting human action). Recognize that they cannot be separated. It is a logical necessity for regeneration to precede faith, but regeneration and faith are essentially simultaneous events. It is not possible for a person to be regenerated and not immediately and willingly believe in Jesus (chapter 49).

*The Greek word *paliggensia* (translated as regeneration in Titus 3:5) occurs only one other place in the New Testament (Matthew 19:28) where it refers to the renewal of the creation in the new heaven and earth.

38. Justification

For all have sinned and fall short of the glory of God, and are justified by his grace as a gift, through the redemption that is in Christ Jesus, whom God put forward as a propitiation by his blood, to be received by faith Romans 3:23–25a

Bucks are not model fathers like the mythical *Bambi* but are promiscuous fornicators who will mate with as many does as possible and never lift an antler to aid in raising or protecting their progeny. Of course, bucks do not have sins that need forgiveness, but humans do. The doctrine of justification makes Christianity unique among all world religions by providing a means for God to grant converted sinners forgiveness without being an unjust judge, thus freeing converted hearts of guilt from their unrighteous past.

In the Roman Catholic view of justification, God actually imparts righteousness that internally changes the recipient's moral character. The recipient adds further merit to this righteousness based upon their disposition and cooperation. God gives people varying amounts of justification according to the amount of imparted righteousness and their own merit. But a Roman Catholic can never be sure if they have enough justification except in the rare case of a revelation from God.

Luther and the other reformers rightly understood that justification is God's act in which he judicially declares the new believer to be righteous in his sight. This declaration must logically follow conversion, but occurs simultaneously with conversion in time. Notice that declaring one to be righteous does not actually mean the person is righteous but only that they are counted as righteous. Protestants believe justification is how God pardons sinners and accepts them as righteous for Christ's sake. God's wrath against a believer's sins has been propitiated or satisfied by the death of Christ on the cross. The Old Testament sacrificial system hinted at this through the annual ritual of the Day of Atonement, *Yom Kippur.** But Jesus truly satisfied God's wrath once and for all on the cross because of his infinite value as God's Son (Chapter 56) and perfect obedience to the Father. The sins of believers were placed on (imputed to) Jesus so that his death paid the price for their sins, and Jesus' perfect adherence to the Law (sinless life) was credited (imputed) to believers. This double imputation occurs at justification and allows God to count those who have faith in Christ to be righteous. This is just (honorable, legal, righteous and so on) because God knew He was going to send Jesus to enact this double imputation. So when people trusted God by faith before Jesus died (chapter 5), they could be counted as righteous because God knew what he was going do in the future. Once Jesus died God is just to declare sinners righteous based upon His death (Romans 3:25b–26).

Today the Protestant understanding of the doctrine of justification is under attack by what is called "the new perspective on Paul." Led by N.T. Wright, this "new perspective" is at odds with both the Roman Catholic and Protestant understanding of justification by claiming that Paul meant the gospel is merely the proclamation that Jesus is the crucified and risen Messiah of both Jews and gentiles and the only true Lord of the world. As a result the gospel is not about how people get saved and justification is not how someone becomes a Christian but a declaration that they are a Christian. For a detailed biblical response to this "new," but incorrect view of justification see *The Future of Justification: A Response to N.T. Wright* by John Piper.

---

*Jews still celebrate *Yom Kippur*. However, with the destruction of the temple in A.D. 70 they no longer have a place to make sacrifices and atone for their sins.

39. Sanctification

For those whom he foreknew he also predestined to be conformed to the image of his Son, in order that he might be the firstborn among many brothers. Romans 8:29

The first time I saw this image I knew this would be the picture for the chapter on sanctification. Sanctification means literally to set apart to God for his use. The concept of sanctification is succinctly defined in Q&A 35 of the Westminster Shorter Catechism as: *the work of God's free grace, whereby we are renewed in the whole man after the image of God, and are enabled more and more to die unto sin and live unto righteousness.*

Regeneration is an instantaneous act bringing a person from spiritual death to spiritual life and evidenced by a profession of faith in Christ. It is entirely God's work. Sanctification is the ongoing process by which a regenerated person increasingly desires to be more like Jesus, to glorify God through good works, to pray and worship, and to grow in faith and knowledge of God's word. Sanctification is not entirely God's work, but also requires human effort, dependent on God (Philippians 3:10–14). In other words, sanctification is an ongoing cooperative effort of God and the believer. The apostle Paul exhorts Christians to *work out your own salvation with fear and trembling* (Philippians 2:12). When Roman Catholics say works are required for justification they often have sanctification in mind. However, works of sanctification do not justify, but give evidence that a person is truly a Christian (Ephesians 2:8–10).

Sanctification is a fight of faith. Some Christian denominations claim that perfect conformity to Christ can be obtained in this life, but this is untrue. The regenerate person never completely eradicates the sin nature. Rather, the new nature in the regenerate person is at war with the old sinful nature. The new nature does not win every skirmish in this struggle. What is significant is that the regenerate person hates when he sins, because his desire is to be like Christ (Romans 7:14–25). Through persistent struggle and with the help of the Holy Spirit, victory over some recurrent sins can be achieved (Romans 8:13). As the work of sanctification progresses in the believer, the conscience becomes more sensitive, and the perception of sin becomes more exacting, such that behaviors that were previously not recognized as sin become known for what they are. But in all these struggles, grace is always available to forgive when there is real contrition for sin.

This leads to a final point. Some teach today that it is possible to be saved but not sanctified (see also chapter 94). They claim that you can go to heaven, but not desire or try to conform to the image of Christ. In other words, Jesus can be a savior without being Lord. However, this idea is fatally flawed. A truly regenerate person desires to follow Jesus' example and submit to His teachings. (John 14:23–24)

So why did I see sanctification in this picture? The fawn is trying hard to conform to its' mother's example. They are in almost perfect lock-step. This is what sanctification aspires to, near perfect conformance to Christ's behavior. Of course in this life we will never be perfect (notice the head and tail positions are slightly different). Take the picture for what it is, a simple child-like desire to follow, as closely as possible, Christ's example so that the Christian can escape from the dangers of sin in this fallen world. That is sanctification.

40. Baptism

Do you not know that all of us who have been baptized into Christ Jesus were baptized into his death? We were buried therefore with him by baptism into death, in order that, just as Christ was raised from the dead by the glory of the Father, we too might walk in newness of life. Romans 6:3–4

This tranquil scene of a deer crossing a stream reminds me of John the Baptist (not the Apostle John) baptizing Jesus in the River Jordan (Mark 1:9). Christian baptism is not the same as the baptism of John the Baptist, which was a preparation for the coming of the Messiah and His judgment (Luke 3:7–18). Rather Christian baptism is an initiation ceremony pointing to a relationship with Christ. It symbolizes having sins washed away by passing safely through the waters of judgment, and uniting the recipient with Jesus' death, burial and resurrection. There are three main views concerning baptism.

Roman Catholics believe baptizing infants brings about their regeneration while most Lutherans believe that baptizing an infant mysteriously creates faith in the infant's heart. But both of these views are in conflict with the clear New Testament teaching that salvation is by the believer's expressed faith alone in Christ alone by grace alone. While a cursory reading of certain passages (like Mark 16:16) may seem to support the notion that baptism is required for salvation, the dominate theme in the New Testament is that baptism was the way new believers first publicly professed their faith in Jesus.

Baptists and some other Protestants believe baptism should be reserved for those who have professed faith in Christ and should be done by immersion in water rather than sprinkling. They argue that the Greek word translated as "baptize" means to be immersed or put completely under water. Mark 1:10 says Jesus came up out of the water, so it is most probable Jesus was baptized by immersion. The image of going under and coming out of the water beautifully depicts death, burial, and resurrection to new life with Jesus. They further argue that baptism is for believers, as evidenced by the accounts in the Book of Acts in which belief always preceded baptism.

Most other Protestants baptize infants (paedobaptism) but do not believe it causes regeneration. They argue that baptism is the New Testament equivalent of circumcision (Colossians 2:11–12). Hence, baptizing infants of believers welcomes them into the covenantal community of believers. They contend that the book of Acts does not necessarily support the Baptist view since: 1) it reports on an era in which no one could have been previously baptized as an infant; 2) it contains household baptisms following faith of at least some family members, and infants could have been part of the household. These Protestants must baptize infants by sprinkling since infants cannot be immersed. For professing Christians who were never baptized, some of these churches baptize by sprinkling and some by immersion.

Who is correct? There is no good biblical support that baptism causes regeneration. Chapter 96 will further investigate paedobaptism and believer's baptism. For now, remember that sacraments are to testify to grace. Baptism should be a comfort to the believer and a source of peace as conveyed by the picture in which God says to the believer: *Fear not, for I have redeemed you; I have called you by name, you are mine. When you pass through the waters, I will be with you; and through the rivers, they shall not overwhelm you;...For I am the Lord your God, the Holy one of Israel, your Savior.* (Isaiah 43:1–3 excerpts)

41. The Lord's Supper

And he took bread, and when he had given thanks, he broke it and gave it to them, saying, "This is my body, which is given for you. Do this in remembrance of me." And likewise the cup after they had eaten, saying, "This cup that is poured out for you is the new covenant in my blood." Luke 20:19–20

During the celebration of the Passover meal no food was to be eaten after the sacrificed lamb. But at that point during the Last Supper, Jesus shocked his disciples by eating bread and announcing that the third cup of wine in the Passover meal (traditionally representing the sacrificed Passover lamb's blood) is His blood. Thus Jesus declared He is the ultimate and final Passover lamb, ushering in a new ceremonial meal (Eucharist or Lord's Supper). Christians generally agree that the Lord's Supper looks backwards in remembrance of the crucifixion and forward as a foretaste of the great marriage feast in heaven with Christ and the church (Revelation 19). But Christians are divided over what happens during the Lord's Supper into four camps.

Roman Catholics teach transubstantiation: Christ is physically present in the Eucharist and the bread and wine actually become Christ's body and blood even though they appear to be bread and wine. In effect the mass becomes a bloodless sacrifice of Christ.

Martin Luther taught consubstantiation: Christ's body and blood are added supernaturally to the elements so that He is physically "in, with, and under" the elements which remain bread and wine. A common analogy is that water in a sponge is "in, with, and under" the sponge, but is not the sponge.

Calvin articulated the Reformed understanding that the bread and wine are only symbols of Christ's body and blood. However, Christ's divine nature is omnipresent so the believer enjoys spiritual fellowship with Christ during the Lord's Supper and is also linked to Christ's human nature though his body is in heaven.

Zwingli agreed with Calvin that the bread and wine are symbolic but shied away from seeing the presence of Christ in the sacrament to avoid any potential heresy in understanding Christ's dual nature.

Who is correct? All the Reformers rejected the Roman Catholic view that communion in any way repeats the sacrifice of Christ. To believe this diminishes the all-sufficiency of Christ's death by adding the priest's work. Both transubstantiation and consubstantiation must be logically rejected for two reasons: 1) Christ's human nature is not omnipresent. His body is in heaven seated at the right hand of the Father (Ephesians 1:19–21). Since communion is celebrated simultaneously in many locations, Christ cannot be, physically, in each location simultaneously but his divine nature can be there, spiritually. 2) Jesus was alive and partaking in the highly symbolic Passover meal when he said, "This is my body." So he must be speaking metaphorically that the elements are symbols, not his actual body and blood. Therefore, only the Calvin or Zwingli views are biblically tenable. In 1529, Luther and Zwingli met to resolve their differences. No agreement was reached, and to this day Lutherans remain separated from other Protestants over the Lord's Supper.

There are similarities between the tender and intimate relationship of a doe and her fawn and Christ and believers. For as the fawn is comforted and intimately joined to the doe by ingesting physical nourishment through her milk, so believers are comforted and intimately joined to Jesus by having a spiritual meal with Jesus through the Lord's Supper. The fawn is nourished physically but believers are nourished spiritually by their remembrance of Christ's broken body and shed blood using the symbols of bread and wine.

42. Heaven

But, as it is written, "what no eye has seen, nor ear heard, nor the heart of man imagined, what God has prepared for those who love him" 1 Corinthians 2:9

Any picture I could possibly use for this chapter would be inadequate to communicate what heaven is like. This mule deer buck stares out over a great chasm much as we ponder the chasm separating this life and eternal bliss in heaven. No matter how good you think heaven will be, it will be better in reality! I do not know exactly what heaven will be like, but I know I will not be disappointed.

What is often not understood is that there are actually two *"heavens"*: one during the present fallen world (the intermediate state) and one for eternity (the new heaven and the new earth). Heaven is generally considered to be the place where God dwells. Wayne Grudem defines heaven as the place where God most fully makes known his presence to bless. Notice that heaven is a place not just a state of mind. Right now we do not know where heaven is but following the judgment heaven and earth will be somehow united as the new heaven and the new earth (Revelation 21:1–4). Much debate has taken place over whether the new earth is a completely new creation or if it is a restoration of the original creation. It seems most probable that the original creation which God proclaimed to be "very good" (Genesis 1:31) will be restored. However, the new heaven and earth will be better than Eden because there will be no possibility of falling.

"Our death is not a satisfaction for our sin, but only a dying to sins and entering into eternal life" (Heidelberg Catechism Q&A 42). Christians die physically as a consequence of the fall (disease, aging, war and the like), but do not fear death because Jesus' death paid the price of their sin. Death is the unbeliever's enemy, sending him to hell, but the Christian's friend, ushering him into the presence of God. A Christian's soul and body are separated at death. Their soul is perfectly sanctified and they immediately enter what theologians call the intermediate state, a conscious existence of worship in the presence of God (Revelation 4). Roman Catholicism teaches that at death the soul enters purgatory where the soul is additionally sanctified to become fit for the intermediate state, but there is no biblical warrant for such a doctrine. Neither is there any opportunity for saving faith after death (Luke 16:19–31). The intermediate state is neither final nor ideal. We were created physical and spiritual beings and are incomplete without a body. However, the intermediate state is far superior to the present life since the believer is with Jesus (Philippians 1:23).

Christians should eagerly anticipate Jesus' return to earth in triumph, and the uniting of their soul with their resurrected body to live forever in the new heaven and the new earth. Our image of heaven is usually this restored creation. It will be a physical reality, probably with incredibly beautiful deer, woods, mountains, and so forth. We will not have an ethereal existence, clothed in white robes while we strum harps and float on clouds. We will recognize our Christian friends and the earth itself will be restored without any corrupting influences of the fall. God has been merciful to restrain the effects of the fall such that the present earth is not completely devoid of beauty or joy. Hence, we have some sensual foretaste of heaven and, through the Holy Spirit indwelling believers, a veiled spiritual experience of the eternal reality. Beyond this we must wait in faith, remembering as the Shorter Westminster Catechism teaches: "the chief end of man is to glorify God and enjoy him forever."

43. Hell

***...Depart from me, you cursed into the eternal fire prepared for the
devil and his angels.*** (Matthew 25:41)

The Greek word translated as hell in the New Testament is *gehenna*. It
occurs only 12 times in the New Testament, 11 times spoken by Jesus. Jesus
repeatedly states hell to be a place of fire. *Gehenna* literally refers to the
valley of Hinnom next to Jerusalem where a continuous fire was maintained
to burn the city's garbage. It had also been a place of Jewish apostasy where
the Jews worshiped Molech, the chief god of the Ammonites, and sometimes
included the sacrifice of children. Against this historical backdrop, Jesus'
words in Matthew 25:41 have particular impact as to the horror of hell.
Biblical images of hell as a place of flames and eternal torment are symbolic
images and the reality is probably much worse than the symbols.

Stories abound of people seeing a bright light in near death
experiences. The buck fawn in this picture has that "deer in the headlights"
look as he stares into the bright light of the sun as it has just cleared the
horizon causing the background to appear aflame in the glorious light of

sunrise. For this deer the question is whether those bright spots reflected in his eyes are the sunrise or an oncoming truck. One day everyone will see a similar bright light, but is it the glory of heaven or the flames of hell? The Bible says it all depends on whether or not you have been saved by faith in Jesus Christ.

When a deer dies, it goes out of existence because it has no soul. But when an unbeliever dies, his body and soul are separated and his soul goes directly to hell. To the 21st century scientific mind, the doctrine of hell is pure foolishness. Even among some professing Christians, hell is regarded as too horrible a doctrine to be the creation of a loving God and many dilute the doctrine to say dead people simply go out of existence, or after a time of punishment are annihilated, or that hell is simply the absence of God. But hell is not an idea made up by coercive clergy to convert people to Christianity. Jesus declares hell to be a place of conscious, unending torment for unbelieving souls (now), and the final abode of resurrected unbelievers, Satan and the fallen angels (Matthew 25:41). There are different degrees of punishment in hell just as there are different degrees of reward in heaven. The degree of punishment is determined at the final great white throne judgment (Revelation 20:11–15). Once in hell, there is no escape. Hell is not like jail where an unbeliever can serve time as corrective punishment, and be released to heaven. (Luke 16:22–24)

To our feeble human mind the idea of infinite punishment seems unjust. This is because we fail to recognize the extent of our sin. In our normal experience the more valuable the offended subject, the greater the required punishment. As a result we can kill a mosquito without any consequences, we will be fined or go to jail for poaching a deer, and may forfeit our life if we commit murder. However, when we sin against God we have offended the infinite God which in turn demands infinite punishment. Anything else would make God less than the God of the universe, since he would not be upholding His infinite value if the punishment for offending Him was less than infinite. To make matters worse everyone in the universe has offended God (Romans 3:23) and deserves to go to hell. If God were merely just, hell would be everyone's eternal destiny. But God is also loving and merciful and has provided a way by faith in Jesus to transfer the believer's sins to Jesus and credit Jesus' sinless life and death on the cross to believers, satisfying God's wrath toward their sin. That's the good news of the gospel!

44. The Millennium

Scripture reference: Revelation 20

I didn't get this buck's picture the first time he appeared just as many people have failed to get the "picture" of who Jesus is from his first appearance. The second time the buck appeared, I got his picture just as when Jesus comes again everyone will get the "picture" as every knee bows and every tongue confesses Jesus is Lord (Philippians 2:11). Exactly how this will happen is a hotly contested doctrinal point among Protestants. There are four views.

Amillennialism (AM) was the predominate view up to the mid–19th century. AM teaches that Revelation 20 does not describe a literal 1,000 year millennium but the present "church age" reign of deceased believers souls with Christ in heaven until the second coming. At the end of the "church age" the gospel will have been preached to all nations, there will be a large scale conversion of Israel, the tribulation (unprecedented persecution of the church) will occur and the antichrist (antithesis of Jesus empowered by Satan and worshipped by the world) will appear. All the dead will be resurrected followed by the rapture in which resurrected believers and glorified (perfected resurrection body) living believers are lifted up to meet Jesus in the sky. History will end with the second coming as Jesus descends to the earth (along with all believers) and conducts the final judgment.

Historic premillennialism (HPM) dates to the second century and essentially expects the same sequence of events as AM to occur, except that only deceased believers are resurrected at the second coming. However, HPM teaches that the millennium is a literal 1,000 year reign of Christ and believers on the earth *following* the second coming. Near the end of the millennium, Satan is loosed to deceive the nations. At the battle of Gog and Magog Satan is defeated and cast into the lake of fire to end the millennium. Deceased unbelievers are resurrected and the final judgment is conducted.

Dispensational premillennialism (DPM) began with the Dispensation movement that tried to preserve historic Christianity against the tide of 19th century liberalism. It has been popularized by the *Schofield Study Bible*, Hal Lindsey's *The Late Great Planet Earth* and Tim LaHaye's and Jerry Jenkins' *Left Behind* series of novels. DPM differs from HPM in that the second coming occurs suddenly without precursors prior to the tribulation. The church will be raptured and spend seven years in heaven with Christ. During this time the tribulation takes place and the antichrist appears. After the tribulation, Christ returns to earth with the church, the battle of Armageddon occurs, Satan is bound and the 1,000 year millennium begins.

Postmillennialism (PM) teaches the present age will gradually become the millennium as much of the world's population, including many Jews, are converted to Christianity. Christian principles and standards will become the accepted norm for nations and individuals. In this optimistic, but not widely held view, sin will not be eliminated but minimized, resulting in an unprecedented, worldwide utopia for a long time. Christ will return to a Christianized world following a limited tribulation that will not harm the church.

Who's correct? AM and HPM are biblically the most defensible positions, but it is probable that none of the views are entirely correct. For readers interested in the many nuances of each view beyond the scope of this book, *The Bible and the Future* by Anthony Hoekema and Wayne Grudem's *Systematic Theology* are excellent resources.

45. The Doctrines of Grace –
The five points of Calvinism

…even as he chose us in him before the foundation of the world, that we should be holy and blameless before him. In love he predestined us for adoption through Jesus Christ, "according to the purpose of his will…" Ephesians 1:4–5

No topic engenders more debate, misunderstanding and enmity among Protestants than the Doctrines of Grace. The controversy centers on predestination and how people actually come to saving faith. To understand the details we need to go back to the 5th century and the great debate between a British monk named Pelagius and Saint Augustine. Pelagius argued that you are on your own before God. Adam's fall was not transferred to every human being, nor could Christ's death transfer to you to atone for your sins. Augustine taught that before the fall, Adam was able to sin (choose what was unpleasing to God) and able to not sin (choose what is pleasing to God). Notice that Adam was not created as a sinner but with the ability to sin. The effect of Adam's sin, not the first sin itself, is called original sin, meaning that Adam and all his descendents (everyone) are born as sinners with only the ability to choose to sin and, hence, are unable to choose to not sin. When a person is "born again" (receives the Holy Spirit and believes in Jesus) they are still sinners, but are restored to their pre-fall state of being able to choose to sin or not sin. Thus, "born again" people still sin because they retain their old sinful nature that wars against the indwelling Holy Spirit (chapter 115). According to Augustine, when a "born again" person dies they are only able to *not* sin and, therefore, unable to sin. To make a long story short, Augustine prevailed and Pelagius was declared a heretic.

From the 5th to the 16th century various forms of "semi-Pelagianism arose claiming people did not totally lose the ability to not sin. According to this view, everyone has a spark of goodness enabling them to choose by "free will" to be "born again." God may assist their choice, but, ultimately, they make the decision. Enter Martin Luther, an Augustinian monk, who was convinced scripture clearly taught we do not choose God, but God chooses us by grace alone. At about the same time, John Calvin observed that the Bible teaches double predestination: God chooses to save some people and chooses not to save the rest. At any rate, predestination was a central doctrine in the spread of Protestantism. In the early 17th century, a Dutch theologian named Arminius resurrected semi-Pelagianism (known today as Arminianism) raising five objections to the prevailing views of Luther and Calvin. The issue was serious enough that the synod of Dort was called in 1618. A year later, they declared Arminius to be in error, answering his five objections with the Doctrines of Grace commonly called the five points of Calvinism. The acrostic TULIP arose as a memory aid for the five points: **T**otal Depravity, **U**nconditional Election, **L**imited Atonement, **I**rresistible Grace, and **P**erseverance of the Saints. Today Arminianism is the dominant doctrine among evangelical Christians. Churches that describe their theology as reformed or denominations called "Reformed," and traditional or conservative Anglicans, Episcopalians, and Presbyterians, and many Baptists usually embrace all five points.

Today many Christians fail to "see" the biblical warrant for one or more of the five points just as some readers will fail to see the doe in the picture, and some Christians claim to be four point Calvinists, viewing one of the points as unwarranted or unimportant like the diminished fifth point on the buck's rack.

46. Total Depravity–
We are morally unable to believe in God on our own.

"No one can come to me unless the father who sent me draws him. And I will raise him up on the last day." John 6:44

The concept of total depravity dates to the 5th century and is credited to Saint Augustine. It does not mean that unbelievers are as bad as they possibly could be. In fact unbelievers are capable of being loving, merciful, honest and a host of other virtues. What total depravity means is that the fall has affected all dimensions of our being, so that unbelievers are totally unable to do anything by their own effort to effect their salvation. Total depravity teaches that before the fall, Adam could choose good or evil with respect to salvation. Once the fall occurred, Adam still had the power of choice (free agency), but Adam and all his descendants lost the ability to choose "good" with respect to salvation because they no longer desired God.

Today most Protestants are Arminians and reject total depravity, believing a person decides by their "free will" to believe in Christ. This concept of "free will," sees the fall as not so complete that humans were rendered unable to decide to believe in Christ on their own. A common Arminian illustration is that the unbeliever has a terminal illness. They are offered a glass of medicine that will cure their disease. If they decide to drink the medicine, they will get well. God provides the medicine (Jesus) and even entices them to drink it, but they must cooperate by taking the medicine. Arminians understand the Greek word *helkō* translated as "draws" in John 6:44 to mean woo or persuade, and often attempt to evangelize unbelievers by luring them to church with secular enticements like coffee bars, and "good" music, like a deer hunter uses scents or a grunt call to lure deer. Once the unbeliever gets to church, Arminians hope to persuade the unbeliever to "choose" to believe in Jesus by rational arguments.

But according to total depravity this is impossible because an unbeliever is incapable of choosing to believe in Jesus. The unbeliever still has free agency, but the Arminian marketing strategy cannot work because unbelievers are spiritually dead and don't want to believe in Jesus. Total depravity teaches we are all born spiritually dead, and allergic to God. Unbelievers are not very sick (as in the analogy above), they are spiritually dead and cannot do anything to resuscitate themselves. It is God alone, who by grace does all the work, and must get all the credit, because the unbeliever is as spiritually dead (totally disinterested in God) as the pictured buck is physically dead. An unbeliever is just as incapable of getting to heaven by their own efforts, as the pictured, dead buck is incapable of getting up the hill unless the hunter drags him.

Who is correct? *Helkō* occurs seven other times in the New Testament, translated as: "drag" (James 2:6); "dragged" (Acts 16:19, 21:30); "draw" (John 12:32); "drew" (John 18:10); and "haul" (John 21:6, 11). There is a forceful, compelling power implied in the meaning of *helkō*. God, literally, must drag or haul (not lure, woo or persuade) your dead, spiritual carcass (unregenerate soul) to himself. However, God doesn't drag unbelievers to salvation, kicking and screaming like a lassoed, live, wild deer. Instead, God first changes the unbeliever's dead heart into a new creation (2 Corinthians 5:17) which desires Jesus, as evidenced by a freely chosen profession of faith. Our fallen nature chafes at the idea that we are unable to effect even a tiny part of our salvation, but that is what the Bible teaches (Ephesians 2:1–10).

47. Unconditional Election-
God's gracious, sovereign, choice of the elect.

though they were not yet born and had done nothing either good or bad – in order that God's purpose of election might continue, not because of works but because of his call – she was told, "The older will serve the younger." As it is written, "Jacob I loved, but Esau I hated." What shall we say then? Is there injustice on God's part? By no means! For he says to Moses, "I will have mercy on whom I have mercy, and I will have compassion on whom I have compassion." So then it depends not on human will or exertion, but on God, who has mercy. Romans 9:11–16

I do not know if these young bucks were twin brothers like Jacob and Esau. (Incidentally, Esau was a skilled hunter, Genesis 25:27.) Due to the low light, I could only get one deer in focus at a time. Why did I choose to focus on the 7 pointer and not the 5 pointer? At the time my reason probably was the slightly larger rack. The hunters among my readers likely have experienced a similar situation when two legal deer were available and they chose to shoot one and allow the other to live. Unconditional election is similar to the hunter's choice, though God's choice is not based upon merit in the elect versus the reprobate.

Unconditional election teaches that before creation God had selected whom he would bring to saving faith by mercy (the elect) and those whom he would bring to justice in hell for their sins (the reprobate). God does not make the decisions randomly, nor is his choice based upon some present or future foreseen merit in the elect versus the reprobate. We are all sinners deserving hell. The wonder is that he chooses anyone! Ultimately, God's reasons for choosing one person for election and another for hell are not ours to know.

The Bible teaches God is good and there is no sin in him, so his decisions are always right and good. Because God is the creator of all things, he has the right to choose as he pleases (Romans 9:19–24). If two deer approach a hunter and one is killed (reprobation) and the other by mercy is allowed to live (election), the surviving deer may realize its companion is dead, but it is incapable of philosophically pondering why it received mercy and its colleague did not. It does not demand an explanation or suppose it could understand the explanation. Unlike deer we suppose we are capable of understanding why God does what he does and in this arrogance further suppose that God has to answer to us to justify his choices.

Consider then that a human hunter compared to a deer has incredibly greater capacity for wisdom, knowledge and logical analytical thought. But great as this gulf is between a deer and a human, the gulf between God and a human is incomprehensibly greater. On this side of heaven all the "elect" can do is express grateful and humble thanksgiving to have received mercy. We are not owed an explanation, nor could we understand it. Of course, the immediate reaction to unconditional election by most people (elect and reprobate) is to consider that God is unfair! The Apostle Paul anticipates this charge and his answer is: we have no right to even ask this question. *But who are you, O man, to answer back to God? Will what is molded say to its molder, "Why have you made me like this?" Has the potter no right over the clay, to make out of the same lump one vessel for honored use and another for dishonorable use?* (Romans 9:20–21) In the final analysis it comes down to this: if total depravity is true, then the only way anyone could be saved is by unconditional election. If you still struggle with unconditional election, humbly ask God to show you this truth in the Bible.

48. Limited Atonement –
Who did Jesus die for?

"...so Christ, having been offered once to bear the sins of many, will appear a second time, not to deal with sin but to save those who are eagerly waiting for him." Hebrews 9:28

Atonement means the work Christ did in his life and death to earn the elect's salvation. Jesus had to do this work in his human nature since he was atoning for human sin, and die a criminal's death since he bore all of the elect's sin against God. So what did God intend that the atonement would accomplish? Does it merely make ***possible*** the salvation of everyone without guaranteeing that anyone will be saved, as Arminians claim? Or does it ***guarantee*** that some people (the elect) will be saved as Calvinists claim? Arminians believe that Jesus' death could cover **all** the sins of **all** people who had lived, were living, or would ever live. Logically this is untenable because there is one sin the atonement cannot cover–unbelief. For if unbelief was also covered by the atonement, then everyone would go to heaven whether or not they believed in Jesus. Of course this is universalism (everyone is saved and goes to heaven) which is rejected by both Arminians and Calvinists. Arminians believe unconditional election means God elects those whom he foresees will choose to believe in Jesus. If Arminians applied the same logic to the atonement that they apply to election (the atonement only applies to those who will believe in Jesus) there would be no issue because they would be in agreement with Calvinists.

Another way people often misunderstand limited atonement, is to infer that the value of Christ's death was limited (only sufficient for the sins of the elect and insufficient for the sins of everyone). This is untrue. Christ's death was of infinite saving value, because Christ is of infinite value and, hence, his death and forsaking by the father is of infinite value in satisfying the wrath of God. It is the Arminian view that limits the power of the atonement, seeing in it only the possibility of salvation when assisted by human free will, as opposed to the Calvinist view of the absolute certainty that the atonement actually accomplishes the elect's salvation. Hebrews 9:28 says Christ bore the sins of *many not all*! You must believe to be saved, so Christ did not atone for the sins of unbelievers and the atonement is limited or *effectual* only for the elect. Hence, the biblical and logical view of the atonement is that it is limited to the elect but guarantees their salvation, rather than making salvation possible for everyone, but without any guarantees. In the final analysis the Arminian view robs God of some of his glory since there is no guarantee anyone will be saved to praise him for eternity in heaven, and the believer can take a little credit for being smart enough to choose to believe in Jesus.

Does the rut merely make it *possible* for *all does* to bear fawns, or does it virtually (though, not absolutely as in limited atonement) *guarantee* that all *fertile* does (the elect in this parable) will bear fawns? God has designed deer and the rut such that fertile does come into estrous in November. If they do not conceive, they will come into estrous again in December and again in January if breeding was unsuccessful in December, thus, virtually guaranteeing that all fertile does bear fawns. Individual does do not initially desire to mate and flee from their prospective suitor (as in the picture) just as unbelievers may initially flee from Jesus. But, through shifting hormones, at the right time to assure conception, God changes each fertile doe's disposition so that she willingly chooses to mate, just as God must first change the heart of the unbeliever, causing the person to be "born again" and enabling them to willingly choose to believe in Jesus.

49. Irresistible Grace –
The effectual call of God

And when the Gentiles heard this, they began rejoicing and glorifying the word of the Lord, and as many as were appointed to eternal life believed. Acts 13:48

  Bucks are almost irresistibly drawn to a doe during the rut. Countless scent and sound products claim to duplicate this irresistible calling to a buck. I put out a scent wick one afternoon late in the rut. The warnings on the product made me wonder whether it was even safe to be near it, unarmed as I was! Near sunset, the pictured buck walked down the trail I was watching with a stiff wind at his back. As he passed under the wick, he stopped, looked up, sniffed once, and nonchalantly proceeded down the trail. So much for an irresistible scent! My most spectacular experience of the irresistible call of a doe left me awestruck. A doe suddenly burst by me 5 feet away, hotly pursued by four bucks. The fourth (pictured in chapter 51) and largest attempted to narrow the gap, leaping over me as I lay in the blind, and clipping the top of my blind with a forefoot. While that's a better depiction of an irresistible calling, it is not nearly as irresistible as God's call through irresistible grace.

Irresistible grace does not mean exactly what may be supposed on first hearing the term. Believers and unbelievers are often able to resist the will of God. This is a result of the sinful nature that completely rules the unbeliever and is not totally eradicated in the believer. But Acts 13:48 is a clear demonstration of irresistible grace. Paul and Barnabas had preached boldly to the Jews and converts to Judaism in Pisidian Antioch. Many, but not all, believed. The next Sunday almost the whole city came to hear Paul and Barnabas (Acts 13:43–44) and all the elect Gentiles believed. Irresistible grace might be better titled effectual calling, meaning that when God, who spoke all creation into existence by his word (Genesis 1), calls to faith, an unbeliever whom he had chosen before the world was made (Ephesians 1:3–10), the call is irresistibly effective, changing the disposition of the unbeliever's heart, so that he earnestly desires Christ and trusts in Him by faith immediately. This change of disposition is called regeneration, being born again (John 3:3). Hence, faith is the result of regeneration, not the cause of regeneration.

Most Protestants believe that somehow the sinner initiates regeneration by coming to faith in Christ through a cooperative action of the unbeliever aided by God's grace. Roman Catholics do not deny that grace and faith are necessary elements of regeneration (as is commonly supposed by Protestants) maintaining instead that regeneration is not by faith alone by grace alone in Christ alone. Rather, Roman Catholics believe that regeneration is initiated by baptism and reinstated by acts of penance whenever regeneration is lost through sinful acts. Thus, many Protestants and all Roman Catholics add some form of human action to initiate regeneration (in opposition to Ephesians 2:8–9). This robs God of his sovereignty, since it is then incumbent on God to bestow regeneration due to the initiating human act. It robs God of his full glory since the human might rightly boast that he was wise enough to make the smart choice and believe in Christ while his foolish, unbelieving, colleague did not. In these views, God of course still gets almost all of the credit and glory for regeneration through Christ's work on the cross, but He does not get it all. Like most new Christians, I was an Arminian and thought I had made a decision on my own. But when I first heard the Doctrines of Grace I was immediately convicted beyond anything I have ever experienced for taking credit for what God had done in calling me to faith. Please prayerfully ponder the implications of God not being totally responsible for your regeneration.

50. Perseverance of the Saints–
God assures the preservation of the elect's salvation.

My sheep hear my voice, and I know them, and they follow me. I give them eternal life, and they will never perish, and no one will snatch them out of my hand. John 10:27–28

I learned that within a month of taking this picture this buck was killed by a professional sharpshooter as part of a herd thinning project in the Twin Cities metropolitan area. A deer is not guaranteed life. They are totally dependent on their wits to avoid a sudden death. We humans are not that different. Only death and taxes are sure, the cynic quips. But for those whom God has irresistibly called, there is absolute security of eternal life with Him. It depends on God alone and not on human effort. That's the good news of the doctrine of perseverance of the saints.

A simple statement of the doctrine is: "Once saved, always saved." You cannot lose your salvation. The biblical case for this doctrine is very strong (John 6:37–40; 17:2, 6, 9, 24; Romans 8:28–39). The argument is also, logically, very strong since if God unconditionally elects a person and brings him to faith through His irresistible grace, then surely He would not allow him to fall back into a state of unbelief and end up in hell. If this were the case, then God is not truly sovereign (unable to keep a person from falling away from faith) and not truly trustworthy, since He promises something (regeneration) that He is unable or unwilling to guarantee forever. Since we know by definition God is totally sovereign, and certainly is trustworthy, it must be that salvation cannot be lost. Otherwise, God would be the impotent, laughing stock of the universe, unable to always and permanently overcome the sin nature in whomever He chose to be with Him forever.

Roman Catholics and Arminian Protestants believe that salvation can be lost. This is a logical result of their belief that salvation requires some human action and, therefore, can be lost by lack of human action. They argue that if salvation cannot be lost, people might reasonably live very sinful lives, since they are guaranteed entrance into heaven. Their argument seems strongly buttressed by the common occurrence of people who appear to be true Christians falling away from faith. The Reformed answer is very simple. In regeneration, God has completely changed the disposition of the totally depraved heart by the indwelling of the Holy Spirit. Thus, a person who is truly "born again" will not permanently desire to "eat, drink, and be merry." The Holy Spirit guides him to desire a life of progressive sanctification (chapter 39) grounded in the desire to please Christ. The idea that a person can be a "carnal" Christian enjoying salvation without obeying Christ is fallacious (John 3:36). Of course, believers fall into sin from time to time, but true believers will be convicted by the Holy Spirit and brought back to a state of humble obedience to Christ's teachings. People who appear to be Christians and then abandon the faith, dying in a state of unbelief, were never elect in the first place. So, how do you know if you will persevere to the end? The answer is simple, by your own power you will never persevere to the end and you will make shipwreck of your faith. But, if you are a child of God by unconditional election, then God will preserve your faith to the end by the power of His indwelling Holy Spirit. Recognition of your helplessness in effecting your own salvation, faith alone in Christ's atonement for your sin, and a desire to live a life in accordance with His teaching, are His gracious assurances to you that you are His.

51. Is there free will?

"...None is righteous, no, not one; no one understands; no one seeks for God. All have turned aside; together they have become worthless; no one does good, not even one." Romans 3:10–12 *And you were dead in the trespasses and sins in which you once walked, following the course of this world, following the prince of the power of the air, the spirit that is now at work in the sons of disobedience - among whom we all once lived in the passions of our flesh, carrying out the desires of the body and the mind, and were by nature children of wrath, like the rest of mankind. But God, being rich in mercy, because of the great love with which he loved us, even when we were dead in our trespasses, made us alive together with Christ –by grace you have been saved* Ephesians 2:1–5

Since the second century free will has meant the ability of all people to choose any of the moral options available in a given situation. Arminians specifically understand free will to mean people are able without the indwelling of the Holy Spirit to choose to believe in Christ. This buck and his kindred do not have free will but they routinely make decisions as free agents. Free agency is a characteristic of all living creatures with a brain, including humans, meaning we choose what we will do in a given situation based upon our desires, inclinations, conscience, or a myriad of other things. Jonathan Edwards taught that we always choose what we think will make us happiest but as unbelievers our choices are never godly. According to Augustine, Adam had free will and free agency before the fall as do true Christians today. But, after the fall unbelievers have only free agency because total depravity makes them unable to choose what is morally pleasing to God. So if there is a moral option an unbeliever is incapable of choosing then by definition they do not have free will. Free will exists in Christians, but unbelievers do not have it, because they are spiritually dead (Ephesians 2:1–5).

Despite Augustine prevailing over Pelagius, Luther over Erasmus and the synod of Dort's rebuttal of Arminius, the unprecedented attack on scripture that began with 18th century "enlightenment" thinking (God is no longer necessary to explain the universe) resurrected free will to center stage. Interestingly, while "enlightened" Europe turned from God, at the same time in the United States the Great Awakening (the greatest revival in U.S. history) took place. Today Evangelical Christianity is far more widespread in the U.S. than Europe, but it has been decidedly in the free will camp. Recently there has been a resurgence of what Time Magazine (March 12, 2009) called "The New Calvinism," one of the top ten ideas influencing the 21st century. But this Calvinism isn't new. It is just traditional reformed theology.

So are Arminians biblically correct that there is such a thing as free will? There are 23 references in the Old Testament to freewill offerings. We still have the concept today in which people give money or goods as a special offering for a worthy cause in a church service or at a benefit for a particularly unfortunate person with limited resources. But there are no biblical references specifically to free will that state an unbeliever has the ability for making God-honoring moral choices. However, Arminians draw free will from several texts which we will examine in the next two chapters. For now we observe the referenced scriptures were written to believers (see Romans 1:7; Ephesians 1:1) and leave no room for free will in unbelievers. We are spiritually *dead* and can do nothing to cause our salvation, nor do we desire things pleasing to God as unbelievers. Christians have chosen to believe in God by free will, but it is only by God first graciously changing their hearts to desire Christ.

52. Does God want everyone to be saved?

This is good, and it is pleasing in the sight of God our Savior, who desires all people to be saved and to come to the knowledge of the truth.(1 Timothy 2:3–4) *The Lord is not slow to fulfill his promise as some count slowness, but is patient toward you, not wishing that any should perish, but that all should reach repentance.* 2 Peter 3:9

This yearling buck was trying to steal the large buck's doe. Finally, the large buck had enough, laid back his ears and approached the yearling, who foolishly stood his ground. Since the large buck could not engage his antlers with those of the smaller buck, he placed his forehead against the yearling's face and gave a firm push. The smaller buck got the idea and withdrew. Much was at stake for the large buck, yet he tempered his aggression proportional to the threat. There is a lesson here for Christians. Truth matters. However, true Christians should always strongly, but civilly, defend their doctrinal positions.

God's sovereignty and glory are at stake in the Arminian/Calvinist debate. Arminians claim the referenced scriptures teach God values an unbeliever's right to freely choose Christ as a higher priority than God's sovereignty. Arminians reject total depravity, reasoning God elects those whom He knows will believe on their own (impossible because of total depravity). By this interpretation Arminians exonerate God of the charge of being unfair for not electing everyone, because if a person does not believe, it is his own fault or the fault of Christians for not arguing persuasively enough for the gospel.

The meaning of the referenced passages depends on the contextual meaning of "all." If I say in a group, "we are all here," everyone knows I do not mean every person in the world, but every person in the group. So if the "all" in both referenced texts really means everyone, then God desires universalism, a position rejected by Arminians and Calvinists. Worse yet, if God desires everyone to believe and not everyone believes, then God is not sovereign since He is unable to accomplish what he desires. This leaves us with a psychologically conflicted God who sits in heaven wringing his hands, wishing everyone would be saved but willing to let everyone go to hell rather than exercising his sovereignty by saving His predestined elect. This cannot be right! We need a better explanation.

In 1 Timothy 2:3–4 the context is an exhortation to pray for salvation for people from *all* socio-economic classes. It is unreasonable to think that Paul means in 1 Timothy 2:3–4 that God desires every person to be saved but leaves it up to each individuals "free will" since Paul also wrote Ephesians 1:4–5 *...In love he predestined us for adoption through Jesus Christ, according to the purpose of his will.* Rather, Paul is encouraging Timothy to earnestly pray for salvation for people in all walks of life since we do not know who is elect and who isn't and God selects the elect from every class, race, tribe, and so on.

The question in 2 Peter is: why hasn't Jesus returned? The *you* in 2 Peter 3:9 must be the *you* in 2 Peter 3:1 who he calls *beloved.* So who are the beloved? In 2 Peter 1:1 he addresses the letter *To those who have obtained a faith of equal standing with ours by the righteousness of our God and Savior Jesus Christ:* namely the believing elect. Therefore, Peter's answer is that Jesus has not returned because not all the unbelieving living elect and unborn elect have been saved.

Though Calvinism is offensive to many, it is biblical just as the doctrine of hell offends many, but also is biblical. Will you trust in human reason or scripture (Proverbs 3:5–7; 14:12)?

53. Does God elect those who will believe?

For those whom he foreknew he also predestined to be conformed to the image of his Son, in order that he might be the firstborn among many brothers. And those whom he predestined he also called, and those whom he called he also justified, and those whom he justified he also glorified. Romans 8:29–30

Exactly how sovereign is God? He is certainly omniscient and omnipotent but how far does He extend His omnipotence? Did God simply omnisciently know that this buck, by his own volition, would present itself to be photographed at 10:58 am CST on November 4, 2005 and hence, ordain it to be so? Or did God know it because he independently, sovereignly predestined it to be so? More importantly, just how sovereign is God with regard to who will believe in Jesus and who will not? Stand back and watch the Christian fur fly.

Romans 8:29–30 is often referred to as the golden chain of salvation. In it Arminians find their proof text that God does not choose the elect but, rather, by His omniscience foresees who will believe in Jesus by their own free will and thus elects these people before the creation of the world. Ironically, the Arminian proof text turns out to be a proof text for the Doctrines of Grace. To see this let's begin by asking: are all or only some of those foreknown, predestined, called, justified and glorified? Obviously, *all* must be correct because if it is only *some*, then not everyone who God foresaw would believe in Jesus would actually come to faith, hence showing God is not omniscient.

No true Christian doubts that God knows in advance who will believe in Jesus. If He doesn't, then He is not omniscient. The question is how does He know? Is it because He perfectly foresees the future or is it because He causes the believers to come to faith? Arminians believe *foreknew* in Romans 8:29 implies the meaning of the following bolded text, interpreting the verse to say *those whom he foreknew* **would believe in Jesus by their own free will** *he also predestined*. They see God as omniscient with respect to actions or events not people. Yet the most literal reading of the text is that those He *foreknew* are people (not actions by people) because biblically *to know* implies intimacy not just factual knowledge (Genesis 4:1).

The problem with the Arminian understanding centers on the word *called*. Called cannot mean the general call an evangelist makes in exhorting everyone to receive Christ as their Savior. This call goes out to everyone but not everyone who hears the general call believes. It is only the call of irresistible grace that is so efficacious that everyone who receives this call believes and is justified. But if the Arminian understanding were correct, this irresistible call is not allowed, only the general call is allowed or else free will cannot be preserved. As a result the Arminian understanding collapses under its own inconsistency. Romans 8:29–30 is a strong argument for the Doctrines of Grace since God does indeed elect only those he knows will believe, because He has decided that He will irresistibly call them, justify them and glorify them. So certain is the elect's salvation that Paul uses the past tense (predestined, called, justified, glorified). It is a done deal, whether or not the person already believes or has even been born. Some of you will chafe at this, hoping to preserve your autonomy over God's sovereignty by looking for a hole in my arguments. Some of you will mock this as the ultimate stupidity. Some of you may despair since you do not believe, but your current unbelief is no guarantee that God will not call you out of darkness into His marvelous light (1 Peter 2:9). But the believing, called elect, will worship saying, "Hallelujah, all praise and glory to God!"

54. Catholic, Evangelical or Reformed?

for I did not shrink from declaring to you the whole counsel of God.
Acts 20:27

Historically, there have been three classifications of doctrine: "catholic," "evangelical" and "reformed." In this context catholic does not mean Roman Catholic, although Roman Catholics are doctrinally catholic. Instead catholic means universal, and refers to the minimum set of beliefs required to be considered a true Christian such as creation, the fall, the attributes of God, the Trinity, the dual nature of Jesus, the virgin birth and incarnation, the atonement, the ascension, the resurrection, a literal heaven and hell, a future second coming of Christ, a final judgment, and the restoration of the creation.

At the time of the reformation Protestants were called evangelicals because of their desire to recover the original gospel through belief in justification by faith alone and the authority of Scripture. Today's evangelicals maintain the original Protestant distinctives and add to catholic doctrine the five *solas** (chapter 33) and the sacraments of baptism and the

Lord's Supper. They are also actively involved in evangelism both within their culture and in overseas missionary work.

Reformed begins with evangelical and adds the full endorsement of *sola gratia* and belief in the five Doctrines of Grace. The collage of a grey squirrel, a Rocky Mountain goat and a whitetail deer is a simple parable of these distinctions. All are mammals (four chamber heart, young are born alive, have hair and produce milk), two are also ungulates (having hooves), but only one is a deer (growing antlers that are shed annually). So, all deer are mammals and ungulates, and all ungulates are mammals, but not all mammals are ungulates nor are all ungulates deer. Similarly, all reformed believers are also evangelical and catholic and all evangelicals are also catholic, but all catholics are not evangelical nor are all evangelicals reformed. In this parable to be "reformed" is to declare the "whole counsel of God" (Act 20:27) since it professes the whole entirety of biblical doctrine.

Today there are at least three other competing doctrinal classifications that profess to be Christian. Liberal theology is the oldest of the three dating to the 18th century. Its primary distinction is a rejection of the supernatural. Therefore, it cannot affirm even a catholic profession of faith and simply sees Jesus as a great role model and moral teacher but not divine. It must be rejected as not truly Christian.

Charismatic or Pentecostal theology is an early 20th century phenomenon. Their theology is usually solidly evangelical. Its primary distinctive is a "supra-biblical" emphasis on spiritual gifts such as prophecy and speaking in tongues. However, Charismatics and Pentecostals are usually true Christians.

In the later part of the 20th century a new movement has arisen. Known by names such as emergent, its basic premise is that the traditional church is no longer relevant. This movement has been primarily among evangelicals, but has included reformed and catholic congregations as well. Experience is valued over doctrine with the idea of making the church look like the world with the hope that the world will come to church and be saved. This "shopping mall" church experience tends towards self-help, practical teaching but in some congregations can also be biblically solid and gospel grounded.

*Many evangelicals are Arminian and do not fully accept *sola gratia* since they believe there is some human effort or choice involved in salvation because of their understanding of "free will" (chapters 49, 51–53).

55. What is the Gospel? Part 1

...for all have sinned and fall short of the glory of God, and are justified by his grace as a gift, through the redemption that is in Christ Jesus, Romans 3:23–24

I have always wanted to photograph trophy bucks, so when I saw this buck I took his picture for the pure humor of these pathetic antlers. But in God's providence there are no mistakes and I have slowly learned to be obedient and take pictures even if I don't think I need the picture. God knows what I need and so he gave me a perfect deer to photograph to start the discussion of one of the most widely used verses in explaining the gospel which is simple enough for a child to understand and profound enough to challenge the greatest intellect.

We must be very clear about what we mean by the gospel. The gospel is the essence of the Christian faith, setting forth God's gracious solution to the greatest problem facing humanity. In Romans 1:18–3:20 Paul has established that everyone (Jew and gentile) has sinned, by rejecting God and his glory. Notice that sin is mainly a failure to honor God first and foremost, rather than mainly being about doing wrong. So the referenced text begins by simply reiterating that everyone is guilty of sin. As a consequence of this sin everyone has fallen short of the glory of God. The translation *"to fall short of the glory of God"* is traditional, but sometimes confusing. It does not mean no one is fit to spend eternity in the presence of a completely holy God who hates sin, because we are not as glorious as God is. Even in heaven we will never be as glorious as God even though we were created in his image and will no longer sin. It would be more clear and correct to say for all have sinned and *lack* the glory of God. The Greek word *hamartanō* translated as sinned literally means to miss the mark. There is an allusion to archery in which the arrow misses the mark by falling short of the target. In this case the target is the perfect adherence to the moral law. The glory of God in this case is best understood as the honor or excellent reputation of God. So even though we are made in God's image, because of sin we are more spiritually impotent and ugly compared to what we would be like without any sin in the image of God than this buck's antlers are compared to the most magnificently imaginable set of antlers.

So that's the problem: *for all have sinned and fall short of the glory of God.* Now comes the solution: *and are justified by his grace as a gift, through the redemption that is in Christ Jesus.* Notice that the solution has nothing to do with us, but is all about what God has done! The wording may seem difficult, but it makes sense if we understand what justified, grace, gift and redemption mean. *Justified* is a legal term meaning to be declared just (just as if you had never sinned) not that you are just (sinless). It is the opposite of condemned. *Grace* means unmerited favor; something completely undeserved. A gift is not worked for, earned or deserved for then it would be a payment. A gift can only be received, and in this case the gift is so costly that no person could ever pay for it. *Redemption* is commonly used to mean an exchange; i.e. if you redeem a coupon you exchange the coupon for something, like a product, service or discount. Redemption is not free. Someone else somehow bore the cost of the product, service or discount you received. In the context of the gospel redemption is essentially the paying of a ransom. But what is the ransom or redemption that is in Christ Jesus? How do I receive it? Why is God justified in accepting this ransom? Stay tuned for part 2.

56. What is the Gospel? Part 2

...whom God put forward as a propitiation by his blood, to be received by faith. This was to show God's righteousness, because in his divine forbearance he had passed over former sins. It was to show his righteousness at the present time, so that he might be just and the justifier of the one who has faith in Jesus. Romans 3:25–26

The buck in this photo lost his life when he recklessly pursued a doe past a waiting hunter. This is a common tale, but in it is a parable of the gospel. For during the rut bucks often lose their lives in an effort to give life to the next generation of deer, just as Jesus gave his life so that those who trust in him might have eternal life with God.

We now get to the very heart and soul of the gospel. The redemption that is in Jesus, that is the ransom he paid, is the satisfaction or quenching of God's wrath against sin by his blood. This is called propitiation. Therefore, the redemption or ransom that takes place is that God punishes Jesus for the sins of all who trust in him while crediting all who believe in Jesus with Jesus' sinless life. The vehicle for you to be justified is a gift by grace and received by faith. *Now faith is the assurance of things hoped for, the conviction of things not seen.* (Hebrews 11:1) Trusting in Jesus for salvation, loving him and praising him for the propitiation by his blood, and not merely intellectually assenting that Jesus' death pays the price of our sins, is the essence of faith. You cannot generate that faith in yourself. I can give you many good arguments for trusting in Jesus, but in the end a miracle of God (gift by grace) is required for your salvation. So there it is my friend, the gospel (good news): You are guilty of infinite, egregious contempt for the glory of God. God's full fury (wrath) is aimed at you and you rightly deserve to spend eternity in hell. **BUT** by grace, as a gift received by faith, God can declare you just by crediting you with Jesus' righteousness (justice and righteousness are synonyms meaning God always acts in accordance with what is right and is the final arbiter or measuring rod of what is right). God has punished Jesus by killing him on the cross for all your sins before and after you came to faith in Jesus. So if you confess your sin and helplessness to save yourself, believe in Jesus and trust in Him alone for your salvation you will be saved!

At this point two questions arise: 1) Is God unfair to only be gracious to some people and not everyone? (This question was answered in chapter 47); and 2) How could God allow sin to go unpunished prior to the death of Jesus? It might seem that before the cross, God could only be just if he sent everyone to hell. Yet, God had allowed sinful people into heaven. How could God do this without compromising his holiness and righteousness? The answer to this theological problem is given in the reference text. God always knew Jesus would die to propitiate the sins of believers so he was and is completely just in looking forward to the cross prior to the crucifixion and backwards to the cross after the crucifixion. The Old Testament sacrificial system (chapter 8) required blood to cover or atone for sins. That sacrificial system only pointed to Jesus. It did not actually propitiate God's wrath (Hebrews 9:11–15; 10:1–4). But Jesus' death did quench God's wrath against sin, because he had led a sinless life, and, as the son of God, was of infinite value. Therefore, his shed blood was of infinite value to cover the infinite transgression against God's glory once and for all for every believer from Adam to the end of time.

Now it is time to get personal. If you are not a Christian what is keeping you from believing? If you are a Christian are you hesitant to tell unbelievers about the gospel because you are not confident you can answer their questions or objections? Part III of this book addresses many common questions and objections of unbelievers.

Part III: Apologetics and Evangelism

For we are the aroma of Christ to God among those who are being saved and among those who are perishing, to one a fragrance from death to death, to the other a fragrance from life to life. 2 Corinthians 2:15–16a

So far I have focused on what Christianity believes. But from now on I will argue for the truth of Christianity, knowing that to a mind hostile to God no amount of argument, however logical, will be effective apart from the intervention of the Holy Spirit. Two subjects are covered in Part III: **Apologetics** (defense of Christianity against other belief systems that oppose it) and **Evangelism** (proclamation of the good news of the gospel). I have written this section as though I am witnessing to an unbeliever and have three main purposes: 1) to empower true Christians with solid answers to unbelievers' questions; 2) to witness to professing Christians who have been fed a watered down gospel that may be no gospel at all; 3) to provide intellectually challenging, thought provoking answers to non- Christians who may, in God's providence, "stumble" upon this book.

When a person is indwelt by the Holy Spirit and believes what the Bible teaches, he recognizes he formerly was destined for hell and powerless to save himself but now is destined for eternal happiness with God. His new found joy overflows, but when he tells the good news to an unbeliever, the unbeliever normally raises a large number of objections. Thus arises the need for apologetics as soon as evangelism has told its story. But if no one believes apart from the sovereign intervention of God, why go through all this effort of evangelism and apologetics? There are at least three reasons: 1) God's job is to change the heart, while the Christian's job is to proclaim the gospel to unbelievers; 2) Christians need to be able to still the voices of unbelief through logical argument. As John Calvin observed, the objective is proof not persuasion; 3) Christians need assurance that their faith is grounded in rationality and truth.

This brings us to the pictured ten-pointer. He knew something was not quite right and tried very hard to figure out what was that strange thing in a seemingly harmless pile of sticks. Stretching out his neck, and holding his nose high in the air he hoped for a confirming odor as he pondered all his sensory inputs about 25 feet from my blind. To a deer, human scent within their comfort zone is offensive, causing them to flee. It makes no difference if the human is attempting to kill it or is trying to feed it. Telling an unbeliever about the gospel is very similar. Unbelievers express offense at the gospel for a variety of reasons that are never the true reasons for their offense. The true reason for their offense is that the unbeliever hates God (Romans 1:30) and wants nothing to do with him whether the evangelism approach is they will go to hell if they are not saved, or they will be eternally happy with God in heaven if they are saved. Jesus said, *and blessed is the one who is not offended by me* (Matthew 11:6) because only believers are not offended by Jesus. So the parable is that to believers, the gospel is like the marvelous fragrance of fresh apples and corn to a starving deer. But to perishing unbelievers, the same gospel is like human odor to a well-fed deer causing the deer (and by analogy the unbeliever) to flee. So if you are a Christian, do not shrink back from sharing the gospel for fear of offending. The gospel will be offensive to unbelievers, but their offense is a small price to pay for God using your witness to bring some to saving faith in Jesus.

57. Did God create the universe?

For the wrath of God is revealed from heaven against all ungodliness and unrighteousness of men, who by their unrighteousness suppress the truth For what can be known about God is plain to them because God has shown it to them. For his invisible attributes, namely, his eternal power and divine nature, have been clearly perceived, ever since the creation of the world, in the things that have been made. So they are without excuse. Romans 1:18–20

When I look at this fawn's picture taken on a sunny fall day I can hardly help but worship. I see God everywhere, in the grass that arose out of light and air and water and soil and became part of the fawn through digestion in its stomach. In turn, the fawn could become part of a wolf through digestion in a wolf's stomach. It is obvious to me as a believer that God created everything we see. I did not always think this way and many are still not so fortunate. Why is there anything? is perhaps the oldest and most fundamental question to have been pondered over the ages. More often than not an unbeliever will defend his unbelief with the assertion that the universe was not created. For if the opening declaration of the Bible can be proven to be untrue then the whole business of faith is simply a fairy tale by logical extension. On the other hand, proving God created the universe will not silence every objection of unbelief, but it is a huge step in that direction.

Before continuing, we should ask if it is possible by human reason to know that God created the universe. The apostle Paul states the answer to be an emphatic yes in the referenced text. Students of philosophy will recall that Immanuel Kant's famous book, *Critique of Pure Reason,* divided the world into *phenomenal* (things observable by the senses, i.e. empirical) and *noumenal* (things not observable directly by the senses like the essence of something, the self and God) realms. According to Kant there is a wall separating the *phenomenal* and *noumenal* realms that cannot be crossed, making it is impossible to know by human reason and observation if God exists and, therefore, is the creator of all things. If this were true then Kant would have destroyed all possibility to be sure of the existence of God. So, if Kant is right then Paul is wrong. But if Paul is right (I am sure he is!), then Kant is wrong. They could not both be right because either you can or cannot know God created the universe. If they are both right we would have a contradiction, namely you can know and not know that God created the universe at the same time and in the same relationship. The odds are that most readers of this book have been more influenced by Kant than by Paul even if they have never heard of Kant prior to reading this paragraph. Beginning with Kant, the last 200 years has seen an unprecedented attack on the veracity of the Scriptures, primarily focused on trying to establish that there is no supernatural realm: i.e., the world ticks merrily along following some fixed set of discoverable natural laws that combined with chance and time account for everything we see.

An even more fundamental question is does anything exist? If nothing exists then clearly God didn't create anything. Most reasonable people start with the assumption that something exists. However, if someone challenges whether anything exists, we have Rene Descartes' famous statement, "I think, therefore, I am." Descartes was a mathematician and wanted to see if there was absolute certainty in anything. He started out doubting everything. But he discovered that if he doubted then he must exist since if he didn't exist, he logically could not doubt his existence. Once we set aside the possibility that nothing exists, there are only three possibilities as to why there is a universe. Of course people can and have invented many scenarios for at least two of the possibilities. The next chapters will address each of the possibilities.

58. Three Possibilities

If any of you lacks wisdom, let him ask God, who gives generously to all without reproach, and it will be given him. But let him ask in faith, with no doubting, for the one who doubts is like a wave of the sea that is driven and tossed by the wind. James 1:5–6

The three deer in this picture were focused on something moving toward them in heavy cover. The wind was at their backs so they could not smell the source of the sounds they were hearing. The picture is a good parable of the dilemma faced by a person sincerely trying to figure out if the universe was created by God or if it came about some other way. Just as the three deer may each have hypothesized a different interpretation for the single observable fact of something noisily moving toward them, so humans have proposed three different hypotheses for the single observable fact that the universe exists. In the case of the three deer, the source of the noise soon revealed itself to be a startled deer fleeing toward them. They had absolute empirical evidence that all three could agree was the sound made by another deer. With respect to the question of the origin of the universe we will also end up with absolute empirical evidence, though it will not be as explicit as literally seeing God, or being able to perform experiments in which something comes from nothing. So before we begin ask God to give you the wisdom to know the truth about the origin of the universe and for faith to believe His answer.

If once there was nothing, there can never be anything. This is the foundation of all rational thought that out of nothing, nothing comes. Descartes showed that something definitely exists. So if there is anything, then something must have eternal being because out of nothing, nothing comes. There are only three options that have ever been proposed for the origin of the universe. They are as follows:

1. The universe is self-existent and eternal; it does not have a beginning or an end.
2. The universe is self created having arisen from nothing without an outside cause; it had a beginning and may have an end.
3. The universe has been created by a self-existent, eternal being. It has not always existed; it had a beginning.

The usual way to proceed is to show that two of the three options are impossible, leaving the third option as the only logical choice. This approach only works if two conditions are met: 1) we know all the possibilities; and 2) the remaining one is logically possible. No one has ever developed a fourth option. Certainly, people have proposed many ways that any of the three options could have arisen, but in the end these different ways have always boiled down to one of the three options. If you think you have a fourth option, you have either revolutionized rational thought, or you have a scenario (maybe new) to explain how one of the three classical options arose. With respect to the requirement that the remaining alternative must be logically possible, only two of the three can meet the criteria: options 1 and 3. The second option is irrational since it violates the fundamental law of logic that 'out of nothing, nothing comes.' On a second front, self-creation is contradictory because for something to create itself it must first exist. Therefore, it must exist and not exist at the same time and in the same relationship, thus violating the law of non-contradiction. So rationally the choice comes down to options 1 or 3. The trouble is that option 2 is exactly what modern science proposes via evolution and the big bang. The following chapters will scrutinize each of the three options.

59. Is the universe eternal?

Of old you laid the foundation of the earth, and the heavens are the work of your hands. They will perish, but you will remain; they will all wear out like a garment. You will change them like a robe, and they will pass away, but you are the same, and your years will have no end." Psalm 102:25–27

As magnificent as this buck is (drool and all), we know he will not live forever, because the "fall" of Adam and Eve extended to the creation as a whole (Romans 8:20–21). Our experience confirms Psalm 102:25–27 that physical change is inevitable, tending always towards decline and imperfection. However, God made man in his own image (Genesis 1:27). So inwardly, to one degree or another, every person craves the security of the eternal that only faith in God can satisfy even though we are painfully aware that everything physical is temporal, gradually or rapidly wearing out, whether it is your body or your vehicle. No time of year so graphically portrays this truth as autumn as evidenced by the background in this picture, clothed in the brown garb of decaying leaves that only weeks before were part of green and living plants.

Since Old Testament times, Jews and later Christians and Muslims have believed the biblical account that God created the universe. But all this changed with the scientific revolution of the 18th and 19th centuries. Unbelief took refuge in the discoveries that unlocked many of the laws of physics, reasoning that if humans could figure out how nature worked, then maybe God wasn't necessary anymore to explain the origin of the universe. Perhaps there was a "naturalistic" explanation, and the first attempt was the idea that the universe was eternal thus eliminating the need for a creator.

The concept of an eternal universe is not irrational. It violates no law of logic. The trouble is that it does not square with the observed data. With advances in 20th century astronomy it became increasingly difficult to believe in an eternal universe. The evidence of an expanding universe that seemed to be moving away from a single point in space reasonably pointed to a created universe. Despite the evidence for creation from this scientific discovery of the expanding universe, science turned to the "big bang" theory ignoring the cause of the "big bang" as an unnecessary detail.

For those who wished to escape both the logical error of the self-created universe (big bang) and the more obvious answer of creation by an eternal being, the concept of an oscillating universe arose. According to this theory, the universe expanded out from a single point in space only to eventually collapse back to the single point and then expand outward again. This cycling could go on forever and we simply find ourselves in an expanding era at the present time. Unfortunately, this "scientific" hypothesis falls victim to empirical science itself. During the 19th century the second law of thermodynamics was discovered which, essentially, says you cannot have a perpetual motion machine. There is always some loss of usable energy (due to the fall!). From this came the concept of entropy or the ability of a system to do work. A detailed discussion of entropy is beyond the scope of this book, but is routinely covered in college physics. The net effect is what interests us here, and that is that based upon empirical "scientific" data, the universe is running down (wearing out) just as the referenced text asserts. An infinite number of expansion and contraction cycles are not possible. Therefore, based upon empirical scientific evidence we must reject the hypothesis that the present universe is eternal. God is eternal but the present universe is not, just as the Psalmist declared about 3,000 years ago.

60. Did the universe create itself?

The fool says in his heart, "There is no God." Psalm 14:1a

This curious yearling buck walked right up to me and peered into my blind. Foolish behavior is legendary among yearling bucks during the rut as they normally make up 75% or more of the total bucks harvested annually. It is no wonder that "young bucks" is used as a derogatory term for foolish young men, arrogant in their ignorance.

The idea that the universe has created itself has already been shown to be logically untenable. It should, therefore, be unnecessary to devote any more time to this idea, except that this is exactly what modern science contends is true. How exactly does science claim that the universe is self-created? The primary answer is the big bang theory in which proponents commonly use language such as the universe "exploded" into existence 18 billion years ago. Some even go so far as to speak of a moment of "creation." However, they do not mean that an eternal being was the cause of this "creation", but that somehow by time and chance the "creation" simply occurred. These scientists avoid the inherent problems with an eternal universe, preferring the empirical evidence for the universe having a beginning. But they dodge the how and the who of the cause and in effect claim the universe created itself. Once there was nothing and suddenly there was a universe. The theory of evolution then starts with the earth and all the necessary elements for life and supposes again that time and chance are the causes of life developing on the earth. Separate chapters will be devoted to a critique of science, evolution and the supposed "causal" forces of time and chance.

If empirical evidence suggests that the universe "exploded" into existence, why is there such reluctance to believe the obvious answer that an eternal being is the cause? The simple answer is sin, or in other words, unbelief. Sin is the idea that a person will be happiest apart from God. From the time we are first able to think and articulate our thoughts, we are by nature opposed to God. We want our own way and do not want any authority over us, especially an authority so powerful that it could speak the universe into existence. Of course, people know that if there is a creator God they obviously will be held accountable to Him, and that no one can measure up to God's standards. So they hide behind a haughty intellectualism wishfully hypothesizing that God does not exist so that they can do as they please without any fear of adverse consequences.

Unbelievers often accuse Christians of being "young bucks," arrogant, ignorant, foolish, weak people who need a mythical super-power to get them through this scary life, and so they have invented a god. But if this were so, why would they invent the Christian God who spoke the universe into existence and sends all those who are not perfectly committed to him to eternal punishment beyond our imagination? Indeed, the Christian God is far scarier than the things believers are supposed to be afraid of in the first place (see *If there's a God why are there atheists?* by R.C. Sproul). When atheist Richard Dawkins was asked what he would say if he met God, he echoed Bertrand Russell's answer to the same question, saying he would ask God why He hadn't made his existence obvious? However, God has blatantly made his existence obvious in the creation so no one has an excuse to not believe in Him (see chapter 57 and Romans 1:18–20). By hypothesizing a universe that does not require a creator, it is unbelievers who are the "young bucks" ignorantly, arrogantly and foolishly denying the evidence to their eternal jeopardy as Psalm 14:1 declares.

61. God Created the Universe

In the beginning, God created the heavens and the earth.
Genesis 1:1

Deer do not think about how or why. They strive to be for as long as they can. Light and trees and other deer are a reality, their origin being of no significance. Deer were created by God, but not in His image. We humans are created in God's image and so we ponder the how and the why.

The third and final possibility for the universe is that God created it. There is nothing illogical about the existence of an eternal being. But does creation of the universe out of nothing by God violate the fundamental law of logic that out of nothing, nothing comes? Does this law refute not only the big bang theory, but also creation by God? Without God there would be nothing, and out of nothing, nothing comes. But with an eternal being (God) able to do far more than we can think or imagine (Ephesians 3:20), there is something, so that out of God everything comes! Unbelievers must not arrogantly assume they will be able to understand how God created the universe for the statement to be true. On the other hand, since unbelief is irrational, believers should not suppose the best logical arguments will lead unbelievers from unbelief to belief.

Unbelief (that an eternal being created the universe) often justifies itself by trying to square the concept of "eternal" with the law of cause and effect. This axiomatic statement says every effect has an antecedent cause, and every cause produces an effect. The question that naturally arises is what caused God? This question is based upon two misunderstandings. First, the concept of eternal is not understood because to be eternal means that there is no beginning. Once a "thing" has a beginning, it is not eternal, and a cause is required. For example, the eight ball goes into the corner pocket because it was struck by the cue ball, which was struck by the cue stick, to which the player imparted a force. So it goes on and on, each cause becoming an effect requiring another cause. I have purposely used this example because the skeptic philosopher, David Hume, claimed to have disproved the law of cause and effect with this example, arguing that all we were seeing was a *customary relationship*. This of course would have thrown all of scientific inquiry into chaos if it was true, because much of science rests on the law of cause and effect. In fact Kant's work was motivated by a desire to rescue science from Hume's arguments.

The second misunderstanding is the supposition that the law of cause and effect says *everything* has a cause. It says every *effect* has a cause. If something is eternal it is not an effect because it is outside the realm of time. As far back as you can ever go you never reach a point where the eternal being did not exist. Aristotle realized this in what he called the *unmoved mover*. One of the great questions in the ancient world was why did things move? Aristotle realized than an infinite regress would result in an example like Hume later used. To escape this quagmire, you had to have an uncaused cause or an unmoved mover. The first is logically untenable because the movement of the eight ball had a cause, hence, working back we have an unbroken chain of effects, all of which must have causes that have the property of motion. However, an unmoved mover would solve the problem. Thus, Aristotle reasoned out the logical necessity of God's existence. This was a great insight in the development of Western philosophy. But by the time Aristotle realized the logical necessity of God, the entire Old Testament had been written affirming in its opening line that God created the universe.

62. Evolution: Fact or Fairytale?

And God said, "Let the earth bring forth living creatures according to their kinds." Genesis 1:24a

Look at this magnificent buck. Do you really think that deer are an accident of chance? Do you think their senses of sight, smell, hearing, taste and touch and their ability to interpret these senses in a logical way enabling their survival just happened? Did antlers suddenly one day sprout from a buck's head or were they always part of the design? Did deer and other ruminates have only one stomach once upon a time in a land far away across the sea and then, suddenly, a deer had three? In Genesis 1:11–27 days 3–6 of creation are summarized with God speaking into existence plants, the sun and moon, water borne creatures, birds, and land animals including humans. According to modern science, the big bang made planets, stars, galaxies, and the elements. In essence the way was prepared for life to evolve. All the basic materials for life were there: water, air and the chemical elements. Evolution says that simply given enough time, random formation of compounds eventually resulted in the fundamental, chemical building blocks of life that in turn formed into single cell plants and animals that formed into increasingly more complex creatures, culminating in human beings. Notice two stark contrasts between Genesis and evolution. First, Genesis says the way life originated was that God created every "kind" of plant and animal, which in turn reproduced only its own "kind" but never a new "kind." Each type of creature was created in its entirety. One never proceeded from a prior creature. Second, Genesis says humans are distinctly different from the rest of creation, being made in the image of God. Humans have an eternal soul and are not merely very intelligent, hairless apes. Certainly this is plausible. An eternal being who could speak galaxies into existence would have no trouble speaking a deer or any other living thing into existence. But is evolution also plausible? Could random chance over a sufficient period of time account for the diversity of life we see around us? The rational answer to this is no, and the reasons will be further discussed in the next chapter. For now, consider the following three points of evidence:

1. As science reveals more and more of the intricate structure and operation of living organisms, it becomes increasingly hard to believe that there is not "intelligent design" behind life. Suppose a professional geologist knew nothing about Mount Rushmore. Then one day he stood before the monument. Would he say, "That is an interesting piece of differential weathering," or would he say, "A skilled sculptor created this?" Yet, this is the very thing science does with evolution. Science must continually remind itself that though the structures of living creatures literally scream that they are created and not evolved, the fairytale of evolution must be defended while denying the substantial, logical, empirical evidence for creation.

2. Consider the evidence from reproduction. A given species can only reproduce the same species due to the construction of the genetic code. A new species cannot evolve from an existing species! Extreme mutations would be needed to make a new species out of an existing one, yet the general rule of even minor mutations is that they are deleterious and not an advantage for survival.

3. The fossil record shows sudden explosions of new species without any extinct intermediate species, just as Genesis says, instead of a slow, progressive advance in the number of species with many extinct intermediate species as evolution would predict. The conclusion is inescapable: empirical observation supports creation not evolution!

63. Time and Chance

All things were made through him, and without him was not anything made that was made. John 1:3

Given enough time, could random chance result in all the diversity of life that we observe? If I just sit in a given location long enough, will I eventually be in the right place at the right time to photograph a trophy buck? No, to see a deer, there has to be a deer to be seen. On average I see a different buck every two days in an area with a large population of bucks, during the times of greatest buck activity, and doing all that I reasonably can to overcome the seeming randomness of deer activity. Let's test the hypothesis of chance and time being the primary causal forces in photographing a buck like the one in this picture. How long would I have to wait in Manhattan's Central Park to take a similar picture of a wild deer? The question seems ridiculous, but it is not as ridiculous as the hypothesis that time and chance would produce a deer on a planet completely void of life. I would be much wiser to look for a deer in Central Park then wait for one to evolve out of nothing. Five hundred years ago, finding a deer in what is now Central Park would have been relatively easy. Today, I would start my search in the Central Park Zoo!

Getting life out of no life by chance and time is irrational and impossible. Experiments have shown that you might get the formation of short lived organic compounds out of a hypothetical, primordial earth, but that is long way from a deer. Chance is simply not a causal force. It is a mathematical concept to help assess likelihood when we don't know what is going to happen. The weather forecast says there is a 30% chance of snow tomorrow. We don't know if it will or will not snow tomorrow. If we knew all the factors involved we could state with certainty whether or not it would snow. Whenever we talk of chance it simply means we are ignorant of what will happen! For example, there is a 50% chance that a coin will land heads or tails. If I flip a coin 1,000 times, I'll get heads about 500 times. But if I flip it once, all I can say is it might be heads or it might be tails. However, a machine could be built that could be set to always produce heads or tails by controlling all the variables. On the other hand, objective observation shows that randomness leads to disorder not order. For example, take some molten silver and randomly throw it into the air every second for a trillion years and you will never get a U.S. silver dollar. Intelligent, purposeful effort is needed to convert molten silver into a coin to flip or to make a deer out of a lifeless planet. A man can make a silver dollar but it takes God to make a deer (John 1:3).

One of the biggest scientific problems today for evolution is biochemist Michael Behe and his concept of irreducible complexity. A "new" species must have all of its necessary parts at the same time. It cannot survive while waiting for a missing part. His example is a mouse trap. If one part is missing, the trap will not work. A new species would be very different from the species it supposedly evolved from, with a system of new parts and behaviors that must all arise in a critical number of creatures of each gender, at the same time in the same location, to enable reproduction without variation. But this compounds the improbability of the improbability of even getting one of the required improbable parts! Charles Darwin was correct that natural selection (time and chance) will tend to result in larger deer with heavier coats in cold climates and smaller deer with lighter coats in hot climates, but it will never bring about amoebas from no life, fish from amoebas, frogs from fish, dinosaurs from frogs, birds and rats from dinosaurs, and deer and humans from rats as evolutionists assert!

64. Natural Selection

And God said, "Let the earth bring forth living creatures according to their kinds – livestock and creeping things and beasts of the earth according to their kinds." And it was so. Genesis 1:24

When Charles Darwin studied finches on the Galapagos Islands he was observing natural selection. Natural selection is a scientific fact. The problem is that Darwin didn't fully understand biology or the Bible. Genesis 1:24 says God created "kinds" (categories of animals). Exactly how "kind" fits into today's system of scientific taxonomy is debatable though a kind is probably a family. To see how this all works, consider the taxonomy of the deer family (Cervidae) comprised of four subfamilies, two of which exist in North America. Subfamily Cervinaes, Genus *Cervus*, subgenus *Cervus* include the species *Cervus Canadensis* (elk), the second largest member of the deer family. Subfamily Odocoileinae/Capreolinae contains Genus *Odocoileus* (deer), Genus *Rangifer* (caribou) and Genus *Alces* (moose), the largest members of the deer family. God created Genus

Odocoileus containing the two species *Odocoileus virginianus* (whitetail deer) and *Odocoileus hemionus* (mule deer). The point of Genesis is that God creates "kinds" and "kinds" reproduce themselves. They do not reproduce into different "kinds." Scientifically, we know that a species can "evolve" (natural selection) into a subspecies, and a given species can mate with another species within the same Genus or Subgenus to produce a hybrid. Hybrids are fertile and can reproduce, but their survival strategies are defective and they can survive only in captivity, not in the wild. For example, hybrid fawns of whitetail and mule deer experience at least 50% mortality in captivity. In the wild these hybrids are occasionally observed, but there is no evidence to support that they survive long enough to reproduce into a viable sustaining population.

There are at least 17 subspecies of whitetail deer all descendents of *Odocoileus virginianus virginianus* found in eastern North America. The doe in this picture is from Missoula, Montana and is the subspecies *Odocoileus virginianus ochrourus*, though in this photo she looks remarkably like the subspecies *Odocoileus virginianus borealis* from Minnesota that comprise most of the photos in this book. All of these subspecies are explained by genetics and natural selection. But why is there such a great diversity of animals from amoebas to elephants? Darwin supposed that since finches with big beaks were more abundant in dry climates and smaller beaks in wet ones, that this potential to adapt could explain how fish, frogs, dinosaurs, snow geese, caribou, and humans all proceeded from a common ancestor. This would require a long list of missing links, the absence of which Darwin said would invalidate his hypothesis. The fact is that these missing links do not exist in the fossil record. Nor does animal husbandry give any record of a new species arising from mating within a given species or the mating of two different species. In fact, genetics precludes that two very different species could mate to form a third species, for example fertilizing fish eggs with frog sperm to get a lizard. You say, "What an absurd example." You are right – it is absurd! Yet some such mechanism is required to proceed from fish to frogs to dinosaurs and, eventually, to humans as natural selection-based evolution hypothesizes, but genetics disallows. Genetics explains why "kinds" always reproduce themselves and not other "kinds" as the Bible says. Once again we are left with the scientific evidence corroborating the Bible not refuting it! In the final analysis, as an engineer I reject evolution simply on the grounds of it being bad science, and as a Christian I reject evolution because it is blasphemous.

65. A Critique of Science

...and you will know the truth, and the truth will set you free.
John 8:32

Science is not the objective final arbiter of truth as the 21st century secular mind believes, but rather suffers from three inherent, fundamental limitations. First, science is limited in scope due to its dependence on empirical data. By its very nature science is incapable of investigating the supernatural because of the need for empirical data. Unfortunately, what has happened is that the belief has arisen that since science does not and cannot deal with the supernatural, the supernatural does not exist. In a way Kant was correct to say that we cannot determine if God exists by observation. Kant was trying to save science from the morass created by Hume's attempt to show that the law of cause and effect was invalid. Kant is correct if he meant that by scientific method (with its dependence upon empirical data and experimentation) we cannot prove empirically if God exists or doesn't exist. However, by scientific investigation of nature we can learn that nature has order that defies a random, purposeless cause.

The fall is the second limitation, manifesting itself in two obvious ways that pervert all human activity. First, we are all fallible and prone to make "honest" mistakes. Second, we all sin. Hence, science cannot be completely objective, and is motivated by the full spectrum of human sin (pride, greed, contractual or dissertation deadlines, "publish or perish" pressures, and the like) rather than the pure search for objective truth. This strikes at the heart of the fallen, modern mind's desire to make science its god. Corrupt people can and will and have manipulated data to achieve whatever results they desire.

Scientific method is comprised of four steps: 1) collect sufficient representative data; 2) form a hypothesis explaining the data; 3) verify the hypothesis by empirical experimentation; 4) use the "law" resulting from validation of the hypothesis to deduce what will happen in a new situation. The third limitation of science is the inherent and frequent inability to do steps 1 and 3 well even when setting aside the limitations of the fall. As a result hypotheses are often based upon an insufficient data set and may address issues that defy experimental verification. Step 1 manifests itself in issues like Newton's laws of motion which work well at low velocities, but Relativity is required at speeds approaching the speed of light. Step 3 results in limitations like proving that time and chance can produce a new species out of an existing species. This would require a ludicrous experiment like sequestering a large population of chimpanzees and observing them for millions of years to see if a human or some other creature ever results! Yet, this is exactly what would be necessary to prove the hypothesis. Because of these limitations, what we often see passing for science today is that a hypothesis is declared a law without proper verification. Verification by computer simulations simply passes the problem on to the simulation, since now you must first verify that the simulation is valid by experimentation.

In a way, the deer in this picture used scientific method. She observed that there was always spillage from my bird feeder (a hypothesis). Dutifully she tested it all winter, appearing at various times. Similarly, your pet has no doubt observed your behavior prior to feeding time. Every time the pet sees this behavior it concludes you are about to feed it. Science is capable of discerning much more than a deer or your pet, doing much good and expanding knowledge when used within its bounds. But you must not allow science to become an idol of arrogant, but futile human reasoning, supposedly supplanting God.

66. Are you 98% chimpanzee?

For not all flesh is the same, but there is one kind for humans, another for animals, another for birds, and another for fish.
1 Corinthians 15:39

This young buck paused from his frantic search for does to eagerly slurp water from a puddle. The muddy mixture he was standing in and drinking from reminds me of the "primordial ooze" that evolution peddles as the origin of the basic building blocks of all life. School teachers are fond of asserting evolution to be true because humans and chimpanzees have 98% of their genes in common*. But is it true?

A common biology textbook analogy is that DNA is equivalent to letters, genes to words, a chromosome to a book and a genome to a collective volume. Humans have 23 pairs of chromosomes comprised of about 23,000 genes (this number varies as more are discovered) that include over 3 billion DNA parts. So, does it follow that if chimpanzees and humans have 98% of their genes in common that humans must have descended from chimpanzees? Of course not! Such reasoning fallaciously assumes evolution is true, so that if two things are mostly made up of the same parts there must be a relationship between them in which one is derived from the other. But is this true in our common experience? Let's look at three simple examples.

1. Leveraging the gene/word analogy, the following two sentences contain exactly the same words, but radically different meanings and no logical relationship that one results from the other. *Jesus hates sin but loves sinners.* and *Jesus hates sinners but loves sin.*

2. The periodic table of elements is defined by the number of electrons and protons in an element. At room temperature 2 = helium, a gas; 79 = gold, a solid; and 80 = mercury, a liquid. But these radically different elements have the same building blocks.

3. An engineer can take a heart pacemaker and by making small changes to the microprocessor software, turn the pacemaker into a motion activated ignition system for a bomb. Of course this didn't happen by random chance over millions of years nor did the bomb ignition descended from the pacemaker or vice versa. Rather the engineer (an intelligent being) intentionally programmed one product to sustain life and another to take lives. This is exactly what God does by changing the information contained in the DNA to make a chimpanzee or a human, though they have very similar organs (heart, liver, blood, bones, and so on).

Therefore, in God's creation and human designs, identical words/ parts in two different things implies nothing about progression from one to the other, or that there is any relationship between the two things.

In the end it comes down to this: if you deny God is the creator of everything and believe evolution is true, then the *98% of genes in common* argument may appear to validate your position. But, if you correctly believe God created the universe then you will see, instead, that a very intelligent creator used parts that are essentially the same to make creatures as diverse as chimpanzees, deer and humans. However, the real difference is not the physical but rather that humans are made in the image of God with an eternal soul that no mere animal has. That is why the apostle Paul says there is human flesh and animal flesh. There is not a progression of fish to birds to animals to humans as evolution would hold, but distinctly different types of flesh created by God for very different purposes (Genesis 1).

*Recently (2012) the number has dropped significantly. 98% was based upon the 2-3% of the genome that codes for proteins. But the "ENCODE Project" has discovered that the non-coding regions of the genome function like an operating system in a computer. This 97+% of the genome is very different in a human and a chimpanzee.

67. Can science answer every question?

For it is written, "I will destroy the wisdom of the wise, and the discernment of the discerning I will thwart." 1 Corinthians 1:19

The primary cause of photographing this deer was God. But could the myriad of secondary causes that had to occur to take this picture have been predicted so that I would have known a nice buck would appear at this place about noon on November 4th? For many years I sought to scientifically unpack the mystery of deer behavior into some universal law(s). But I was on a fool's errand for there are no discernable laws, only general tendencies somehow dependent upon multiple factors. These factors make it more probable to see a buck at noon on a sunny November 4th than in a blizzard at 2 PM on November 20th (see appendix B). Through these efforts I learned that scientific method cannot answer every question. In fact, scientific method only works for a given area of inquiry when three things are true. 1) There actually is a governing universal law. 2) The law is simple enough that it can reasonably be discovered. 3) Free agency (choices) cannot be a factor, because choices may be irrational or simply personal preferences that are not repeatable and do not conform to any law.

Scientific method is very effective for discovering the basic laws governing physics and chemistry. For example, Ohm's law, V=IR, governs the operation of electricity. (Voltage = V; Current = I and Resistance = R) This law is simple and it always works so it was easy to gather V/I/R data sets and hypothesize that V=IR. Gathering other data sets to verify the law was also easy and soon people were using the law to distribute electrical power and invent useful tools like the computer I am using to write this book. Scientific method worked so well it started finding its way into other arenas. But what if scientific method is applied where there are no laws to discover or the laws are very complex? Many disciplines (sociology, economics, psychology and the like) are like deer behavior, without universal laws, and only general tendencies that can be described statistically but cannot absolutely predict what will happen in a given set of circumstances like Ohm's law does for electricity. Worse yet, these tendencies may change dramatically under a new set of factors like severe weather for deer or the unexpected failure of a large bank when trying to predict future stock prices. In these cases doggedly using scientific method will yield bogus laws whose application will predict bogus results.

When laws exist but they are either complex or interact with behaviorally driven factors, it is nearly impossible to ever collect enough representative data. In some biological systems, laws like genetics can result in complex predispositions which when mingled with behavioral preferences produce the effect under scrutiny. For example, cigarette smoking is linked to lung cancer but no one (except God) can say with certainty who will smoke and if they do, who will get lung cancer. The best that can be determined is the percentage of a given demographic that will smoke and get lung cancer at a given exposure. We cannot determine why the statistics occur so we cannot predict specific individual outcomes. In physical sciences, confirmation of truth is usually obtained by independent experiments yielding the same results. However, in some biological studies a broad spectrum of results may occur for supposedly the same experiments because the subjects in each experiment have different attributes that are unintentional and indiscernible. It would be very convenient to use scientific method if every effect we saw was governed by a universal, independent law, but God has designed a universe more complex than humans can ever entirely figure out. Scientific method is a good tool in the right applications but it is not the magic hammer that turns everything into a nail as some suppose.

68. Other Proofs for the Existence of God

The heavens above declare the glory of God, and the sky above proclaims his handiwork. Psalm 19:1

Does a deer's life have any purpose? Deer are born, reproduce, die and are eaten by other creatures (a result of the fall) only to have their genes carried forth in subsequent generations of deer that live, reproduce, die and are eaten in an endless cycle leading nowhere. Indeed, the present reality renders all life meaningless if there is no God. That is why arguing for the existence of God is so important. If there is no God, then we and deer are just hopeless, helpless, protoplasmic accidents on a one-way trip to meaninglessness. Much of 21st century western civilization believes this. But if God exists, then there is purpose in everything. As God orchestrates His grand plan, He maximizes His glory by redeeming a remnant of fallen people to worship and enjoy Him forever in a perfectly restored creation, my backyard being an imperfect Garden of Eden to this deer.

Chapters 57–61 argued that the universe was created by God, using the law of cause and effect and the basic laws of logic. This is called the

Cosmological argument, one of three classical arguments for the existence of God. Anselm, the archbishop of Canterbury from 1093–1109, developed the *Ontological* argument that has given scholars headaches for over 900 years. The essence of his argument is that *God is that being than which no greater being can be conceived.* According to Anselm such a being must exist in reality as well as in the mind. (See college level philosophy books for further study.) The *Teleological* argument is essentially that the necessity of a creator God's existence is undeniable because of the amazing order and apparent design in everything we see (Romans 1:18–20). The more sophisticated people and science become, the more obvious is God's existence. The "uneducated," jungle-born native has sufficient evidence to know all he can observe with the naked eye was created by God. The 19th century scientist armed with a simple microscope saw a world of living, dividing cells and had more evidence. Today, scientists know of the incomprehensible vastness of space, and the amazing chemical factories and complex mechanical parts comprising living cells, and have even more evidence that God exists.

Yet, all unredeemed people hate God and suppress the fact that He exists because they know He is holy, and they are not. He will hold them accountable for their sin. As Dostoyevsky wrote, "If there is no God, all things are permissible." They prefer the despair and meaninglessness of life as espoused by Nietzsche ("God is dead") and Jean-Paul Sartre who saw freedom as freedom from morality. They glory in Immanuel Kant whom they credit with disproving the existence of God. However, Kant did not prove atheism but embraced agnosticism, claiming the existence of God could be neither rationally proved, nor disproved. Surprisingly Kant developed what is called Kant's moral argument based upon what he called the *categorical imperative* (all people have a sense of what is right, requiring a moral obligation to duty). Kant began by asking what must be true for society to survive, and for life to be meaningful, or at least, bearable? He concluded there must be perfect justice. Kant knew justice is never perfect in this fallen world, so a future world is required with perfect justice. But perfect justice requires a morally perfect, omniscient, omnipotent judge who knows all the facts and always reaches perfect decisions that he can always enforce. Ironically, Kant discarded the classic arguments for an amoral creator God he said could not be rationally proven, only to postulate the perfectly moral, biblical God. Try as it will, unbelief cannot triumph over the fact that God exists!

69. Cosmos not Chaos

Where were you when I laid the foundation of the earth? Tell me, if you have understanding. Who determined its measurements – surely you know! Or who stretched the line upon it? On what were its bases sunk, or who laid its cornerstone when the morning stars sang together and all the sons of God shouted for joy? Job 38: 4–7

God's stinging cross examination of Job in Job 38: 4–7 makes it clear that we mortals have no capacity to look back in time to the instant of creation and deduce how the universe came into being. The obvious point is that God is the creator and worship is our only sensible response. In 1980 Carl Sagan's bestseller, *Cosmos,* was published. The book began with a profound observation that we have cosmos not chaos. Sagan spoke better than he knew. For if random chance was the cause of the universe we would expect disorder (chaos) not order (cosmos). Sagan tried to argue that random chance has somehow resulted in order. It is hard to understand why so learned a man would think this way except that he was blind to the things of God and desperately tried to suppress the truth that the presence of cosmos necessitates a creator God (Romans 1:18).

Science could never make sense out of the nonsensical chaos of a randomly operating universe. An ordered universe operating in accordance with a marvelous but monotonously repeatable set of immutable governing laws is needed to make scientific discovery possible. If science is to supplant God as creator it must explain how a random chance universe (randomly, changing from one behavior to another with time and location) would finally "get it right" and suddenly stop being random, operating according to a set of immutable laws governing everything we see. What would sustain this order so that it did not fall back into chaos? Of course this is a rhetorical question begging a resounding response that none of these things make any sense at all when we appeal to our empirical experience. It is because we have a Creator that we have a cosmos not chaos. God not only created the universe, but He also actively sustains and governs it. He is not a "watchmaker god" that wound up the universe and let it go as the 18th century Deists like Benjamin Franklin wished to absolve themselves of being accountable to God.

Human scientists and engineers must deal with the world as God created it, seeking to discover the laws that govern it and constrained in what they can accomplish by its fallen state. But God had no restraints. He created the periodic table of elements, the laws of physics and everything else as he wished. Humans must accept their limitations and concede they will never add to or change the laws of physics. Purposeful, human intelligence did create the technology needed to capture and view this image of a magnificent rutting buck making his rounds just before sunrise. However, only a fool would think random chance and not a photographer caused the buck to be in focus against the blurred background. Similarly, only a fool would think the buck and the entire cosmos are a random chance accident of fate without a purposeful, intelligent, sustaining Creator. But unbelievers are sometimes so enamored by technology and the triumphs of scientific inquiry in bringing into focus the marvels of creation, that the Creator becomes just the blurred background. As W.C. Fields neared death, a visitor found him reading the Bible and expressed surprise that Mr. Fields was investigating the Bible. But Mr. Fields retorted that he was only looking for loopholes. The Bible, reason (the cosmological argument) and empirical observation (the teleological argument) all declare God is the cosmos' Creator. Yet, unbelievers doggedly persist in searching for a scientific loophole to justify their unbelief. May this not be true for you.

70. Intelligent Design

For what can be known about God is plain to them because God has shown it to them. For his invisible attributes, namely his eternal power and divine nature, have been clearly perceived, ever since the creation of the world, in the things that have been made. So they are without excuse. Romans 1:19–20

Many animals have a vomeronasal organ (sometimes called the 6th sense) that enables them to analyze pheromones (chemicals produced by members of their species). By curling his upper lip (flehmen response), pheromone scent molecules are drawn back to the buck's vomeronasal organ under his upper lip, allowing him to determine the presence or absence of estrous from a doe's urine, and how long ago the urine was passed. Could such a marvelous organ be the result of random chance, or does it point to an intelligent based design?

David Hume and Immanuel Kant are perhaps the most widely recognized critics of the classical arguments for the existence of God. Yet both of these men admitted they were most impressed by the teleological argument that Paul presents in Romans 1:19–20. By the late 20th century, a movement had begun within the scientific community called intelligent design that essentially espoused the teleological argument. Birthed by the tremendous strides science had made in understanding the operation and reproduction of living cells, many secular scientists realized it simply was no longer reasonable to believe that random chance and not some intelligence was behind it all. The name intelligent design, while redundant, was necessitated because there remain hard core atheistic scientists like Richard Dawkins who persist in saying, in essence, that biological systems are very complicated and give the appearance of design, but nevertheless, are the result of random events.

Perhaps the tipping point that launched the intelligent design movement was the realization that DNA was not really about matter but about information. Cells know how to operate and faithfully reproduce themselves because the DNA contains a complex, sequenced chain of information like a computer program that regulates the cell. Coherent, sequenced information always has intelligence as its source. The truth of this is self-evident. (Computer programs always have a programmer) To escape this logic some opponents have gone as far as to argue extraterrestrial beings came to earth and "intelligently" created life, but this only pushes the question back to how did these space aliens come into being? The main point is that the creating intelligence cannot be part of the creation. Therefore, God must be transcendent and beyond the realm of the physical reality we observe. But transcendence is not about location as many suppose, but about "being"; i.e., God is the eternal, creator of the universe as shown by the cosmological argument.

Today the trend is definitely in the direction of accepting intelligent design. Christians have been quick to embrace intelligent design, and this has created two problems. First, it appears to unbelievers that intelligent design is a religious explanation, not a scientific one based upon empirical evidence. This will no doubt remain fertile ground for many foolish arguments and policies, especially within the domain of public education. The second problem is more dangerous. Christians must not be too elated over intelligent design because it does not explicitly credit the biblical God as the intelligence behind creation. There remains much work to be done in the fields of apologetics and evangelism to bring unbelievers from the point of just affirming the empirical necessity of God to the point of saving faith in Jesus Christ.

71. A Leap of Faith

Now these Jews were more noble than those in Thessalonica; they received the word with all eagerness, examining the Scriptures daily to see if these things were so. Acts 17:11

In a steeple chase, a horse will trust its rider and blindly jump a thick hedge, but a deer is unlikely to jump a barrier like this deep narrow ditch, if it cannot see what is on the other side. Only as a last ditch effort (pun intended) will a deer blindly leap a barrier, hoping the unseen alternative on the other side is better than their present reality. Unbelievers often suppose Christians foolishly leap before they look, blindly and ignorantly trusting in the existence of a heavenly paradise on the other side of death, free from the ugly realities of life in a fallen world. In Acts 17:11, the Apostle Paul commends the converts at Berea because they not only eagerly received the word, but they also, carefully studied the Scriptures to be sure Paul's teaching was true. If the Bible really is the word of God, then it is capable of standing up to the most rigorous, sincere investigation.

Having spent 14 chapters arguing that logically everything we see was created by God and didn't "just happen," unbelievers are faced with a serious problem. If evidence, reason, and even other religions like Judaism and Islam support the opening claim of the Bible that God is the creator of everything, then is the rest of the Bible true? Recognize that if God is the sovereign, creator of the universe, then every other claim in the Bible is easy for God. Parting the Red Sea, virgin birth, resurrection or any other supernatural claim in the Bible that you wish to not believe, suddenly is child's play for a God who spoke the universe into existence! But there is a second reason unbelief fights creationism so vigorously. If God exists as creator, then God is extremely powerful and you are extremely vulnerable. What does this all powerful God require of you and what can He do to you if you do not comply? Hence, unbelief ignores reason and evidence for God's existence, foolishly hoping that there is no God and no consequences for unbelief and sin. While unbelief rants that Christians stupidly hope for a better reality after death, unbelief makes the real leap of faith, hoping that there is no reality at all after death. *The fool says in his heart, "There is no God."* (Psalm 14:1a)

Once the truth of creation is conceded, unbelief usually will attack the veracity of the Bible next. The evidence for creation is provided to **everyone** through general revelation and is sufficient to send **everyone** to hell (Romans 1:18–22), but it is insufficient to show anyone that the only way to God is through faith in Jesus Christ (John 14:6). Only the Bible provides this information. Serious examination of the Bible will immediately show it is unlike any other book. The 66 books of the Bible were written over a period of about 1,500 years by at least 40 different authors from all walks of life and yet, it all fits together into a unified consistent story of a perfect creation that fell and ultimately will be restored for eternity. This is in effect a biblical teleological argument for the Bible's authentication, namely, that this consistency defies human ability when contrasted to human efforts of a single author (the Koran or the Book of Mormon that are riddled with contradictions and inconsistencies). No ancient book was so carefully preserved, nor has there ever been a book subjected to more critical, scholarly review. Even in our modern scientific age and despite claiming creation, virgin birth, and resurrection, the Bible is the number one bestseller of all books worldwide, every year. But the Bible is not the only book claiming to be the word of God. How can you be sure it is the one and only true word of God?

72. Is the Bible reliable?

But the Helper, the Holy Spirit whom the Father will send in my name, he will teach you all things and bring to remembrance all that I have said to you. John 14:26 *All Scripture is breathed out by God and profitable for teaching, for reproof, for correction, and for training in righteousness* 2 Timothy 3:16

One thing that is *fairly* reliable is that during the rut, you are likely to see a dominant, breeding buck like the one above who strutted by me as the drizzle was about to turn to snow. So is the Bible *fairly* reliable or is it absolutely trustworthy? When 2 Timothy 3:16 was written the New Testament had not been completed so *All Scripture* must mean the Old Testament. However, Jesus says in John 14:26 that the Holy Spirit will teach all things and enable the New Testament authors to remember all that Jesus said. As a result, based upon Jesus' authority, the New Testament was also divinely inspired. In addition the Holy Spirit indwells all Christians, and enables them to believe and understand the Bible. Logically, since God inspired the Bible's authors (though not as secretaries taking dictation), He also assured it was inerrant and infallible*, having no higher authority than itself (Hebrews 6:13) to validate its claims. However, unbelievers, incapable of believing and understanding the Bible (1 Corinthians 2), incorrectly reason all of this to be a circular argument formulated as: *The Bible says it is the word of God. Therefore, it is the word of God.*

Unbelievers make a truly circular argument about the Bible. They think the supernatural is impossible, so the Bible's supernatural claims are untrue, and hence the Bible is untrue. Unbelievers usually raise five objections to biblical reliability.

1. *Conflicts with science:* These have already been extensively covered and will not be discussed further (chapters 57–70).

2. *Historical inaccuracies:* This is a foolish objection given the vast body of ever-increasing historical and archeological evidence supporting the veracity of the Bible.

3. *Self-contradictions:* By contradictions, people usually mean differences exist, mainly within the Gospels, concerning the same subject. Of course different authors may emphasize different aspects of a subject, but different perspectives give the reader a better picture of the subject than any one individual account. Application of the rules of logic to these supposed contradictions always results in the conclusion, that the Bible contains mysteries but not contradictions.

4. *Offensive language:* The Bible criticizes us and leaves no room for us to criticize it. Sin is taken seriously and we live in an age that does not. As a result, the punishment for sin and the definition of sin described in the Bible seems unrealistically harsh and offensive to an "anything goes" 21st century mindset. But, within everyone's psyche, the Bible's view of justice and morality rings true, even though, our fallen nature tries to suppress this truth (Romans 1:18–25).

5. *Miracles and myths:* 21st century people have a severe allergy to miracles. But, since God is the omnipotent creator of all things, it is easy for God to cause a miracle. The mythological objection often arises because some miracles have certain similarities to Greek or Roman mythology. By applying the rubric of guilt by association, the unbelieving mind can quickly and erroneously convince itself that the Bible is filled with myths. This will be addressed in chapter 74.

For a more detailed defense of the of the Bible's trustworthiness, the reader is referred to *Evidence That Demands a Verdict* by Josh McDowell and R.C. Sproul's booklet, *Can I Trust The Bible?*
*Inerrant means the original text was without error and allows for minor copying errors in later copies. Infallible means it was impossible for the original text to err.

73. Was Jesus wrong about the Parousia ?

The Olivet Discourse Matthew 24–25, Mark 13 and Luke 21

Deer do not have a calendar to predict when the rut will occur. They simply follow the physical and behavioral "signs" driven by hormonal changes in bucks and does that ultimately culminate in the rut. Humans however are prone to predict specific times. Many false predictions of the Parousia (Second Coming) have occurred throughout history, but did Jesus also wrongly predict the Parousia?

The so called "Olivet discourse" begins (Mark 13:2) with a prediction by Jesus that Jerusalem, including the temple will be destroyed. The disciples responded to this unthinkable prediction with two questions: When will it happen and what will be the signs that precede it? Liberal theologians claim that Jesus' statement in Mark 13:30 that *"this generation will not pass away until all these things take place"* is wrong because *all these things* include the Parousia which has not occurred. Therefore, Jesus and the Bible are flawed. Jesus is just a "pretty good" role model and moral teacher, but he is not God despite his remarkable prediction of the destruction of the temple in A.D. 70. On this argument liberals primarily base their objection to the inerrancy of the Bible. But are they correct and is it this simple?

There are three kinds of future statements in the Synoptic Gospels that seem to apply to the Parousia. Some texts like Matthew 10:23, 16:28 and Mark 13:30 speak of things to happen within one generation (about 40 years). On the other hand, the Parables of the Weeds, the Mustard Seed, and the Leaven in Matthew 13, the Parables of the Ten Virgins and of the Talents in Matthew 25 and the Parable of the Ten Minas in Luke 19, all suggest long periods of time. Finally, a third group of statements say that the exact time is unknowable even to Jesus in his human nature (Matthew 24:36, 24:43–44 and 25:13).

In addition, a prophecy will often include elements to be fulfilled by events that will happen relatively soon and other elements that are either figurative or will not happen for a long time. For example, nearly the same words in Matthew 24:29 are contained in Isaiah 13:9–13. In this case the consensus is that Isaiah is predicting the Babylonian captivity which came to pass without any of the dire astronomical upheavals included in this prophecy. In the case of the Olivet discourse, there is also consensus that it predicts the destruction of Jerusalem and the Temple by the Romans in A.D. 70 in which over a million Jews were slaughtered. Interestingly, secular historical accounts record that the Christians followed Jesus' instructions in Luke 21:21 and fled from Judea, and Jerusalem to escape the Roman inflicted holocaust even though this was completely contrary to the usual practice of fleeing to a walled city to escape an advancing army as did the Jewish population to its demise.

The net effect is the liberals are incorrect. The Olivet Discourse does not exclusively predict either the destruction of Jerusalem and the Temple in A.D. 70 or the Second Coming. Rather, the passage is best seen as predicting both the end of the Jewish age in A.D. 70 (within the lifetime of many of Jesus' followers) and the end of history at the Parousia which Jesus says will occur at an unknown time. In addition, many of his followers also lived to see his transfiguration, resurrection, ascension and his resurrected body, all of which heralded the coming of his kingdom. For a more detailed investigation of these complicated and controversial passages, the reader is referred to chapters 10 and 11 in *The Bible and The Future* by Anthony Hokema, and *The Last Days According to Jesus* by R. C. Sproul.

74. Miracles: Fact or Fiction?

Therefore we must pay much closer attention to what we have heard, lest we drift away from it. For since the message declared by angels proved to be reliable and every transgression or disobedience received a just retribution, how shall we escape if we neglect such a great salvation? It was declared at first by the Lord, and it was attested to us by those who heard, while God also bore witness by signs and wonders and various miracles and by gifts of the Holy Spirit distributed according to his will. Hebrews 2:1–4

The soft crunch of leaves alerted me to the possibility of a deer approaching from the heavy cover behind my blind. Materializing out of the grey November dusk, this buck's sudden appearance was definitely not a miracle, but just an example of his highly honed stealth. But are there miracles at all? Since the 19th century, liberal theologians and secular scientists have railed against the possibility of miracles. Their reasoning is that if miracles are impossible, then the Bible is untrue. But if miracles are possible, are the biblical miracles true, heralding a great purpose, or are they just myths about a cosmic conjurer pulling stuff out of his hat willy-nilly?

In the original languages, the Bible does not use the word miracle, but, instead, words like wonder, mighty work, or sign to describe an event that cannot be explained as an improbable, but normal operation of the natural world. Biblical miracles are basically confined to three eras: 1) Moses and Joshua; 2) Elijah and Elisha; and 3) Jesus' life and the apostolic witness following his resurrection (by far the greatest concentration of miracles). By the very definition of miracles, it is scientifically impossible to investigate and either prove or disprove a given miracle or miracles in general. However, once the existence of God is accepted, the possibility of miracles must also be accepted, because if God is creator of the universe then there would be no restraints to prevent him from intervening in his creation in any creative way he wishes to accomplish his purposes. Miracles are not magic. Magic creates illusions using the "laws of nature" to fool the observer into thinking the magician has circumvented the laws of nature. Magic seeks to subvert truth in order to entertain an audience or exalt the performer, while God's purpose for a miracle is to authenticate the truthfulness of the messages of God's messengers. Of course, God's miracles always triumph over magicians as in the classic confrontation of Moses and Pharaoh in Exodus 7.

Christians are divided as to whether or not miracles still occur. Some hold that once the New Testament was completed, miracles ceased for there were no more messages from God that needed authentication. Other Christians believe miracles are still possible, often arguing that if miracles ended with the apostles, then the spiritual gift of miracle-working would not be listed in 1 Corinthians 12:10. In either case, there is a balance to be struck. Biblical miracles all lead to the message of salvation as God redeems a remnant from fallen humanity to be his people. But Christians must not be overly zealous for miracles, lest we become like the crowds that followed Jesus to receive free food (John 6:25–34), but did not grasp the message that the miracles validated. Similarly, we must not be like Herod who was hoping to be entertained by Jesus' miracles. (Luke 23:8)

Christianity is defined by the supreme miracles of Jesus' virgin birth and resurrection that attest to the truth of scripture. In the final analysis, it is impossible to be a true Christian without believing in all of the biblical miracles. To reject the biblical miracles reduces Jesus to a superb role model, eliminating any hope of the miracle based salvation promised to all who trust in Jesus alone for eternal life.

75. Show Me a Miracle and I Will Believe

And the Pharisees and Sadducees came, and to test him they asked him to show them a sign from heaven. He answered them, "When it is evening, you say, 'It will be fair weather for the sky is red.' And in the morning, 'It will be stormy today, for the sky is red and threatening.' You know how to interpret the appearance of the sky, but you can not interpret the signs of the times. An evil and adulterous generation seeks for a sign, but no sign will be given to it except the sign of Jonah." Matthew 16:1–4a

While the clouds in the background may look ominous, I was sure they indicated that the strong cold front, with high winds, rain and snow that had pinned me down in my tent 20 miles from a road the previous day had passed. Jesus notes in the referenced passage that unregenerate mortals, including the era's two most prominent Jewish sects, are fairly adept at short-term weather forecasts by interpreting the sky, but are no good at discerning spiritual truth. But Jesus says he will not try to quench their insatiable thirst for authenticating miracles, for there can never be enough proof for the unbelieving heart apart from the sign of Jonah. What is this ultimate sign? Jesus had already revealed it in Matthew 12:39–40: it is the resurrection.

The 21st century unbelieving mind, callused by modern science, also wants empirical evidence if it is going to believe in Jesus. Two millennia ago, people at least thought they could be persuaded by miracles. But today many people don't even believe there is such a thing as a miracle. Through the ages unbelief has prided itself in skepticism which masquerades as objectivity in the quest for truth. But it is foolish to think scientific inquiry can ever empirically establish the existence of miracles. But this is not because miracles do not ever have empirically discernable, physical manifestations.

There are at least three reasons why scientific method cannot establish the reality of miracles. 1) Reality occurs in two realms: physical and spiritual. God is spirit and science works only in the physical. Hence, anything in the spiritual realm is physically indiscernible though its effects may be empirical. 2) Sometimes effects are observed that conflict with established scientific models (laws). But, the overwhelming reason is not that these effects are miracles, but that the observations or models are flawed. For example, observing that time slows down as velocity approaches the speed of light could be erroneous due to a defective clock. However, in this case it's not the observation that is at fault but the model. When Newtonian physics is revised by Einstein's theory of relativity, everything is completely predictable and repeatable. 3) Science can only study repeatable empirical effects. We can study gravity because it follows an ever-present law. An experiment can be performed anytime and anywhere we wish and always yield the same result. But miracles by definition are not always available for observation. If they were, they would not be miracles. So a given miracle may occur only once, or it may be extremely rare, but the frequency will always be insufficient to allow for experiments to authenticate a miracle.

However, there is a miracle that always brings the observer to faith in Jesus: God's gracious and sovereign regeneration of an unbelieving heart. Evidenced by saving faith driven by the testimony of the indwelling Holy Spirit, the unbeliever's hostility toward Scripture and doubts of its truth claims are vanquished. Unbelievers scoff at this answer, because a humanly unbridgeable gulf of unbelief blinds them from supernatural reality. But God is God and like it or not He has ordained the only way for people to come to Him is by faith in Jesus.

76. Is there double truth?

And God made the two great lights-the greater light to rule the day and the lesser light to rule the night-and the stars. Genesis 1:16

I do not think there are any deer in this picture taken as I approached my vehicle at dusk under the soft light of the rising "hunter's" full moon.* Thomas Aquinas (1225–1274) is generally considered to be the greatest theologian between Augustine and the Reformation. Aquinas correctly taught that truth is revealed in three ways: 1) truths exclusively revealed in the Bible like the gospel; 2) truths exclusively revealed through the investigation of nature using scientific method like the laws governing the moon's orbit; and 3) truths revealed by both the Bible and reason like the moon was created.

Long before Islam's military threat to Christian Europe was finally repulsed at the Battle of Vienna (September 11–12, 1683), Islamic philosophers were threatening Christianity by combining Aristotelian logic with Islamic theology to create their "double truth theory" that argued the third category of truths (Aquinas called them "mixed articles") could be true in faith and false in reason, or vice versa. Aquinas sought to refute the double truth theory and correctly reasoned that the Bible (faith) and nature (reason) never contradict one another, because they both have God as their source and both bear witness to Him. Protestants have often misunderstood Aquinas to have taught that the natural world and faith, are separate realms when in fact he taught that nature and faith, while distinct, are ultimately united in God. Nevertheless, contemporary Christianity is plagued today by at least two fallacious double truths.

1. Some people claim to be Christians but accept the big bang and evolution as true. Essentially they say creation is true in faith and false in reason. But Aquinas has shown this is fallacious because any given thing must be either true or false in both faith and reason. Spectacular scientific accomplishments like Neil Armstrong's famous "one small step for man, one giant leap for mankind" may stoke the pride of human achievement and give false solace to unbelievers, but these accomplishments prove nothing about the universe's origin nor do they refute the need for an eternal Creator of the universe.

2. Ironically, despite Aquinas' profound influence on Roman Catholic theology, Roman Catholics have blended Aristotelian philosophy** with Christianity in the Eucharist. Catholics claim in effect that transubstantiation (chapter 41) is not a double truth fallacy because the bread and wine really become the body and blood of Christ (true in faith) while still appearing to be bread and wine (true in reason). However, when Jesus said, "this is my body" and "this cup is the new covenant in my blood" (Luke 22:19–20) he was referring to the bread and wine in the Passover that symbolized the body and blood of the sacrificed lamb. Therefore, what Jesus really said was that in the Lord's Supper, the Passover elements of bread and wine take on the true meaning they always pointed to. Jesus is the "Lamb of God" whose broken body and shed blood take away the sin of the world (John 1:29). Therefore, transubstantiation is a Christianized double truth, being false in faith and true in reason because the bread and wine are really only what they appear to be, just bread and wine.

*Native Americans called the full moon that occurs between mid October and mid November the "hunters" full moon probably because they would have experienced increased success in killing rutting members of the deer family at this time of year.

**Aristotle taught an object's "substance" (what it really is) and its "accidents" (what it appears to be) are separate.

77. How do we know what is true?

...these things God has revealed to us through the Spirit. For the Spirit searches everything, even the depths of God. For who knows a person's thoughts except the spirit of that person, which is in him? So also no one comprehends the thoughts of God except the Spirit of God. Now we have received not the spirit of the world, but the Spirit who is from God, that we might understand the things freely given us by God. And we impart this in words not taught by human wisdom but taught by the Spirit, interpreting spiritual truths to those who are spiritual. The natural person does not accept the things of God, for they are folly to him, and he is not able to understand them because they are spiritually discerned. 1 Corinthians 2:10–14

Deer do not usually notice me lying in my blind. Occasionally, a deer becomes curious about the slight motion or sound from operating the camera and takes a closer look as this fawn did. Once a yearling doe came to me and smelled and licked the bottom of my right boot. Still unsure about what I was, she placed her forehead against the bottom of my left boot and pushed rather forcefully against the resistance of my extended leg. Smelling and licking the bottom of my left boot still did not satisfy her curiosity, so she stepped into the blind, knocking over a 3 inch diameter cross stick, to sniff the lens hood. For several seconds her black, moist nose pondered the situation 15 inches from my face before she carefully backed out of the blind.

Founded by British philosopher John Locke (1632–1704), modern empiricism is one school of epistemology, the branch of philosophy concerned with the origin and nature of knowledge. Locke argued that we come into this world as a blank slate without any *a priori* (prior to experience) knowledge. According to Locke all knowledge is learned through experiencing the world through the five senses and subsequent reflection upon these experiences. In the United States we know of Locke primarily for his political theory (all law is based upon natural law which is based upon the law of God) that heavily influenced the Founding Fathers. Locke was not the first to consider sense perception as the basis of all knowledge, but his work at the end of the 17th century was perfectly positioned for the subsequent scientific revolution that buttresses the 21st century mindset that only the empirical exists. Of course our senses are very prone to err as people have realized all the way back to the founding of philosophical thought. For example, a perfectly straight oar appears bent when dipped into the water. My point is that sensory experience is ultimately inadequate to empirically establish what God has ordained can be known only by faith. It is only through the indwelling presence of the Holy Spirit that the believer attains the full assurance of the truth of Scripture and of the resurrection (1 Corinthians 2:10–14).

The sensory capabilities of a deer are vastly superior to a human's. Yet, the yearling doe could not perceive me by sight, sound, smell, taste, or touch. But just because the doe could not perceive by her senses that I was a human did not mean I am not a human. Similarly, just because unbelievers cannot "perceive" the things of God with their five senses does not mean the supernatural does not exist or that Christianity is untrue.

Enter Bishop George Berkeley (1685–1753) and his famous maxim, "To be is to be perceived." This has lead to foolish questions like, if a tree falls in the forest and there is no one to hear it, does it make a sound? What Berkeley showed was objective reality exists apart from human empirical perception because God is the great perceiver. Hence, truth is reality as known by God not as perceived by man.

78. Is the Trinity irrational?

"In the unity of the Godhead there be three persons, of one substance, power, and eternity: God the Father, God the Son, and God the Holy Ghost: the Father is of none, neither begotten nor proceeding; the Son is eternally begotten of the Father; the Holy Ghost eternally proceeding from the Father and the Son."
Westminster Confession (2.3)

A person who knew virtually nothing about deer, might conclude their behavior was irrational. For most of the year interaction between mature bucks and does is essentially nonexistent. Then for a few weeks in the fall, bucks aggressively seek does who vigorously flee from them. But each doe eventually, and willingly accompanies a buck for about 24 hours (as pictured), mating several times with him. This fickleness is not irrational but is driven by hormonal changes in both bucks and does, though the exact cause(s) are debated (Appendix B). But despite this general understanding of the causes, it is still a mystery as to the exact day an individual doe will mate.

Atheists, members of other world religions, and cults like Mormons and Jehovah Witnesses all charge that the Trinity is irrational. Worse yet, Liberal "Christian" theologians have strayed far from a historic understanding of the Trinity, thus appearing to validate the charges leveled by non-Christians. Against this backdrop, the long held position of both Roman Catholic and conservative Protestant scholars is that the Bible clearly teaches the Trinity is true. On this point there has been amazing agreement throughout church history as articulated in the catechisms and confessions of faith (the Westminster Confession being one example) spanning a broad range of Christian denominations. Like the preceding deer parable, the root cause behind the charge of irrationality is a limited understanding.

To determine if the Trinity is irrational we must first acknowledge the incomprehensibility of God as the starting point of all theological discussions. God is transcendent, being ultimately beyond fallen human comprehension. That does not mean we cannot know Him at all, but rather, while we can know much about Him, there is a limit to our knowledge. We must not expect to understand everything because only unbridled arrogance would ever assume that human understanding could equal God's understanding. Next we must distinguish between objective truth (which can be shown to be true), nonsense (which can be shown to be untrue), mystery (something obviously true but not completely explainable) and paradox (appears untrue but can be shown to be true). Finally, we need to consider the perspective of God, Christians, and unbelievers.

An unbeliever is incapable of understanding the Trinity (1 Corinthians 2:10) so it appears to them to be nonsense or a contradiction. But it was shown in chapter 30 that the Trinity is not a contradiction as defined by the classic rules of Aristotelian logic. So while unbelievers think the Trinity is false, they are unable to prove it violates the rules of formal logic. Ultimately the Trinity is a paradox for unbelievers because it appears untrue to them but from God's omniscient knowledge, the only thing that really counts (chapter 77), it is absolutely true. An unbeliever's only hope for knowing if the Trinity is true is to be one of the elect and eventually be brought to saving faith. As Christians they will then see the Trinity is absolutely true based upon their trust in Scripture's truth (chapters 30 and 71–77). But because of the incomprehensibility of God, at least on this side of heaven, Christians will not fully understand or be completely able to explain the Trinity, and aspects of it will remain a mystery.

79. Why must God be triune?

Father, I desire that they also, whom you have given me, may be with me where I am, to see the glory that you have given me because you loved me before the foundation of the world. ...I made known to them your name, and I will continue to make it known, that the love with which you have loved me may be in them, and I in them. John 17:24, 26

Christianity is the only world religion that correctly understands God is triune. The necessity for God to be triune can be deduced by leveraging Scripture's unambiguous revelation of God's plan of redemption and from two additional statements of truth: 1) The axiom that love must have its object and cannot exist apart from its expression; 2) God's ultimate goal is to preserve and display His glory which He loves infinitely (chapter 2).

Let's suppose that God is not triune, but is monotheistic as understood by Jews and Muslims as a single eternal person. This would mean that before creation God would have been incomplete having no way to express love because he had no one to love. He would have been like the pictured yearling doe, who despite her innate ability to love (chapter 100) had no fawn to lavish her love upon. God could have created the universe to declare his glory (Psalm 19) and populated it with people to worship Him. But this solution would not work for two reasons: 1) God could not have the infinitely perfect relationship with humans he could have with his equal, just as a person has a deeper loving relationship with another person than they can ever have with their dog; 2) Because of the fall, humans hate God and are morally unable to save themselves (chapter 46). They must be born again in order to delight in God and be in the presence of a perfectly holy God.

A triune God is not obligated to create the universe since He could have been eternally glorified in the infinite and perfect mutual love of the Father, Son, and Holy Spirit. But the Trinity glorifies God even beyond creation's declaration of His glory because it allows Him to redeem sinners so that they can love and delight in Him forever. Jesus not only quenches God's wrath against the elect's sin and preserves God's holiness, but removes their sins from them and transfers Jesus' perfect obedience to them (chapters 105–107). This is accomplished by overcoming the elect's enmity toward God by indwelling them with the Holy Spirit. Thus the elect can be in God's presence forever as adopted children sharing in the love of the Trinity (chapter 110).

Islamic or Jewish monotheism is relegated to a works-based salvation that saves no one from hell. The Islamic accounting system of more good works than sins results in imperfect people with sins still on their record. Muslims are essentially Pelagian (chapter 45). They see no need for a perfecting atonement and are satisfied with their simplistic, uninspired, carnal heaven of an eternal orgy of unlimited sex and binging on delicacies. The fall makes the original Jewish understanding of salvation by perfect obedience to the law impossible. Apart from the veiled, substitutionary system revealed in the Old Testament sacrificial system (chapter 8) and consummated in the perfect, one time sacrifice of Jesus that Jews reject, no one can be saved. Modern Judaism has less hope than Islam, having degenerated into an organization to preserve Jewish history, culture and ethnicity. Its only hope is that hell does not exist because it has no hope of heaven. But God's glorious solution of a monotheistic Trinity maximizes His refulgent glory in three ways: 1) His love and delight in Himself within the Trinity; 2) the creation's declaration of His glory; and 3) the adoration of the elect whose "chief end is to glorify Him and enjoy Him forever" (Westminster Catechism Q&A 1). In the final analysis, the impossibility and irrationality is not that God is triune but that God could be God apart from being triune.

80. Are the Son and Holy Spirit eternal?

He was in the beginning with God. John 1:2

Artists love to paint family scenes of a large buck with a doe and fawns. The truth is that capturing such an image is nearly impossible because does only tolerate a mature buck's close proximity just prior to mating. By then the fawns have usually been temporarily driven away. The buck above was pursuing the buck fawn's mother early in the rut. She fled with her doe fawn leaving the buck fawn behind and enabling me to capture this image of a mature buck and a fawn.

Both the Nicene and Chalcedonian Creeds that defined the Trinity and various Bible translations and confessions of faith say the Son was eternally begotten of the Father. How can the Son be eternal and begotten? Doesn't begotten mean the Father existed first and then the Son appeared? Hence the Son is not eternal just as if the deer above were father and son, the buck would be older than the fawn. Part of the problem lies with translation and interpretation of the Scriptures. The Greek word *monogenēs* is the culprit. Literally, *monogenēs* means one descendent or offspring.

Traditionally it has been translated as "only begotten Son" in John 3:16 and other passages. The ESV more accurately translates *monogenēs* as "only Son" in John 3:16. The Greek word for beget is *gennao* meaning to bring forth and is usually translated as born. For example, in John 3:3 "born again" is "*gennao* again". In Hebrews 11:17, referring to Abraham offering Isaac, the Greek word used is *gennao,* and is correctly translated traditionally as "only begotten son." In Acts 13:33, Hebrews 1:5 and 5:5 *gennao* is used in quoting Psalm 2:7 *"You are my Son, today I have begotten you;"* However, in these passages the Father is declaring that Jesus is God's Son at the conclusion of Jesus' fulfillment of his role in redemption, within the time domain and in his human nature, not his eternal personhood in the Trinity. So while the original Greek does not say the Son was begotten, the church has historically interpreted the Scriptures to imply the Son was begotten.

Our normal experience teaches two things: 1) begetters (parents) always exist before the begotten (baby) arrives; 2) the begotten is always of the same essence of the begetter(s). Hence humans beget humans, deer beget deer, and so on. Scripture makes clear that the Son (Jesus) is eternal with the Father (John 1:2) and exactly of the same essence (Hebrews 1:2–3). By our normal experience it is easy to see God would beget God but what about eternally begotten? C.S. Lewis explained this paradox as analogous to what happens when we imagine something. The act of imagining and the resulting image occur simultaneously but are logically sequential since the imagining precedes and is the source of the image. So there never could have been a time the Father existed apart from the Son, nor did the Son ever derive his life from the Father as a creature does.

The problem of the Holy Spirit proceeding from the Father and the Son is much easier to understand. One might wonder if God could be "biune" (two in one) and comprised of just the Father and the Son. The answer is that the infinite love and delight of the Father and Son in each other flows out as the person of the Holy Spirit. So if the Father and Son are eternal then the Holy Spirit is eternal. To help explain this Daniel Fuller compares the Holy Spirit to the esprit de corps of a military unit (*The Unity of the Bible* Chapter 8). The idea is that the unit's devotion to their purpose and one another takes on a separate nature of its own. Of course human organizations are not perfect, but the perfect "esprit de corps" of the Father and Son, completes the perfect, eternal Trinity in the person of the Holy Spirit.

81. If God exists why is there evil?

The Rock, his work is perfect, for all his ways are justice. A God of faithfulness and without iniquity, just and upright is he. ..Vengeance is mine, and recompense, for the time when their foot shall slip; for the day of their calamity is at hand, and their doom comes swiftly... For I lift up my hand to heaven and swear, As I live forever, if I sharpen my flashing sword and my hand takes hold of judgment, I will take vengeance on my adversaries and will repay those who hate me. I will make my arrows drunk with blood, and my sword shall devour flesh—with the blood of the slain and the captives, from the long haired heads of the enemy. Deuteronomy 32:4, 35, 40–42

The virile buck in chapter 72 seemed self-confident of his invincibility. Two days later I saw him again. Looking exhausted, humped-up and moving slowly, he bled from wounds on both ears. This picture and story are an inadequate parable of the terrible wrath that awaits the critic who smugly supposes that in the problem of evil, they have the trump card against the folly of Christianity. If they only were destined for a sound thrashing by a dominant buck they would not be in such a pitiable, desperate position. But the thrashing that awaits them eternally increases in intensity as meted out by the omnipotent God of creation for their arrogance in calling him to task.

Simply stated, the "problem of evil" is as follows: since evil exists, God cannot be both good and omnipotent as Christianity claims. For if evil exists and God is good, then God is not omnipotent because he cannot eliminate evil. On the other hand if God is omnipotent and evil exists, then God cannot be good to allow evil. There are four kinds of evil: 1) physical evils such as disease, earthquakes, and the like; 2) spiritual evil of Satan and demons; 3) moral evil manifested by sin of every kind; and 4) the eternal evil of hell. When evil is defined it is usually expressed as either the opposite of what is good (immoral), or a lack of good such as failing to obey God's laws. Despite the fact that evil is real (not an illusion), it cannot exist independently. It is dependent upon the existence of good which it then somehow corrupts! Physical and moral evil resulted from the fall. Spiritual evil existed prior to the fall since Satan tempted Eve. The eternal evil of hell is necessitated by God's justice to deal with Satan and his minions, and the rampant human moral evil resulting from the fall.

The problem of evil has an unstated, invalid assumption, that God's goodness and omnipotence cannot coexist with evil. The story of Joseph powerfully refutes this assumption. "*As for you, you meant evil against me, but God meant it for good.*" (Genesis 50:20a) While Scripture often declares that God brings about all four kinds of evil, it never says God does anything evil, blames God for evil, or claims God takes pleasure in evil. Rather, God uses evil for His glory and our good. The most evil act ever, Jesus' crucifixion, was orchestrated by God for the good of the elect (Acts 2:23–24; 4:27–28).

God is entirely good and omnipotent (sovereign) over all things including evil. His wrath proclaims His absolute goodness and omnipotence because of the infinite force He levels, eventually and eternally, against all forms of evil. God governs everything, working through secondary causes to accomplish His purposes. God's holiness makes it impossible for Him to do evil, but humans may intend evil (Joseph's brothers) in carrying out these secondary causes (God's plan to save Jacob's family from the famine). Our fallen minds cannot understand the mystery of how God can hold us accountable, and be sovereign but not culpable for evil, but to God there is no confusion.

82. If God exists why is there suffering?

Indeed, I count everything as loss because of the surpassing worth of knowing Christ Jesus my Lord. For his sake I have suffered the loss of all things and count them as rubbish, in order that I may gain Christ... (Philippians 3:8)

Like the problem of evil, the problem of suffering questions how God can be both good and sovereign since suffering exists. I had seen this doe and two fawns several times before this picture was taken six days after a bow hunt ended near my blind. Most likely the buck fawn's flesh wound would not prove fatal. The picture is a parable of two ancient suffering questions: 1) Why do some suffer much and others very little? (Why was only one deer shot?); and 2) Is suffering always bad or can it sometimes be God's mercy, acting as a wake-up call? (Why did the arrow careen off his rib cage rather than fatally penetrating his chest cavity?) In this case there is probably a logical answer for these questions. I had noticed previously that his mother and sister were very vigilant to sound and movement in the trees while he was oblivious to them, so he probably blundered too close to a tree-perched hunter and by God's grace was given a valuable lesson.

At its root, suffering is the result of the fall. When sin entered into the world it extended to the whole creation so that suffering is pervasive. To explore suffering, we must distinguish between Christians and non-Christians and the Old and New Testaments. About 80% of the words translated as some form of suffering are in the New Testament. Suffering usually appears in the Old Testament as a consequence of sin (*an idle person will suffer hunger,* Proverbs 15:19). The New Testament focuses mainly on Christ's suffering for the elect's sins and how Christians are united with Christ through suffering. Some Christians claim suffering is always the result of some specific sin, or at the other extreme, that true believers will not suffer. Both claims are false. Certainly people may sometimes suffer because of a specific sin, but usually suffering cannot be linked to a specific sin, seemingly occurring randomly as disasters, accidents, diseases, and the like. Sadly, many Christians take this secular view, talking in terms of tragedy and random chance, instead of the biblical approach couched in God's sovereignty. There are no tragedies in God's economy. Hurricanes, terrorist attacks and pandemics, can all result in great suffering, but they are also gracious reminders of God's infinite wrath against sin and the need for personal repentance. (Luke 13:4–5).

God is good and sovereign. He continually orchestrates events to achieve the greatest glory so that His holiness, justice and righteousness are satisfied. No one escapes suffering for his sins. Unbelievers receive justice and suffer to one degree or another during life as a result of the fall and sometimes for specific sins. Ultimately, they will suffer for eternity in hell, because they did not believe in Jesus while on earth. Christians receive mercy and are spared from eternal suffering, because Christ's sufferings are an acceptable substitute to satisfy God's wrath for their sins. Nevertheless, Christians are called to suffer in this life. This accomplishes at least 3 purposes: 1) it unites them with Christ (Romans 8:17); 2) it glorifies God because they do not turn against God because of their sufferings (1 Peter 4:16); and 3) it puts a human face on Christ's sufferings for unbelievers when they see Christians suffer for bringing the gospel to them (Colossians 1:24). Like deer, we want to avoid suffering, but unlike deer we also ponder the ancient questions. However, the question is not *if* you will suffer, but *when*, you will suffer. By God's grace, through the Holy Spirit, Christians should not ask "why me?", but "why not me?" seeing their suffering as insignificant compared to the splendor of spending eternity with Christ (Philippians 3:8).

83. Is Christianity a crutch for the weak?

But he said to me, "My grace is sufficient for you, for my power is made perfect in weakness." Therefore I will boast all the more gladly of my weaknesses, so that the power of Christ may rest upon me. 2 Corinthians 12:9

This doe's left rear leg had been broken and healed in a contorted fashion. She had a very pronounced limp when she walked, but could run remarkably fast when pursued by a buck. Perhaps with a crutch, she might have walked more easily! If you agree that Christianity is a crutch for weak people, then you have no real understanding of the cataclysmic problem Christianity addresses. Christianity is not a crutch for weak people to hide behind like science is a fool's crutch to rationalize God does not exist. Rather, Christianity is a high tech trauma center, resuscitating dead people (Ephesians 2:1–10)! Christians have not invented a fairytale god to help them cope with the difficulties of life that normal people easily deal with as Freud asserted. No, Christians are people for whom God has graciously opened their spiritual eyes enabling them to see the utter hopelessness of their situation apart from Christ and the immeasurable greatness of His power to redeem their lives forever.

By way of analogy, suppose the doe in this picture not only had a crippled rear leg, but that she could neither see, nor hear, nor smell her impending doom as she hobbled toward a pack of ravenous wolves. A crutch would not help her! A savior is needed who can intervene and destroy the wolves. However, that would not be of much value if the savior could not also restore her crippled leg and her sense of sight, hearing and smell so that she could perceive the danger she was in and give thanks to this savior. If God has not opened your eyes and ears to the reality of his wrath against all unrighteousness, then you are like the doe in this analogy. You cannot see that you have a one-way ticket to hell. You may comfort yourself that you do not murder, or rob banks, or physically commit adultery. But that is not how God reckons righteousness. The slightest offense against God (for example, thinking that any worldly pleasure will make you happier than coming to saving faith in Christ) will condemn you to everlasting torment in hell. (To recall why this is appropriate, see chapter 43) However, embracing Christ as your savior, humbling yourself before him, confessing that you are weak and need His power in your life, will secure for you unimaginable joy forever in His presence. Christ is the savior who defeated Satan (wolves in the parable) when he died for the sins of all who would put their trust in him, thus allowing their entry into the presence of God in heaven where only the perfectly righteous can dwell. Christ defeated the final enemy, death, when he rose from the grave securing for all who trust in Him eternal life in fellowship with God.

Perhaps God has graciously opened your eyes and ears to the reality of Christ and heaven and hell and that you have come to saving faith in Jesus Christ. If so, praise Him! For others I pray this parable might be the beginning of your realization that you need a savior, and that you might earnestly desire to come to know that Christ is real and the Bible is true. However, I know that many will consider this to be foolishness. You may judge me to be arrogant, ignorant, insane, narrow-minded and a host of other uncomplimentary adjectives. Do not lose heart. I, also, once thought the same things before God opened my mind to my need of a savior and the truth of the gospel. I needed far more than a crutch for I was dead. I needed to be made alive to see the danger I was in and the excellency of Christ to rescue me. May God grant you eyes to see and ears to hear the gospel!

84. Are all Christians hypocrites?

"Woe to you, scribes and Pharisees, hypocrites! For you are like whitewashed tombs, which outwardly appear beautiful, but within are full of dead people's bones and all uncleanness. So you also outwardly appear righteous to others, but within you are full of hypocrisy and lawlessness." Matthew 23:27–28

In ancient times an actor was called a *hypocrite.* Actors often play roles in which the characters they play, say and do things that do not reflect the actor's true beliefs. When we watch an actor play the role of a noble character it is easy to confuse the role with the actor's true character and beliefs. Similarly, bucks sometimes act out elaborate ruses to try to mate with an unreceptive doe. This buck walked away to try to convince the doe he had lost interest. Then he circled back, sneaking up on her using the available cover. Overcome by his passion, he stupidly rushed the doe who easily avoided him. The buck tried to use the deception of disinterest in the doe to get what he really wanted (mate with the doe). In an analogous way, Christian hypocrites use the deception of interest in God to get the worldly things that they really desire.

Jesus minced no words about the hypocrites of his day, the scribes and the Pharisees. The scribes were the experts in the Jewish law. The Pharisees were one of several denominations of Judaism. Together they had created an elaborate system of rules that seemed to follow the letter of the Mosaic Law while missing or corrupting its intent. Following the rules had the appearance of righteousness, but it was motivated by their love of human praise, not their love of God. By definition, a hypocrite is someone who does not practice what they preach. A hypocrite intentionally tries to create the illusion that they love Jesus when in fact they love what the appearance of loving Jesus can get them. When unbelievers say Christians are hypocrites they usually are justifying why they are not a Christian. Often the unbeliever's reasoning begins with the perception that a professing Christian has sinned. Assuming Christianity claims that Christians do not sin, the Christian is deemed a hypocrite and the unbeliever concludes they want nothing to do with a bunch of Christian hypocrites! However, Christianity does not claim that Christians are not sinners. Christians retain the old nature, against which the indwelling Holy Spirit wars. Christians hate when they sin and earnestly desire to be free of the sin nature (Romans 7). So, if the unbeliever means that all Christians are sinners, then they are absolutely correct! There is no argument. But usually, the unbeliever has simply equated sinner with hypocrite. All Christians are definitely sinners, but not all Christians are hypocrites.

However, some professing Christians are indeed intentional hypocrites, doing all kinds of "good deeds," but in their hearts they do not love Jesus or have any real desire to submit to him by following his commandments. For a myriad of reasons they receive some benefit to their standing in the world by leading others to think they are a Christian. They greatly dishonor Jesus and true Christians as do the many highly publicized scandals of church leaders who are exposed in every conceivable kind of sexual immorality or financial impropriety. The point of application is that if you profess to be a Christian, then you have to be ever vigilant in your behavior. This is not legalism, but persistent attention to your sanctification so that your behavior does not dishonor Christ. Simply put, you need to be exemplary not only in your moral behavior, but also in speech and work ethic. Christians should always strive to be morally upright, but also the best employee, neighbor, spouse, and the like so that they do not dishonor Jesus in the eyes of the world (Colossians 3:17).

85. Is the church just after your money?

The point is this: whoever sows sparingly will also reap sparingly, and whoever sows bountifully will also reap bountifully. Each one must give as he has made up his mind, not reluctantly or under compulsion, for God loves a cheerful giver. 2 Corinthians 9:6–7

These mule deer bucks appeared at dusk, peacefully sharing the abundant food in a high alpine meadow next to my remote campsite in Glacier National Park. But when food is scarce, a doe will chase her own fawn away to keep the food for herself. People often tend to be more like the hungry doe, despite that in the United States we are usually more like these well-fed bucks. Our fallen nature is simply not generous. In the referenced text, the Apostle Paul uses an agricultural metaphor to exhort the Corinthian church to be generous in taking a collection for the poverty stricken Christians in Jerusalem. This should not be interpreted as a prosperity gospel that the reaping will be material riches beyond their giving. Rather, what generous givers usually reap is rewards in the life to come. Unfortunately, many unbelievers are well aware of TV preachers who have been exposed as charlatans, bilking their followers to enrich themselves. As a result, an unbeliever will often equate appeals from legitimate ministries with the charlatan's ruse. What is the true Christian position with respect to giving?

Many Christians think the Bible says a Christian should give 10% of his income to the local church. This is untrue. Paul says people should give *cheerfully* as they have made up their minds, not reluctantly or under compulsion. Whether someone thinks they should give 3% or 30% of their income, they are free to do so. Essentially, the biblical message is that everything belongs to God (Psalm 50:10). We are only given material wealth to steward. As sanctification advances in a believer, one of the fruits is generosity, not only in money, but also in service (Romans 12:6). Of course, it is always expected that individual Christians as well as churches and Christian based ministries will be good stewards of their resources. But in this fallen world there is often a tension with respect to giving. The average man in the pew will tend to be stingy while church leaders may envision more ministry opportunities than the laity perceive or desire.

Surveys show that fewer than 10% of "evangelical" Christians give at least the 10% guideline that most pastors and churches recommend. This is not commendable and points to how hard it is to be a Christian in an affluent society. The Bible never says it is a sin to be wealthy, but Jesus says, *For it is easier for a camel to go through the eye of a needle than for a rich person to enter the kingdom of God.* (Luke 18:25) This is because being rich causes one to trust in their riches and not in God. Statistics show the less affluent one is, the more they tend to give as a percentage of income. As Jesus said with respect to the poor widow, *For they all contributed out of their abundance, but she out of her poverty put in all she had to live on.* (Luke 21:4) In the end, claiming that churches are just after your money is merely a feeble excuse to remain in unbelief and not go to church. Jesus gives us the true perspective: *Do not lay up for yourselves treasures on earth, where moth and rust destroy and where thieves break in and steal, but lay up for yourselves treasures in heaven, where neither moth nor rust destroys and where thieves do not break in and steal. For where your treasure is, there you heart will be also.* (Matthew 6:19–21) In other words, trusting in the material things of this world will not ultimately satisfy. But when our first priority is pleasing God, material resources will be less important, and it will become easier to battle our fallen nature's propensity to materialism and selfishness.

86. Is church boring and irrelevant?

For the time is coming when people will not endure sound teaching, but having itching ears they will accumulate for themselves teachers to suit their own passions, and will turn away from listening to the truth and wander off into myths. 2 Timothy 4:3–4

Deer accumulate a lot of ticks on their ears and often are seen itching these pests with their hind feet to dislodge them or at least gain some relief from their present discomfort. In the referenced text, Paul is awaiting execution for preaching the Gospel in Rome and exhorts his young protégé, Timothy, to hold fast to true doctrine. He warns Timothy that the itching ears of fallen humans want to dislodge sound doctrine from the pulpit and replace it with what seems exciting and relevant to their fallen minds. Not much has changed in 2,000 years. According to polls the main reasons people do not attend church are that it is boring and they find it irrelevant. There are at least two questions imbedded in that belief. The first is how could something based upon a book completed 2,000 years ago in a pre-scientific era possibly have any value to sophisticated, well-educated people in the 21st century? The second is the more pragmatic question of how will going to church make me happier?

The answer to the first question boils down to the fact that the Bible transcends time. "Modern" thinking has been corrupted by the appearance of scientific progress: a theory is embraced, but later found to be flawed, based upon new evidence. Hence, science tends to be always changing direction on a subject as new data is discovered. Over all, science usually moves continually closer to truth, appearing to be continually improving. Given such a paradigm, 2,000 year old ideas would likely be useless, and the Bible would indeed be boring and irrelevant if it was just another work of man. But, the Bible was done right the first time! It is the inerrant, infallible word of God (2 Timothy 3:16). God is unchangeable and the Bible is the sum total of all the information we need about God and how to live a life pleasing to Him. There is nothing new to be written or discovered in this area, no improvement or progress to be made. Whenever you read of a new idea that rethinks orthodox (historical) Christianity, run for your life, because it will almost always be a contemporary twist on an old heresy. In short, the Bible remains the only tangible, constant anchor in a continually changing world.

Will going to church make you happier in this present life? Probably not if you are an unbeliever, because church is usually boring and irrelevant from this perspective. The unbeliever just wants relief from the "ticks" of this present life because he does not believe there is an afterlife. He is blind to the peril he is in. He does not grasp the wrath of God against his unrighteousness (Romans 1:18; 1 Corinthians 1:18; 2 Corinthians 4:4). The problem the church can solve is to reconcile sinners to God (Romans 5:10). This is the most relevant problem that anyone ever faces! Certainly, the progressive work of sanctification is beneficial in this present life, but on the whole, being a Christian will precipitate many new problems because the world is an enemy of God. To be a Christian is to be joined with Christ in his suffering, death and resurrection (Romans 5:10; Galatians 2:20; 1 Peter 5:8–10; James 4:4). Unfortunately, many churches today have tried to increase attendance by scratching the itching ears of unbelievers. This corruption of the gospel will be further explored in the next chapter.

87. Is Jesus the Lion of Judah or a pet cat?

I know that after my departure fierce wolves will come in among you, not sparing the flock; and from among your own selves will arise men speaking twisted things, to draw the disciples after them. Acts 20:29–30

Jesus is called the Lion of Judah in Revelation 5:5. While the lion is the king of beasts, Jesus is the King of kings and Lord of lords (Revelation 19:16). Unfortunately, many churches have corrupted the gospel as Paul predicted would happen in Acts 20:29–30 to the point that Jesus is not a savior but a role model, not the Son of God but a butler, not the creator of all things but a social activist. Jesus has been reduced to a shadow of the Lion of Judah just as a domestic cat is not the king of beasts but a non-threatening pet, sometimes responding to your beckon call of, "Here kitty, kitty!" How did this happen?

The 18th century Enlightenment saw science as a replacement for faith. Kant's work provided solace for the unbeliever by claiming that the existence of God could not be proven. In the 19th century liberalism tried to "reform" the church into a change agent that would result in a utopian society. Jesus was seen as a very good man and a great moral teacher, but he was not the Lamb of God who takes away the sins of the world (John

1:29). By liberal reckoning, miracles do not exist, so his virgin birth and resurrection could be conveniently dismissed as pre-scientific era myths.

Following World War II, the evangelical movement exploded, especially through the Billy Graham crusades. Being "born again" was the catch phrase. While this was a welcome return to a more biblically correct Christianity, the basic theology of the movement was mostly Arminian, not reformed. It espoused that people must be persuaded to "make a decision for Christ" as opposed to Jesus' statement that the Father, not flesh and blood, reveals that Jesus is the Christ (Matthew 16:15–17). In their zeal to win as many souls as possible, many evangelical churches adopted a Madison Avenue approach to evangelism. Success was measured by growth in church attendance. The assumption was that traditional church didn't work any more and was boring and irrelevant to modern people. Using marketing techniques the church experience was redesigned to conform to what the unbelieving world wanted rather than transforming the world by renewing the world's mind (Romans 12:2). While there is biblical merit to being all things to all people (1 Corinthians 9:22) it must never be at the expense of gutting the gospel or even watering it down. Church was no longer viewed primarily as a time for believers to worship God, but as a time to evangelize unbelievers by drawing them in with clever schemes, and entertainment, hoping that through these things and a watered down gospel presentation they might decide Jesus is the Christ and be saved. By God's grace, not all churches have abandoned the biblical gospel. However, some churches have gone far beyond "cookbook" evangelism methodology, by trying to reconcile what the world loves with what the Bible hates, such as embracing homosexuality or promoting a gospel that claims by becoming a Christian you will enjoy health and wealth and the best possible life on earth. In the final analysis, the more a church abandoned the biblical gospel to avoid being irrelevant to unbelievers, the more it became irrelevant from an absolute biblical perspective.

As C.S. Lewis observed, Jesus could be either a liar, a lunatic or the Lord. However, if he is not the Lord, then he must be either a liar or a lunatic because he could not possibly fulfill the claims and promises he made like the "I am" sayings in chapters 22–29. But could the 19th century liberals have been correct? Is there a fourth choice? Was Jesus simply a very good man and a great moral teacher?

88. Was Jesus merely a very good man?

Scripture Reference: Matthew, Chapters 5–7

19th century liberal theologians began an assault on the Bible which today has evolved into a distorted picture of God and Jesus. According to this view, God is mainly a God of love without offensive properties like wrath that must be propitiated by Jesus' death to save sinners from hell. The supernatural does not exist. Heaven and hell are not real and miracles are just myths. Jesus was a very good man and role model, an excellent moral teacher and a nonviolent social reformer, but he wasn't the son of God. This liberal view of Jesus reached its nadir in the late 20th century with the Jesus Seminar where "scholars" voted on Bible passages as to whether or not they were true statements about Jesus. The net result was like the buck in the picture. You can tell he is a "good" buck, in the sense of a desirable trophy, but you cannot see all the detail you would like to have. The picture was taken at dusk, resulting in a blurry picture just like liberal theology gropes in the darkness of false assumptions and fallen human reason, giving a blurry picture at best of Jesus. You can still see he is morally a very "good" man, but little more.

The Sermon on the Mount (Matthew 5–7) is generally well-loved, even by harsh critics of Christianity. Liberal theologians derive from it the idea that Jesus is merely a good man and a great moral teacher who gives us a bunch of wise principles to live by leading to the idea that Christianity is just redefined Jewish legalism. Obey these rules and if there is a heaven you'll be fine. Yet, within the Sermon on the Mount, a broad range of topics that liberal theologians vigorously deny appear. For example, Jesus so elevates behavioral requirements in Matthew 5 on anger, lust, divorce, oaths, retaliation, and love of enemies that no one can meet the standards and escape condemnation to hell. Not only proper action is required, but also proper intent and thoughts. No one will ever be good enough to be saved by his own doing. Therefore, a savior is needed, not just a role model and teacher.

Matthew 6 contains important teachings on charity, prayer (including The Lord's Prayer), fasting, and greed with the net effect being a call to believe in Jesus to meet all our physical needs. Matthew 7 is well known for the Golden Rule (7:12). Its opening salvo on judging others (7:1–5) has been extrapolated into false teaching by liberals to be tolerant, accepting all kinds of sinful behavior and considering other religions as ways to God. But this is not what the text is about. Rather, it cautions believers to not deny their own sins by focusing on other's sins. It calls for discernment to identify false teachers (prophets) from true teachers and believers from unbelievers based upon their fruits (7:6, 15–20). Liberals conveniently avoid these texts which if applied to themselves would show they are condemning (judging) evangelicals who hold to traditional teachings on the need for atonement, and the reality of heaven and hell. As a result liberals have gutted the gospel to the point that they do not know who Jesus really is. The Sermon on the Mount ends with a solemn warning:

"Not everyone who says to me, 'Lord, Lord,' will enter the kingdom of heaven, but the one who does the will of my Father who is in heaven. On that day many will say to me, 'Lord, Lord, did we not prophesy in your name, and cast out demons in your name, and do many mighty works in your name?' And then will I declare to them, ' I never knew you; depart from me, you workers of lawlessness.' (Matthew 7:21–23) A person is not saved because they think they have done good works. The question is **does Jesus know you?** Thus, the Sermon on the Mount gives the true picture of Jesus that goes far beyond the false view of Him that characterizes Him as a morally very good man who gives us a plethora of rules to live by.

89. Postmodernism –
Is anything absolutely true?

... "I have come into the world – to bear witness to the truth. Everyone who is of the truth listens to my voice." Pilate said to him, "What is truth?"... excerpt from John 18:37–38

Postmodernism is a philosophy that says there is no absolute truth. A quick perusal of articles in the various hunting magazines would lead one to believe that deer are very predictable creatures, following a set of basic rules. However, my experience leads me to believe that postmodernism is at least correct about deer behavior, because I believe there are only general tendencies, but no absolute laws, governing deer behavior. For example, common wisdom says bucks are eagerly attracted to the aroma of estrous doe urine. This ridiculous looking buck crowned with dual burrs and attached cottonwood leaves looks as foolish as postmodernism really is. Detecting the scent of my expensive doe urine collected from a single doe in estrous, he cautiously gave a wide berth to my scent wick before continuing on his way, obviously in quest of a receptive doe!

The context of the referenced scripture is that Jesus was before Pilate, discussing Jesus' kingship. Pilate's question, "What is truth?" sounds like what was known initially in the 20th century as moral relativism and more recently as postmodernism. At the heart of these "isms" is the belief that there is not such a thing as absolute truth. Risking over-simplification, a little historical background is useful. For most of recorded history, the prevailing mindset has been that there is such a thing as absolute truth, but we humans are not usually able to know what it is. There had been a definite theistic bent to this philosophy in western civilization: namely, that the Bible represented absolute truth about the spiritual realm but that the physical realm was mostly unknown. By the 17th century the scientific era had dawned, ushering in what is known as modernism. Modernism's prevailing thought was that the natural world was governed by a set of absolute discoverable laws. By the 19th century there was great optimism that somehow science, government and education would solve all the problems that had beset mankind and that a utopian society was attainable. Then came the 20th century's two world wars and postmodernism. Optimists said World War I was the war to end all wars. But following World War II pessimism prevailed in Europe, while in the United States the Billy Graham crusades resulted in a resurgence of Christianity. At this point intellectuals threw in the towel saying that truth was relative not absolute. With regard to the Bible, postmodernism says if the Bible is true for me, that is fine and if it is not true for you that is fine, also. In short there is no such thing as absolute truth. It was very much like the mood in Israel at the end of the Book of Judges: *In those days there was no King in Israel. Everyone did what was right in his own eyes.* (Judges 21:25) Today politically correct 21st century America believes the only absolute truth is that there is no absolute truth!

Historic reformed Christianity as espoused in this book stands in direct opposition to postmodernism, proclaiming that the Bible is absolutely true. The exclusivity of the claim that Jesus is the only way to God is the ultimate antithesis of postmodern thought. Christians often unfairly characterize postmodernism as believing in no absolute truth. This is incorrect because only the radical fringe of the movement tries to deny the cause and effect reality of the laws of physics. The truth is postmodernists literally worship science. It is the truth about things spiritual, ethical or moral where the idea of "no absolute truth" holds sway because according to postmodernism all religions are equally true or untrue because nothing is absolutely true.

90. Do all world religions lead to God?

Jesus said to him, "I am the way, and the truth, and the life. No one comes to the Father except through me." John 14:6

    I think an elk looks more like a deer than a moose. So if a deer represents true Christianity, then a moose represents other world religions and an elk (in the next chapter) represents other Christian denominations because there are more similarities between Christian denominations than between world religions. At any rate, it is true that moose and deer share some similar characteristics, but any casual observer will note large differences in appearance, habitat, food preferences, etc. Similarly, world religions have some common traits (temples/churches/mosques, "holy" days and writings, "spiritual leaders," belief in a hereafter, etc.) but vary radically in their teaching.

    Nineteenth century intellectuals went beyond saying all religions lead to God and confidently declared God did not exist, culminating in Nietzsche's famous statement that, "God is dead." Yet every discovered culture inevitably had a religion because God created man in his own image

(Genesis 1:26–27). As a result much 19th century intellectual capital was spent trying to explain why religion was a universal human attribute. Freud said it was guilt and fear of nature, Marx thought religion was a ruling class ploy to keep the lower class happy, and Nietzsche said religion arose out of man's weakness. Today the world is offended that Christians claim Jesus is the one and only way to God. The world wants many ways, failing to see how amazing it is that God should provide **any** way at all! The following table compares the major world religions' teachings on several key topics. Clearly, they are radically different. If they all lead to God, then there are many contradictory gods, which would be no God at all. On the other hand, except for Christianity, all world religions, are the same because they all lead people away from the true God!

Religion	God	Jesus	Creation	Salvation
Christianity	One eternal, knowable God in three co-equal persons (Father, Son, Holy Spirit)	Son of God, i.e., both fully human and fully God; Born sinless of a virgin	Triune God created the universe out of nothing	All are born in sin and must be born again through faith in Jesus' sinless life, subsitutionary death, and resurrection
Islam	One God, Allah who is not holy and an unknowable slave master, not a Father	One of many prophets; Muhammad is the last and greatest prophet; Jesus was not crucified.	Allah created the universe	Good deeds must out weigh bad ones at death as judged by submission to Allah and adherence to Islamic teachings
Judaism	One eternal God	False Messiah	God created universe out of nothing	Saved by obeying the Mosaic law
Hinduism	Many paths to one God; A Hindu may believe in one, many, or no gods. Most Hindus accept Brahman as a supreme being who sustains the cosmos.	One of many incarnations of divinity	No point of creation; Universe is eternal, in perpetual cycles of creation and destruction; Space and time are cyclical in nature.	*Moksha,* i.e., liberation from repetitive cycle of birth/death based upon *karma* (past actions and dispositions); Achieved by right action (works), knowledge, or devotion to a deity
Buddhism	Atheistic religion; No God or eternal creator	No human form of God exists since there is no God.	No creation story; Everything is always going in or out of being.	No soul to save; seeks refuge from pain and suffering thru *Nirvana* - bliss thru cessation of thought.

91. Do all forms of Christianity lead to God?

I know that after my departure fierce wolves will come in among you, not sparing the flock; and from among your own selves will arise men speaking twisted things, to draw away the disciples after them. Acts 20:29–30

An elk looks more like a deer than a moose, but there are significant differences between deer and elk. Two are shown in the picture: bulls collect harems and announce their dominance by a high pitched bugle call that signals rivals to stay clear unless they want a good thrashing. By analogy there are significant differences between denominations and cults that claim to be Christians though the disparities are not as extreme as in world religions. The definition of a cult is a group that claims to hold Christian beliefs, but has so corrupted major Christian doctrines as to not be a legitimate Christian organization that trusts in Jesus alone for salvation by grace through faith. The last two centuries have seen a vicious attack from within the church (as predicted by Paul in Acts 20:29–30) of so-called liberal protestant movements that essentially reject the supernatural and try to depict Jesus as a nice guy who implores his followers to good works. These spin-offs of mainline denominations are usually not considered to be cults like Mormons, Jehovah's Witnesses, and Christian Science and are not compared in the table below. Careful study of the following table should protect you from falling victim to major doctrinal errors.

Denomination	God	Jesus	Authority	Salvation
Evangelical or reformed Protestants	One eternal God in three co-equal persons (Father, Son, Holy Spirit)	Son of God, i.e., both fully human and fully God; born sinless of a virgin	The Bible is the final authority.	All are born in sin and must be born again by grace alone through faith alone in Jesus' sinless life, subsitutionary death, and resurrection.
Roman Catholic	One eternal God in three co-equal persons (Father, Son, Holy Spirit)	Son of God, i.e., both fully human and fully God; born sinless of a virgin	The Bible, Church traditions and the Pope	Justification is by faith and works and begins with baptism. Salvation is a cooperative effort of God and human efforts.
Eastern Orthodox	One eternal God in three co-equal persons (Father, Son, Holy Spirit)	No way to know if God is as revealed in Jesus; more focus on Holy Spirit than Jesus	The Bible and Church tradition. There is no systematic theology. Mystical is dominate over the cognitive.	Man's Free will with no room for sovereignty of God's grace; Man is flawed by original sin but not guilty of Adam's sin; Baptism removes original sin; reject subsitutionary atonement
Jehovah's Witnesses	One eternal God named Jehovah; no Son or Holy Spirit	Created by God as the archangel Michael before the world existed	The Bible is the sole authority as interpreted in their leader's books	Faith in Christ, being a Jehovah's Witness, and obedience to Jehovah Witnesses rules
Mormons	God the father was a man and progressed to godhood. He has a physical body. There are many other gods.	First born spirit-child of the heavenly Father and a heavenly Mother; later he was conceived in Mary	Book of Mormon reinterprets and supplements the Bible	God gives eternal life to almost everyone in a heavenly kingdom. To reach the highest heaven requires faith in Christ, and being a Mormon.
Christian Science	All things are ultimately God. Matter does not exist because God is spirit.	A human being and manifestation of divinity as other people can be	*Science and Health and Key to the Scriptures* by Mary Baker Eddy	Cessation of belief in sin, sickness, and death; none of these exist because matter does not exist

92. Are Protestants and Catholics saved?

As we have said before, so now I say again: If anyone is preaching to you another gospel contrary to the one you received, let him be accursed. Galatians 1:9

The doe I was watching suddenly snapped to attention, nervously staring at an approaching line of two feet tall creatures. Much to her relief these creatures materialized into a flock of turkeys instead of a pack of predators as they paraded by to their roosting site. I'll leave it to the reader to decide who is represented by the turkey and who is represented by the deer in this parable! My point is that the turkeys frightened the doe when she wasn't sure if she was seeing ten coyotes or ten turkeys. But once she knew they were turkeys not coyotes, she relaxed. The same can be true in the long and bitter conflict between Protestants and Catholics in which both sides have considered the other to be heretical by preaching a different gospel. On closer examination, the threat may not be as grave as initially supposed since both sides agree on many key tenets of the Christian faith.

In fact evangelical and reformed Protestants have more in common with Roman Catholics than they do with liberal, social gospel Protestants.

Of course, there is substantial difference between Protestants and Catholics about how salvation is achieved. Both cannot be correct so the crucial question is: can both Protestants and Catholics be saved? To answer this question, I'll assume that both sides at least agree the Bible is true, and tells us all that we need to know to be saved. For if the Bible is untrue or inadequate, then the Bible is untrustworthy. And if the Bible is untrustworthy, then Christianity is untrustworthy. Protestants are divided over interpretation of how salvation is accomplished and how the sacraments are to be understood. But these divisions are not over what needs to be added to the Bible, but rather how to interpret what is there. Here is the great divide between Catholics and Protestants because Catholics add church tradition as equal in authority to Scripture, and add works that are necessary for salvation. But if these additions contradict the Bible, then they must be rejected as a different gospel. Otherwise the two equal authorities of traditions and the Bible would be in conflict and could not both be true, so Christianity would collapse under the weight of its own self contradictions. By making works a requirement for salvation, Roman Catholic theologians have contradicted Ephesians 2:8–9 by preaching a different gospel and by Paul's strong words in Galatians 1:9 are in grave danger of being accursed.

Nevertheless, Catholics have always proclaimed and defended many of the great doctrines of Christian orthodoxy such as the trinity, the virgin birth, the resurrection, heaven, hell, the dual nature of Jesus as fully man and fully God, the atoning nature of Christ's death, and the promise of the second coming. In addition, Catholics have always defended human dignity, and ministered to the poor, the hungry and the sick. Finally, Catholics have a long record as staunch contenders for the moral teachings of Christianity, taking leadership roles in the fight against legalized abortion, and the defense of biblical marriage as one man and one woman for life.

God's grace is sufficient to overcome the flawed Roman Catholic teaching on the gospel (chapters 33, 35-39) and generate saving faith in whomever he chooses. I expect there will be many Catholics and Protestants in heaven. However, those who teach the traditional Roman Catholic way of salvation should prayerfully ponder James 3:1: *Not many of you should become teachers, my brothers, for you know that we who teach will be judged with greater strictness.*

93. Do we need priests and a Pope?

For since the law has but a shadow of the good things to come instead of the true form of these realities, it can never, by the same sacrifices that are continually offered every year, make perfect those who draw near. Otherwise, would they not have ceased to be offered, since the worshippers, having once been cleansed, would no longer have any consciousness of sin?...And every priest stands daily at his service, offering repeatedly the same sacrifices, which can never take away sins. But when Christ had offered for all time, a single sacrifice for sins, he sat down at the right hand of God.... For by a single offering he perfected for all time those who are being sanctified. Hebrews 10:1-2, 11–12, 14

As you come to him, a living stone rejected by men but in the sight of God chosen and precious, you yourselves like living stones are being built up as a spiritual house, to be a holy priesthood, to offer spiritual sacrifices acceptable to God through Jesus Christ. 1 Peter 2:4–5

A large, powerful, buck, like the one above may dominate a square mile or two, as a priest rules a parish. But there is no such thing as a "king" of deer that all deer are subject to like Roman Catholics and their priests are subject to the Pope. Old covenant Judaism required priests because sinful people could not approach God and needed an intermediary that could offer sacrifices on their behalf to atone for their sins. The book of Hebrews argues that Jesus is the high priest of a better covenant. Jesus was sinless and did not need to offer sacrifices for his own sin like human priests. Therefore, his death on the cross was a single sacrifice that satisfied God's wrath against sin forever for all who trust in the sufficiency of Jesus' sacrificial death. Christians are the priests in the new covenant and can go directly to God. There is also no need to endlessly offer bloodless sacrifices as in the Catholic mass. So priests are no longer needed and Jesus is the head of the Church, residing in heaven at God's right hand.

Nevertheless, whenever I attend a Catholic mass, I am astonished by how similar the mass is to the Old Testament sacrificial system (Hebrews 10:1–2, 11–12, 14) despite 1 Peter 2:4–5's declaration that all believers are priests who can make spiritual sacrifices acceptable to God through Jesus. Catholic theologians insist Peter became the first Pope in Matthew 16:18 when Jesus changed the Apostle Simon's name to Peter and declared *"And I tell you, you are Peter, and on this rock I will build my church, and the gates of hell shall not prevail against it."* Peter (*Petros* in Greek) is a play on the Greek word for rock (*petra*). Catholics take the rock on which the church will be built to be Peter. But the context will not allow this for clearly the rock is Peter's confession that *"Jesus is the Christ, the Son of the living God."* (Matthew 16:16) Furthermore, if Peter was the first Pope, his first recorded act as Pope (Matthew 16:21–23) was to rebuke Jesus for telling the disciples he must go to Jerusalem to be crucified. Jesus in turn rebuked Peter, *"Get behind me Satan! You are a hindrance to me. For you are not setting your mind on the things of God, but on the things of man."* This "rocky" start to Peter's papacy, coupled with his denial of knowing Jesus (Matthew 26:69–75) stretches credulity of papal infallibility. One might rightly argue that the Holy Spirit had not yet been given, and after Pentecost Peter boldly preached sound doctrine. But if he was the first Pope, why then did he say believers are the priests of the new covenant (1 Peter 2:4–5) and never teach defining Roman Catholic doctrines like salvation by faith and works? Finally, why does he endorse all of Paul's writings, which champion *Sola fide and Sola gratia*, as scriptural (2 Peter 3:15–16)? The reason is simple: Peter was not the first Pope and never affirmed the papacy.

94. Can I be saved without obeying Jesus?

Whoever believes in the Son has eternal life; whoever does not obey the Son shall not see life, but the wrath of God remains on him. John 3:36

Orphan fawns are relatively common around my blind due to the emphasis on harvesting does to control the deer population. Without the leadership and instruction of their mother, surviving their first Minnesota winter is a precarious situation at best. Single orphans, like the one in this picture, are particularly vulnerable since two sets of noses, eyes and ears are better able to perceive danger and find food and shelter.

If you think you can be saved without following Jesus' teachings, you are at far greater risk than this orphan fawn. There is an erroneous idea among some who claim to be Christians that you can be born again but not be obedient to Jesus' teachings. Sometimes they are called "carnal" Christians. There are many facets to this condition. For example, surveys reveal that a very high percentage of Americans claim to be born again. Yet, when the lifestyles of professing Christians are studied the overall averages are not very different from those who make no claims to be Christians. For example, the divorce rate is very similar for people in so called evangelical churches as compared to the society as a whole. To understand this we must remember that what we see is the visible church and God sees the true church. We are often unable to perceive who is a true believer and who is not, but God sees the heart. Hence, in a given congregation there may be many souls that are not saved. Tragically, many of these people are unaware of their peril. They are like this forlorn fawn, mindlessly walking down a trail, and stepping over the gut pile of his mother, en route to the same fate from a well-placed shot.

Why this is so has many reasons. Some people have grown up in the church and never known any other life. They are comfortable in a church setting, know the correct lingo, and may even serve the church with their time, talent and treasure. But, they do not really trust God and are headed for eternal punishment. Other people may belong to a local church for some societal benefit they receive by masquerading as a pious Christian. They may fool their neighbors, but they are spiritually dead in their sins with a one-way ticket to hell. A third category are victims of well-intended but poorly-grounded believers who, in their zeal to make church friendlier to unbelievers, have watered down the gospel to the point that people don't really know that obedience to Christ is the proof of a changed heart resulting from being born again.

The net effect of all this is that in making church less "scary" for unbelievers, some churches have become impotent to the point that no one hears the truth. In these churches people really think that all you have to do is give intellectual assent to some truths, pray a prayer and go to church and you will be fine while living like the rest of the world. They do so at great peril to their souls. It is no wonder that unbelievers think that Christians are hypocrites! John 3:36 leaves no doubt that obedience is required, not because you need faith AND obedience to be saved, but that obedience is the proof of true faith. Later, the Apostle John wrote: *Everyone who believes that Jesus is the Christ has been born of God, and everyone who loves the Father loves whoever has been born of him. By this we know that we love the children of God, when we love God and obey his commandments. For this is the love of God, that we keep his commandments. And his commandments are not burdensome.* (1 John 5:1–3)

95. Is my parents' faith transferred to me?

But to all who did receive him, who believed in his name, he gave the right to become children of God, who were born, not of blood nor of the will of the flesh nor of the will of man, but of God. John 1:12

If the buck and doe in this picture successfully mated, the resulting fawns would contain genetic information from both parents. Deer beget deer and people beget people, but the faith of Christian parents is not transferred to their offspring according to the referenced verse. To be a child of God *you* have to look in obedience to your heavenly Father through faith in Jesus Christ. I once had a long discussion with a woman who claimed she was a Christian because she had been born to believing parents, was baptized as a baby, learned her catechism, and was confirmed into church membership. As an adult, she faithfully attended church every week, so in her mind she had no need to be "born again." Certainly this is not what the Bible teaches and, yet, it is a common view of many professing Christians.

A major theme of the Gospel of John is about being born again or being born of God or becoming children of God. All of these are essentially the same idea and John 1:12 succinctly gives the criteria: you must receive Christ and believe in his name to be a child of God.

At its root, the idea that being born into a Christian family is the ticket to heaven is really the same argument that the Jews put forth in John 8. They maintained that Abraham was their father because they could trace their blood lines back to a patriarch of one of the twelve tribes of Israel. All this proves is that they were ethnic Jews. But Jesus says their heart is stone cold. Their behavior is not at all like Abraham's. They are trying to kill Jesus and, hence, show they are not Abraham's children (John 8:39–40). Of course Christian parents would bestow the advantages of Christian fellowship and teaching on their children, and a true Christian would regularly attend church, BUT a true child of God would trust in faith not human works as the basis for their salvation. Are you like the woman in the previous story? If you are, carefully and prayerfully consider the following words of Jesus:

Truly, truly, I say to you, unless one is born again he cannot see the kingdom of God. (John 3:3) You must be born again to get to heaven.

That which is born of the flesh is flesh, and that which is born of the Spirit is spirit. (John 3:6) Physical birth produces physical life and spiritual birth from the Holy Spirit produces spiritual life.

The wind blows where it wishes, and you hear its sound, but you do not know where it comes from or where it goes. So it is with everyone who is born of the Spirit. (John 3:8) The Holy Spirit sovereignly comes upon the elect. We do not know who will be saved, but we see the effect evidenced by a changed heart that believes in Jesus, just as we perceive the effect of wind.

For God so loved the world, that he gave his only Son, that whoever believes in him should not perish but have eternal life. For God did not send his Son into the world to condemn the world, but in order that the world might be saved through him. Whoever believes in him is not condemned, but whoever does not believe is condemned already, because he has not believed in the name of the only Son of God. (John 3:16–18) The only way to be saved is to believe in Jesus whom God sent to save sinners. But if you do not believe in Jesus, you are condemned to hell.

96. Should we baptize babies or believers?

We were buried therefore with him by baptism into death, in order that, just as Christ was raised from the dead by the glory of the Father, we too might walk in the newness of life. Romans 6:4

     Following the birth of a fawn the doe vigorously licks it to remove odors, consumes the placenta, nurses the fawn and then leads it away from the birth site. The fawn spends most of its first weeks of life flat on the ground to elude predators as the doe watches over it from afar to avoid leading predators to it by her scent. Periodically, she visits the fawn to nurse it and consume its excrement. Her zeal to keep the fawn clean and scent free protects the fawn from a host of predators.

     Chapter 40 did not resolve the intramural debate among reformed Christians over paedobaptism versus believers baptism. However, the gulf between both camps is not as great as is sometimes believed for both agree that baptism symbolizes union with Christ in his atoning death, burial and resurrection; and that baptism symbolizes washing away the recipient's sins even though it does not actually protect the recipient from hell as the doe protects her fawn by cleansing it.

The first mention of paedobaptism is in Tertullian's *Treatise on Baptism* (early third century), though Tertullian did not enthusiastically endorse the practice. However, the titans of Reformed theology like John Calvin and Jonathan Edwards embraced paedobaptism. The 1563 Heidelberg Catechism (Q&A 74) makes clear that paedobaptism is mainly about bestowing the blessing of Christian instruction and fellowship on believers' children as the equivalent New Testament initiation ceremony of Old Testament circumcision. Paedobaptists maintain that the children of a believing parent are *holy* (1 Corinthians 12:7). However, this does not mean that they have a measure of righteousness or are necessarily elect, but that they are "set apart" from the children of non-covenant parents. Nevertheless, churches usually welcome children of nonmembers or unbelievers and make the full range of Christian fellowship, worship and instruction available to them.

Churches that practice believer's baptism usually dedicate babies to God. This dedication ceremony expresses the parent's and the congregation's desire for the child to come to saving faith and their solemn pledge to assure the child receives all the benefits of Christian instruction and fellowship within the parent's church. While this chapter will not resolve the long running controversy, the following points support the practice of baby dedication and believers baptism:

1) It accomplishes the primary paedobaptism objective (Heidelberg Catechism Q&A 74); 2) It reserves the sacraments for Christians by making baptism available only to believers just as the Lord's Supper is reserved for believers (1 Corinthians 11:27–29); 3) It avoids any possible confusion with salvation claims for infant baptism as practiced by Catholics and many Lutherans; 4) It prevents any confusion about the reformed view of limited atonement (chapter 48) since the recipient has declared their faith in Christ. Paedobaptism can only depict the possibility, not the certainty, that the recipient may one day be *united with Christ** as evidenced by a credible profession of faith; 5) It allows baptism by immersion, thus dramatically depicting the spiritual reality that the new believer is united with Christ in his death, burial and resurrection (Romans 6:4); 6) It gives the recipient a public forum (by giving their testimony at their baptism) to glorify God for regenerating them.

*To be united with Christ means Christians receive every benefit of salvation because they are in Christ, Christ is in them, they are like Christ and are with Christ. For further study see Chapter 43 of Systematic Theology by Wayne Grudem.

97. What if you never heard about Jesus?

For the wrath of God is revealed from heaven against all ungodliness and unrighteousness of men, who by their unrighteousness suppress the truth. For what can be known about God is plain to them because God has shown it to them. For his invisible attributes, namely, his eternal power and divine nature, have been clearly perceived, ever since the creation of the world, in the things that have been made. So they are without excuse. For although they knew God, they did not honor him as God or give thanks to him, but they became futile in their thinking, and their foolish hearts were darkened . Claiming to be wise, they became fools, and exchanged the glory of the immortal God for images resembling mortal man and birds and animals and reptiles. Romans 1:18–23

This buck may look rather innocent but he was shadowing the buck in chapter 31, trying to steal a doe from him! It is quite common that younger bucks do the initial chasing of a doe coming into estrous. As the time for breeding draws near, a very large buck usually arrives on the scene, though smaller bucks breed often enough to keep them encouraged. Innocence with respect to deer and the rut is not a very important concept, but are there innocent humans, people who have never heard the gospel? Will they escape judgment?

The question of what happens if someone dies having never heard the gospel is often phrased in terms of concern over the justice of God. For if the only way to heaven is faith in Jesus Christ, and somewhere there is a tribe of people who have no knowledge of Jesus, then how can God be just and send all these people to hell? The answer lies in the referenced text which shows that God has made it obvious to everyone through the creation (general revelation) that he exists. No one can honestly say, "I didn't know there is a God." But because of the fall, all people, to some degree, suppress the truth of God. So even though they are aware that God exists, they choose to ignore him and are guilty of not worshipping him. To make matters worse, various pagan religions have been invented, worshiping manmade images of creatures rather than the Creator. The net effect is that there are no innocent people to be found anywhere. Those who never heard of Jesus are condemned because they didn't perfectly worship God as revealed by the creation, and God is completely just in sending these people to hell. But as soon as the gospel is proclaimed, the unbeliever's problem is compounded. Once they are told about Christ and reject him, they are in double-trouble having rejected both general revelation and the special revelation of the Bible and will be judged accordingly. So is it a bad thing to proclaim the gospel and create double jeopardy for unbelievers? No, because some unbelievers will come to faith in Christ and be saved. In the final analysis God is sovereign. God determined before the creation of the world who would come to faith (Ephesians 1:4–11). No one can come to faith in Christ unless the Father draws them (John 6:44). God has determined that the means of coming to faith is through preaching the gospel (Romans 10:13–15). Thus, proclaiming the gospel is the mandated calling of the church to bring history to an end, ushering in the new heaven and earth where all the redeemed whose names are written in the book of life will enjoy God forever (Matthew 28:19; Revelation 20:11–15). *Oh the depth of the riches and wisdom and knowledge of God! How unsearchable are his judgments and how inscrutable his ways! "For who has known the mind of the Lord, or who has been his counselor?" "Or who has given a gift to him that he might be repaid?" For from him and through him and to him are all things. To him be glory forever. Amen.* (Romans 11:33–36)

98. Why do we evangelize the predestined?

For God so loved the world, that he gave his only Son, that whoever believes in him should not perish but have eternal life. John 3:16 (See chapters 45–50 to review the terms and doctrines in this chapter.)

Thinking the coast was clear, I crawled out of my blind only to find this incredulous young buck standing behind me. Quickly regaining my composure, I took his picture. He stood for a long time trying to reconcile this experience with his misconception that humans are blundering, upright bipods, emitting ominous odors and sounds, not scentless, quiet, and horizontal creatures lying in an innocuous pile of sticks. People also try to make sense of the world in the context of their misconceptions. But like this buck, human misconceptions can be wrong. For example, a common misconception is that predestination (unconditional election) renders evangelism futile. People are either destined to believe or not believe so evangelism has no impact. The error in this thinking is that evangelism is commanded by Jesus (Matthew 28:16–20). God uses the gospel preaching of Christians to bring unbelievers to faith. (Romans 10:13–14). In fact the only hope for salvation when presenting the gospel to an unbeliever is predestination since, due to total depravity, an unregenerate person is incapable of coming to faith on his own (John 6:44).

Another common misconception is that if predestination is true, then people are doomed if they believe on their own but are not elect. This flawed idea begins by rejecting total depravity, erroneously deduces faith results from the believer's efforts and concludes John 3:16 is in conflict with predestination. But John 3:16 says nothing about predestination. It is a limited atonement and perseverance of the saints verse. *Not perishing* is the result of belief (the atonement is only effective for believers) and whoever believes, *has* eternal life, not the mere possibility of it if they persevere on their own. Since total depravity is true, the only way anyone can be saved is by unconditional election, implemented through irresistible grace. The result is John 3:16, limited atonement and perseverance of the saints.

Some argue that predestination is derived only from the epistles (mainly Paul). In this view Paul is seen as a harsh advocate of the Old Testament law not the gentle Apostle John who proclaims a merciful, loving, gracious gospel. However, in the Gospel of John we have all five of the doctrines of grace directly from the lips of Jesus:

Total Depravity: John 6:44, *No one can come to me unless the Father who sent me draws him*;

Unconditional Election: John 15:16, *You did not choose me, but I chose you*;

Limited Atonement: John 3:16 (see discussion above);

Irresistible Grace: John 6:37, *All that the Father gives me will come to me*;

Perseverance of the Saints: John 10:28, *I give them eternal life, and they will never perish, and no one will snatch them out of my hand.*

Finally, in John 10:26 Jesus says to some unbelieving Jews, *you do not believe because you are not part of my flock*. Notice belief results from being part of Jesus' flock (i.e., the elect). If believers actually came to faith by their own doing, the statement would be *you are not part of my flock because you do not believe*. The Doctrines of Grace are often defended by quotations from the epistles, but the epistles only expand and comment on Jesus' gospel teachings, so it might be better to call the Doctrines of Grace "***Jesus-ism***" not Calvinism!

99. Nobody is Perfect.

You therefore must be perfect, as your heavenly father is perfect.
Matthew 5:48

While engulfed in heavy fog on my fourth morning in the blind in 2004, this yearling buck sauntered down the trail towards me. How did his rack become so deformed? Perhaps the left antler was twisted out of alignment when it was in velvet. At any rate, this imperfect rack was not the trophy I was hoping for. But God in His providence never makes a mistake, so I snapped my first digital picture of a deer.

21st century America prefers its information in sound-bites that hit only the subject's high points. Unfortunately, "sound-bites" can leave the reader with a "foggy" understanding. So while this book is essentially a collection of theological "sound bites," I have tried to be as "meaty" as possible in each two-page essay, softening the reader's potential overload with deer stories and photos. The remaining chapters will bring this book to an end with a more comprehensive summary of the gospel than found in chapters 55–56.

Even if the Bible didn't tell us we are imperfect, fallen, corrupt and the like, we would know it from our experience and observation. The buck's antlers are a good example of the old saying that nobody is perfect. Sadly, many people go through life wishfully hoping God is aware of our "minor" imperfections and allows "pretty good" people into heaven. Yet, in the Sermon on the Mount Jesus says, *"You therefore must be perfect, as your heavenly father is perfect."* Can He really mean that you must attain the perfect holiness of God to go to heaven? This verse comes on the heels of Jesus declaring that it is not good enough to avoid committing murder or adultery. One must not even be angry with another person or look at a woman with lustful intent. Furthermore, we are not to retaliate but turn the other check, not to hate our enemies but love them and pray for those who persecute us. The Jews of Jesus' day had defined 613 laws, and it was possible to literally obey each one of them. The common Jewish understanding was that by offering sacrifices when a law was not obeyed and scrupulously trying to obey all of the laws all of the time, people could escape God's wrath. But Jesus set a new and significantly higher standard. It is not good enough to merely avoid all sin literally. Rather one must completely avoid ever thinking (even a little) about anything sinful. By these standards everyone is doomed to spend eternity in hell! So salvation does not boil down to an accounting system of having more good deeds than sinful ones. God really does demand absolute perfection to spend eternity with Him.

Why would God set such a standard? God has perfect holiness. God's holiness certainly means He is morally perfect and completely devoted to his glory (honor). But this popular view of holiness misses to some extent the main point. Rather, God's holiness primarily means He is transcendent. God exists in a separate realm where the sin and evil that pervades the fallen world we inhabit does not and cannot exist. As a result, God cannot allow in his presence anyone who is not perfectly holy in God's judicial sight. By way of a poor analogy, I must be essentially scent-free to be in close proximity to deer, but completely sin-free to be in God's presence. God loves all that is good and conforms to his character. So if a sinful person entered His presence, it would be incumbent upon God to preserve the purity of His holy transcendence, and direct His wrath (intense hatred of any and all sin) against the intrusion. If He did less, He would not be God.

100. Is God exclusively love?

Anyone who does not love does not know God, because God is love.
1 John 4:8

At least five Greek words are translated as love in English. In our common usage love is usually a noun but in the Bible love is usually a verb. *Agapē* and its derivatives occur over 200 times in the New Testament including 1 John 4:8. *Agapē* is the love God expresses and is the highest form of love, ultimately expressed as Jesus' sacrificial death on the cross. It is an exercise of the will, not a feeling and is sacrificial in nature. *Agapē* is unselfish and committed. It loves when all other forms of love quit or where there is no apparent reason for love. It is how God loved the world in John 3:16 and the love Paul speaks of in 1 Corinthians 13. Unbelievers can do works that appear to be *agapē*, but this doesn't please God because these works are not motivated by love for God. Only Christians have the true *agapē* that they receive at regeneration through the indwelling of the Holy Spirit.

Phileō and its derivatives occur about 60 times in the New Testament.

Phileō implies a strong emotional bond and is the basis of friendships and "brotherly love." A person who exudes *phileō* is someone everyone wants as a friend. *Phileō* makes *agapē* pleasurable. A good example of *phileō* occurs in John 11:3 translated as, "he whom you love is ill" and refers to Jesus' *phileō* love of Lazarus.

The other three words are: 1) *Aphilagathos* in 1 Timothy 3:3 and Hebrews 13:5 as "not a lover of money" and "free of the love of money" respectively; 2) *Storgē* implies devotion, or tender, loving affection like a kiss or hug. When combined with *phileō* to form the word *philostorgos*, it occurs only in Romans 12:10 that says, "Love (*philostorgos*) one another with brotherly affection (*phileō*)"; 3) *Eros*, refers to sexual desire and does not occur in the New Testament.

To some degree deer exhibit all five Greek words for love. Does put themselves at risk to defend their fawns (*agapē*). The pictured doe and fawn not only had the strong, but common emotional bond (*phileō*) of a doe and fawn, but also expressed *storgē* in their exuberant and affectionate licking beyond any deer I have ever observed. Of course, anyone who has ever observed a rutting buck knows of their unbridled *eros*. Finally, when food is scarce, does will drive away their own fawns and in essence are lovers (*aphilagathos*) of food. Yet in God's providence, all these forms of love assure the species' survival, including *aphilagathos*, by sacrificing fawns who are less able to survive the rigors of deep snow and cold temperatures. Thus, rather than dividing the limited food between several deer so that none have enough to survive, the doe has it all and lives to bring forth new life in spring. This may seem cruel and unloving at first blush. But as poet and hymnodist William Cowper (1731–1800) observed, "Judge not the Lord by feeble sense, but trust Him for His grace; Behind a frowning providence, He hides a smiling face."

God is love but not exclusively love as is often supposed by many today. For God is also wrathful against sin because of this love (chapter 102). Christians are called to please God by expressing *agapē, phileō,* and *storgē* to other Christians grounded in their love (*agapē*) of God because God first loved (*agapē*) them. (1 John 4:19) It is also *agapē* that loves unbelievers so much that it preaches the gospel, and brings the mercies of food to the hungry, clothing to the naked, shelter to the homeless, and modern medicine to the sick at the risk of being ostracized, humiliated, persecuted, or even killed by those whom Christians seek to serve with the *agapē* gospel.

101. Satan

Beware of false prophets, who come to you in sheep's clothing but inwardly are ravenous wolves. Matthew 7:15

The large buck approaching my blind froze in his tracks and stared intently ahead. Training my lens on the focus of his attention, where a trail emerged from thick brush, I expected another buck to appear, but to my astonishment the coyote above emerged. The serpent (Genesis 3), the dragon (Revelation 12:4), a roaring lion (1 Peter 5:8) and wolves (14 references) are all cited in the Bible as the personification of Satan or manifestation of his evil in the world. But the wolf's cousin, the wily coyote, is the primary wild enemy of the vast majority of deer. Like deer, coyotes are amazingly adept at thriving in small pockets of cover amid the presence of human activity. Coyotes are particularly effective at preying upon new born fawns, and are literally like the dragon (Satan) in Revelation 12:4 who stands before the woman to devour her child (Jesus) as soon as she gives birth.

The name Satan comes from a Hebrew word meaning "adversary" or opponent of God and his people. Satan does not attack unbelievers since they are on their way to hell. He is not omnipresent and can attack only one person at a time, but he has at his command many demons to attack troublesome Christians as is brilliantly and humorously depicted in C.S. Lewis' famous classic, *The Screwtape Letters*. Demon *oppression* is real, but Christians cannot be demon *possessed* because of the indwelling Holy Spirit (1 John 4:4). It is just as wrong to dismiss Satan as a myth from a bygone, unscientific age as it is to attribute every difficulty in life to satanic activity. Indeed, most Christians never reach a point of effectiveness that warrants Satan's personal attack and full fury. Except for Jesus (Matthew 4), perhaps no one has experienced more of Satan's direct attacks than Martin Luther who once threw an inkwell at what he perceived to be Satan. Satan is an enemy on a chain (Job 1–2), but he is still a formidable foe, more powerful than any human except for Jesus. But Satan is not omniscient or omnipotent and is not evenly matched against God. Satan is a fallen creature, unable to triumph over God (Revelation 20:10). Because of the atonement, Satan cannot accuse the elect in God's court room, and Christians have the authority and tools to defeat Satan and demons. (Luke 10:19; Ephesians 6:10–18)

Deception and lies are Satan's stock in trade (John 8:44). His greatest deception is that he doesn't exist. Most people say they "believe" in God, but few believe in the existence of Satan or demons despite over 150 references to them in the Bible. The New Testament gives Satan titles like "accuser of our brothers" (Revelation 12:10), "destroyer" (Revelation 9:11) and "tempter" (Matthew 4:3). Paul observes that Satan disguises himself as an angel of light (2 Corinthians 11:13–15) as do his servants, feigning righteousness while seeking to dishonor Christ and destroy believers and the church (Matthew 7:15). One day the lamb and the wolf will peacefully coexist (Isaiah 11:6; 65:25) when the creation is restored in the new heaven and the new earth. But unlike the creation, Satan will not be perfected, for his eternal destiny is the lake of fire (Revelation 20).

Christians must persevere in their evangelistic and apologetic efforts, because people must intellectually know what they believe and why. But all these efforts are futile, unless people also trust in Jesus alone for their salvation and love the triune God. Mere intellectual agreement with the Bible affords one only the status of demons. *You believe that God is one; you do well. Even the demons believe – and shudder!* (James 2:19)

102. Wrath

Since, therefore, we have now been justified by his blood, much more shall we be saved by him from the wrath of God. Romans 5:9

This little buck's laid back ears, mean in deer body language "I am really angry." But his anger is a proverbial drop in the bucket compared to the wrath of God. Christians often speak of being "saved," but what are they saved from? The Apostle Paul tells us we are saved from the wrath of God. Why would we need to be saved from the wrath of God? Is not God loving? Actually the wrath of God is a direct consequence of God's love. First and foremost, God loves himself as the embodiment of all that is good and right and conforms to his moral character. Consequently, He hates anything that does not love him above everything else. But every person who has ever lived, except for Jesus, has not loved God as they should. *You shall love the LORD your God with all your heart and with all your soul and with all your might* (Deuteronomy 6:5). The bad news is that there isn't anything that anyone can do to make right his estranged relationship with God. Good works, baptism, confirmation, church membership, ordination, and the like, are no guarantee of saving faith in Christ's death nor evidence of submission to him. *For the mind that is set on the flesh is hostile to God, for it does not submit to God's law; indeed, it cannot. Those who are in the flesh cannot please God.* (Romans 8:7–8)

However, Christians do not need to fear the wrath of God because they are justified by their faith in Christ who bore God's wrath that was due them because of their sin. Justification is the opposite of condemnation. When we sin we have offended God and there is nothing we can offer valuable enough to pay the penalty. Only the infinite value of the death of God's only son can cover the infinite penalty of offending an infinite God. As the Apostle Paul says in Romans 3:25, God put Jesus *forward as a propitiation by his blood, to be received by faith.* Propitiation means that the death of Jesus satisfied God's wrath towards the sins of those who trust in Jesus' death to pay for their sin.

> *And you, who once were alienated and hostile in mind, doing evil deeds, he has now reconciled in his body of flesh by his death, in order to present you holy and blameless and above reproach before him, if indeed you continue in the faith, stable and steadfast, not shifting from the hope of the gospel that you heard, which has been proclaimed in all creation under heaven, and of which I, Paul, became a minister.* (Colossians 1:21–23)

This does not mean that because of the death of Jesus God can lawfully love the elect. Instead it means that because of God's love for the elect, God the Father established the new covenant by putting to death God the Son so that the record of the elect's sin could be blotted out. *For I will be merciful towards their iniquities, and I will remember their sins no more.* (Hebrews 8:12)

Wrath is such a negative word conjuring up thoughts of dread and fear. Why would anyone want anything to do with a God who is wrathful? The answer can be seen by considering the consequences of a God who was not wrathful against sin. In this case, he would either endorse sin or at least tolerate it. So now the question turns around to the rhetorical question of why would anyone want anything to do with a God who tolerated or even endorsed sin? Such a God would provide no comfort, nor would He be worthy of worship. God must hate sin to be worthy of our worship and not just hate it a little, but the hate must be so intense that it overflows into wrath.

103. The Virgin Birth is a Fact

Now the birth of Jesus Christ took place in this way. When his mother Mary had been betrothed to Joseph, before they came together she was found to be with child from the Holy Spirit. Matthew 1:18

  This precocious fawn showed up in my neighbor's yard one afternoon for a hosta salad (plants in the background). When we look at a fawn or any other baby mammal, we know that the fawn or baby is the product of their mother's egg and father's sperm. People often talk of the miracle of birth, but strictly speaking the birth of a baby is not a miracle, even though it is a wonderful work of God. True miracles are not the awesome norm, but extraordinary, unnatural events like the Bible's claim that Jesus was born of a virgin (not fathered by Joseph, but conceived by the Holy Spirit), led a sinless life and was resurrected from the dead.

  I am not willing to accept the claim that the virgin birth is untrue because we know it doesn't happen. Mary and Joseph and everybody else in that "unscientific" era also knew virgin birth doesn't happen (Matthew 1:20; Luke 1:34). However, if virgin birth cannot happen, why has the story persisted? Let me suggest that it has persisted because it is true. The fact that virgin birth does not happen in our experience is exactly the point. In the Incarnation (God taking a human nature upon himself), Jesus' conception did not come about in the usual way to make it clear to everyone that Jesus was the Messiah.

Virgin birth is an easy matter when you consider that the only rational explanation for the universe is that it has been created by an eternal being (chapter 61). Now an eternal being that can create the universe out of nothing would surely have no problem causing a virgin birth. The more important question is: why did the Incarnation take place? There are at least two fundamental reasons: 1) Jesus as the incarnate God models what God is like so that we can learn from his example; and 2) the Incarnation is ultimately about the fact that sin had entered into the world through Adam and Eve. God had purposed before he created anything that Jesus would be born of a virgin, live a sinless life, and be crucified to atone for the sins of everyone who would ever believe in Jesus and his resurrection from the dead. The most amazing miracle is not the virgin birth but that anyone could live a sinless life.

How could Jesus have been fully human and born without inheriting Adam's legal guilt and corrupt moral nature? Since Jesus did not have a human father, his line of descent from Adam is different from every other human. But Scripture never claims that the transmission of sin comes only from our fathers. So why did Jesus not inherit a fallen nature from Mary? Roman Catholics claim Mary was sinless but this is not supported by Scripture. A better answer is indicated by Gabriel's statement to Mary: *"The Holy Spirit will come upon you, and the power of the Most High will overshadow you; therefore the child to be born will be called holy - the Son of God."* (Luke 1:35) In other words God somehow *overshadowed* Mary's sin nature so that it was not transmitted to Jesus. This only was true for Jesus because Mary's other children were fallen (John 7:2–5).

If Jesus had not been sinless, then his death could not have atoned for the sins of every person who would truly believe in him. If he had not been able to atone for sins, then no one could ever get into heaven. And, if no one ever got into heaven, then God would not be as glorified as he will be because of the great multitude who will praise him forever (Revelation 7:9–12).

104. How can Jesus have two natures?

For in him the whole fullness of deity dwells bodily, Colossians 2:9

From the point of conception a fawn is fully and exclusively a deer. In Roman mythology there is a group of rural deities called fauns that are part human and part goat. Mr. Tumnus in the *Chronicles of Narnia* was a faun, but of course there are no naturally occurring creatures that have two distinct natures. Yet the Bible says that the Son, is fully God and fully man. Attributes of these two natures are not mixed together as in a faun to create a new creature. The Son did not give up any attributes of God to become fully human, nor did the divine nature relieve the human nature from normal human experiences because: Jesus was born (Luke 2:7); grew to adulthood (Luke 2:40); learned as he grew up (Luke 2:52); and got tired (John 4:6), thirsty (John 19:28) and hungry (Matthew 4:2). Jesus had a human soul (John 12:27) and died (Luke 23:46). In fact, Jesus was so human his neighbors and half brothers failed to see his deity at all and thought he was just another man (Matthew 13:53–58, John 7:5).

But Jesus was clearly different from other humans because he was:

conceived by the Holy Spirit (Matthew 1:20); his virgin birth made it possible to unite the human and divine nature in one person (John 3:16); he is *holy* and did not inherit Adam's corrupt moral nature (Luke 1:35); he was sinless even though he was tempted in every way humans are tempted (Hebrews 4:15) including by Satan (Luke 4:1–13); he was transfigured (Matthew 17); he was resurrected from the dead (Luke 24:39–42); and he ascended into heaven (Acts 1:9–11). Colossians 2:9 makes clear that Jesus was divine. A voice from heaven (God the Father) called him *"my beloved Son"* at his baptism (Mark 1:11); The disciples worshiped him saying, *"Truly you are the Son of God."* (Matthew 14:33); Thomas declared him to be, "My Lord (*theos*) and my God (*Kyrios*)" in John 20:28. (*Theos* is normally reserved for God the Father in the New Testament and *Kyrios* occurs 6,814 times in the Septuagint, the Greek Old Testament in use during Jesus' time on earth, as the name of the Lord.) When he turned water into wine, John 2:11 says it *"manifested his glory"* and when he stilled the Sea of Galilee, the disciples perceived his omnipotence in *"that even the winds and the sea obey him"* (Matthew 8:27).

We cannot completely understand how the Son has two natures. But, we can often gain some understanding of this mystery by distinguishing between the human and divine natures and the person of the Son. A general rule is that whatever one nature experiences is experienced by the person. Here are three examples that demonstrate this principle: 1) The human nature was not manifested until the incarnation. However, the divine nature is eternal so the *person* of Jesus is eternal. 2) When Jesus died, his soul was separated from his body and went to heaven (Luke 23:43, 46). His divine nature did not die but, the *person* of Jesus experienced death, so in some way the divine nature tasted death. 3) From conception Jesus' human nature never existed apart from his divine nature (which is unable to sin). So even though his human nature was like Adam's pre-fall nature and theoretically able to sin, the Son's person could not morally fall. Hence the human nature could not sin.

In the final analysis, Jesus had to be fully man to be the elect's substitute and bring about their salvation (chapters 8, 55, 56, 105–107), and to show us what God is like and how God wants us to live. But he also had to be fully God because only God could reconcile fallen man with God by mediating between sinners and God (1 Timothy 2:5) for salvation is exclusively from God (Galatians 4:4–5).

105. Jesus Was Crucified to Save the Elect

Christ redeemed us from the curse of the law by becoming a curse for us – for it is written, "Cursed is everyone who is hanged on a tree" Galatians 3:13

I hope this picture jolts you out of complacency about the seriousness of sin. Any sin is so grievous to God that nothing less than the death of Jesus can pay the price needed to make a sinner right with the holy, triune God. Our fallen minds think our sins are minor, but it takes only one sin to condemn us to hell. For example, my father and I always proudly hung our deer in an elm tree in the front yard so that everyone who passed by could see our prowess as deer hunters. We were not alone in this sin of not crediting God for our success! In fact in our rural community people usually hung their deer by the yard light to make it easy to see their trophies day or night. The bloody, eviscerated buck hanging in this picture no longer brings to my mind the pride of a successful hunt, but the price that Christ paid for my sin of pride and all my other sins. The ancient Jews would hang criminals convicted of a capital offense on a pole (figuratively a tree) following their execution. This served as a warning of the seriousness of their offense and that such crimes were in fact punished. Of course, the clear implication was that these executed criminals were cursed by God. Jesus hanging on the cross naturally caused those present at the crucifixion to believe that Jesus was cursed by God. This was exactly right. But, He was cursed by God not because He had sinned, but because He took upon himself the sins of all who would ever believe in Him.

The measure of punishment in our common experience is proportional to the value of the offended *being*: You can kill a mosquito and nothing happens to you; Poach a deer and you will be fined; murder a person and your life may be demanded of you. Romans 6:26 says the wages of sin is death. This means that **any** sin we commit sentences us to death. If there were no sin there would be no death. This seems incredibly harsh to our 21st century mindset. However, God is of infinite value so to sin against God requires infinite punishment.

All sin is exchanging our delight in the infinite value of God for delight in something else like money, or sex, or toys, or jobs, or hobbies or anything else people delight in. Since everyone of us has at least at one time delighted more in the things of this world than in God, there are only two options: 1) die and be punished eternally since infinite punishment is required; or 2) die (since everyone has sinned and the wages of sin is death) and somehow have someone else bear the infinite punishment required of us. Since Jesus is the son of God, he is of infinite value. Therefore, Jesus' crucifixion provides a way for God to not count the sin of believers against them, but at the same time quench His hatred of their sins. In this loving transaction, God assigned to the sinless Jesus **all** the sins of every person who would ever believe in Jesus. Through Jesus' death, believers' sins are no longer counted against them, and Jesus' sinless life (perfect adherence to the Law) is credited to believers. As you will recall from chapter 38 the theological term for this is ***justification***, meaning believers have the legal status of being sinless and righteous in the sight of God. However, if mere forgiveness was all the crucifixion accomplished, then the benefit in believing in Jesus would be that you would be put back in the garden with Adam (mere innocence). But by being justified, the believer can also enter eternally into the presence of the holy triune God. So, the crucifixion not only spares the believer the agony of eternal punishment, but, more importantly, allows him into the infinite joy of spending eternity with God in heaven.

106. How did the cross ransom the elect?

For if while we were enemies we were reconciled to God by the death of his Son, much more, now that we are reconciled, shall we be saved by his life. Romans 5:10

The angry buck fawn in chapter 101 is pictured above touching noses with his supposed enemy. In that brief contact the little buck's wrath was somehow appeased and the two fawns were reconciled. This interesting behavior is a poor parable of how sinners are reconciled to God because no one suffered to accomplish the reconciliation. So why was the crucifixion a sufficient ransom for the elects' sins?

It was not absolutely necessary for Jesus to be crucified. God could have been a perfectly happy triune God and exercised his judgment on fallen humanity by sending everyone to hell as he did with fallen angels (2 Peter 2:4). But because of God's gracious love, he chose to save some people to worship him for eternity to maximize his glory. But once this decision was made, it became absolutely necessary for the elect's sins to be transferred to Christ, because infinite punishment of the elect was required for sinning against the infinite God. Eternal punishment was required so the only way for God to allow sinners into his presence for eternity was to design a ransom on their behalf that was infinitely costly so that it could be accomplished quickly.

Much is made in Easter sermons of the physical pain of crucifixion. Indeed it was horrendous, but the Bible never grounds the sufficiency of Jesus' suffering in the physical pain of his crucifixion. Jesus had to physically die and shed his blood because without the shedding of blood there is no forgiveness of sins (Hebrew 9:22). Jesus foresaw the crucifixion's true horror when he said, *"If it be possible, let this cup pass from me"* (Matthew 26:39). For the suffering within his soul of bearing all of the elect's sins would be far worse than the physical pain, because Jesus was perfectly holy. He hated sin and yet on the cross *the LORD has laid on him the iniquity of us all* (Isaiah 53:6). Jesus could not escape the cross because God had always planned to redeem a people for Himself via the crucifixion (Acts 2:23). So Jesus obediently bore the full fury of God's wrath against the elect's sins, facing the pain alone. Not only did the disciples abandon him, (Matthew 26:56) but to compound his anguish, God the Father also abandoned him because God cannot behold evil (Habakkuk 1:13). As Jesus cried out, *"My God, my God, why have you forsaken me?"* (Matthew 27:46) we hear the depth of his suffering. Liberal theologian Albert Schweitzer tried to claim that at this point Jesus was disillusioned and recognized that the Father would not rescue him, but this will not do given the Covenant of Redemption (chapter 4).

Some versions of the Apostles Creed seem to say Jesus went to hell to finalize the ransom following the crucifixion. (*"was crucified, dead and buried, he descended into hell; the third day he rose again from the dead"*) The Apostles Creed originated about A.D. 200 and continued to "evolve" until about A.D. 750. It was never written by the Apostles nor affirmed by a church council. The first record of the statement *"he descended into hell"* appeared about A.D. 390. Scripture does not explicitly address why Christ's suffering was a sufficient payment for the elect's sins. Somehow the "hell" Jesus experienced on the cross of bearing all of the elect's sins, the Father's abandonment and outpouring of the Father's wrath was in God's perfect justice sufficient. The Bible does not say Jesus' soul went to hell, and Jesus' statement to the thief on the cross, *"Truly, I say to you, today you will be with me in Paradise,"* (Luke 23:43) is good evidence that Jesus' soul did not literally go to hell after his death.

107. How did Jesus' life benefit the elect?

...and be found in him, not having a righteousness of my own that comes from the law, but that which comes through faith in Christ, the righteousness from God that depends on faith Philippians 3:9

For as by the one man's disobedience the many were made sinners, so by the one man's obedience the many will be made righteous. Romans 5:19

Sometimes I get to photograph bucks in successive years. This picture was taken in 2011. I believe that this buck was at least six and a half years old in this picture, very old for a dominant buck. He also appears in chapter 49 (2008), chapter 73 (2009) and chapter 10 (2010). Deer are not moral creatures, and they do not have a soul. The fall affected deer so that death is their ultimate enemy. They live and die and that is the end of their existence. But unlike humans made in the image of God, a deer does not have to worry about being reconciled to God or facing eternal punishment. Deer exhibit behaviors that would be sinful in a human context like fighting over mates.

But they do not need a substitute deer to live as their representative to atone for their sins like humans require.

Jesus' atonement accomplished two things: 1) He perfectly obeyed all the requirements of the law and this perfect obedience was transferred to the elect; 2) He suffered in place of the elect by receiving the punishment the elect deserved which in turn God counted as sufficient punishment of the elect. Therefore, the atonement is primarily an event between God the Father and God the Son that secures the salvation of the elect by quenching God's wrath for the elect's sins and fulfilling the righteous requirements of the law.

Isaiah had predicted Jesus would be, "*a man of sorrows, acquainted with grief.*" (Isaiah 53:3) To some extent Jesus suffered throughout his life in his body and soul by living in a fallen world. He was tempted by Satan for 40 days (Matthew 4:1–11, he was opposed by the Jewish leaders (Hebrews 12:3–4), and must have grieved the death of Joseph (his earthly father), as well as the death of his friend Lazarus (John 11:35). But all of these sufferings paled in comparison to the suffering he endured on the cross.

What then, if anything, did Christ's life contribute to the elect's salvation? If all Christ achieved was the forgiveness of the elect's sins by crucifixion, then no one could go to heaven. The elect would have been restored to the innocence that Adam and Eve initially enjoyed, but with the possibility of falling again. What God required was perfect obedience to the law over a period of time, not just the forgiveness of sin. Adam and Eve and the elect could not do this, so Jesus had to live a life of perfect obedience to God's law. Paul's point in Philippians 3:9 is that we need more than a clean slate (no sin) but also a positive moral righteousness. No one except Christ could ever achieve this righteousness so God transferred Christ's righteousness to the elect through the faith of the elect. Of course this faith can only come about by God mercifully **causing** the elect to be "born again" (1 Peter 1:3). The real point of Christ's life-long perfect obedience was not to qualify him as a worthy, sinless sacrifice in his death, because he already had been eternally obedient to the Father in his divine nature. If only a long term perfect obedience was required he could have been sacrificed as a baby instead of living 33 years. Rather he had to establish a record of obedience in his human nature for the elect, whom he represented, that merited God's favor and eternal life with him in heaven. For just as by Adam's sin all humanity became sinners, by Christ's righteousness all of the elect, through faith, become legally righteous in God's sight (Romans 5:19).

108. Resurrection, Life After Death

And if Christ has not been raised, your faith is futile and you are still in your sins. 1 Corinthians 15:17 *But in fact Christ has been raised from the dead, the first fruits of those who have fallen asleep.* 1 Corinthians 15:20

Killed late one Saturday afternoon, this buck's glazed, sunken eye shows he is still dead at noon on Monday. Now, if I were to claim that shortly after I took this picture the buck got up and started browsing on some red osier dogwood, you would likely conclude that I am not in my right mind. You would reach this conclusion because you know from experience that dead deer do not come back to life. However, Christianity makes the apparently outrageous claim that after being dead about the same time as the pictured buck, Jesus came back to life! The gospels say three days because in that era a day was reckoned as any part of a day. Therefore, Friday afternoon and evening, Saturday, and early Sunday morning equaled the three days.

Now, if I persisted in claiming the buck was alive, you would probably seek some credible evidence that the buck was in fact dead. You might interview my friend Bill who killed the buck and ask if he was sure it was dead. Bill would say, "Yes, I drove an arrow through the buck's heart, removed its entrails and hung it in my pole barn to cool down to ambient temperature." In all probability you would take this as expert testimony from a man who clearly knew a dead deer when he saw one. But, if I still claimed the deer was alive, the easiest thing to do would be to produce the body of the dead deer. You could go to Bill and get the body and compare it to the photo on the adjoining page to prove to me the deer was in fact dead. My only recourse would be to produce the buck alive and show it to Bill who could attest that it was in fact the deer he killed.

This is exactly what the Bible claims. First of all, Jesus was dead as attested by the Roman soldiers who were experts in crucifixion, but to make sure, they thrust a spear through his rib cage (John 19:33–34). Then Jesus' body was taken down from the cross and tightly wrapped in a linen shroud with about 75 pounds of a myrrh and aloes mixture before being placed in a guarded, sealed tomb (Matthew 27:59–66; John 19:39). But Sunday morning (three days later) the tomb was empty! Jesus appeared to people intimately acquainted with him like the Apostles and his brother James, and then to over 500 people at one time most of whom were still alive when Paul wrote 1 Corinthians at least 20 years after the resurrection (1 Corinthians 15:4–8). So, many expert witnesses were available to refute Paul's claim and had they refuted it you would not be reading these words now. Finally, all the Jews had to do was produce Jesus' body right after the claim of the resurrection, but they could not produce the body (Matthew 27:62– 28:15). As a result, it is reasonable to conclude that the death and resurrection of Jesus is a historical fact attested to by expert witnesses without any credible historical evidence to the contrary. To those who persist in saying, this is impossible, I say you are exactly right– humanly speaking! But God has attested to the truth of this claim by publicly doing something so spectacular that no reasonable person would try to explain it by natural processes or deny its occurrence. It must be attributed solely to God for His glory and the joy of all believers. Do not be hasty to dismiss the resurrection, since for God, who spoke the universe into existence, resurrecting his Son was a simple act. What is truly amazing is that a human could live a sinless life, not that the sinless Jesus came back to life. The actual impossibility is that a sinless person could stay dead since the cause of death is sin (Romans 6:26).

109. The Ascension

And when he had said these things, as they were looking on, he was lifted up, and a cloud took him out of their sight. Acts 1:9

Five miles of trail and 2,000 vertical feet separated me from a tunnel just below the crest of a glacier carved ridge. I had mixed emotions as I walked, knowing that the tunnel would be the end of a wonderful five day wilderness retreat. Interrupted infrequently by only a handful of fellow sojourners, I had experienced this little corner of creation as is only possible when immersed in it with just a tent and sleeping bag. On the other hand I was eager to be reunited with my wife who was en route to our rendezvous site five downhill miles beyond the tunnel at a busy tourist destination. As I slowly ascended from the lake I had camped beside the previous night, I noticed some strange ripples in the otherwise perfectly still lake. My telephoto lens revealed these ripples to be several deer, seemingly unable to contain their joy as they exuberantly bounded through the shallow water. Their joy reminded me of how the disciples had rejoiced following Jesus' ascension (Luke 24:52). Yet the stunning scene was far more spectacular than the camera could record because immediately beyond the lake a mountain rose up a vertical mile crowned by a freshly snow-covered glacier glistening in the morning sun.

As I walked I pondered if Jesus had mixed emotions as he ascended, leaving the Apostles behind and entering the glorious reality of heaven?* I think not, but my meditation was cut short as I reached the tunnel. After another 250 feet I passed from wilderness to the busy world on the other side. Soon the first group of many day hikers would reach the tunnel as their final destination, having barely tasted the wilderness, while regrettably most park visitors would expend no effort at all, being satisfied with a superficial roadside experience of the park's declaration of the glory of God, much like the modern church's "ho hum" attitude towards the ascension.

Why did the disciples rejoice when Jesus ascended to heaven? The ascension was a coronation that restored Jesus to the heavenly status he relinquished in the Incarnation when he was born as a human baby (Philippians 2:5–11). Since Jesus ascended to heaven Christians know heaven is a real place and can be assured that their final home will be there with Jesus (John 14:1–3). In the ascension the former glory Jesus had enjoyed was restored, his human nature was glorified in a way that had never existed before and he reigns in a new way in a resurrected human body, sitting at the Father's right hand, and ruling on the Father's behalf (Ephesians 1:20–22). While Jesus was on earth he was relatively ineffective, being limited in space and time. But with the ascension, Jesus is once again spiritually omnipresent, and has unlimited availability to help all Christians simultaneously, if need be, wherever they are (John 16:7; Hebrews 4:14–16, 7:25). He does this not only by intercession to the Father but also by intervention, lavishing upon Christians the benefits his suffering purchased on the cross (Ephesians 1:7). Another way he does this is by indwelling all Christians with the Holy Spirit (John 14:16–17) to guide them to the truth (John 16:13), equip them for service (Ephesians 4:8–12), protect them from the desires of the flesh (Galatians 4:16–17), and empower them to advance in Godly behavior (Galatians 4:22–24). If only we Christians truly anticipated the heavenly reality accomplished by the ascension, our joy would overflow like the deer I observed!

*My ascension was backwards from Jesus' because he ascended from life in a fallen world to the glories of heaven whereas I ascended from the glorious and spectacular wilderness to the humdrum of life in the fallen world.

110. Adoption

...In love he predestined us for adoption through Jesus Christ, according to the purpose of his will, to the praise of his glorious grace, with which he has blessed us in the Beloved . Ephesians 1:5–6

During the rut, fawns are usually separated from their mother while the buck is tending the doe. Once breeding is completed the doe searches for her fawns, occasionally, calling to them with soft grunts. Fawns more or less stay in the approximate area where the doe left them and wait for their mother to return. Of all my deer photos this one has been the all-time favorite among non-hunters. In this tender scene, the doe sighted her fawn slowly meandering down a trail, grazing on some still green grass. The doe purposefully approached it and touched noses. This seems to be a method of confirming whether or not this is in fact the does' fawn. In this case the doe had found her fawn and the fawn happily followed mama down the trail. God has wisely designed does to usually not adopt other fawns they may encounter, but only to tenderly care for their own just as God adopts only the elect and tenderly cares for them.

In the New Testament era, wealthy people without children would often adopt a young man of good character to carry on the family name and inherit the family fortune. The Apostle Paul makes the incredible statement that Christians have been adopted into the family of God. The implications of this statement are staggering, since in our common experience, an adopted child is legally equivalent to a natural born child of the parents and receives all the rights and benefits of its natural siblings. But when the adopting parent is God the Father, it means the adopted child becomes a child of God, Jesus' sibling, with all the benefits of relationship that exist within the Trinity. It does not get any better than this. Imagine sharing for eternity in the perfect loving relationship that exists between the Holy Spirit, Jesus and God the Father!

So how does one receive this blessing of adoption? God chooses (predestines) whom he will adopt just as adopting parents choose who they will adopt. People of Paul's era chose whom they would adopt based upon some admirable characteristics in the young man. God, however, does not select people of demonstrated good character to adopt because no one is of sufficiently good character. Instead, He elects sinners, counting them righteous by crediting them with Jesus' perfect character.

How do you know if you have received this blessing? Do you joyfully believe that Jesus is the son of God who paid the price for your sin on the cross, was raised from the dead, is seated at the right hand of God and will come again to judge the world and take all believers to be with him forever? And, is this belief evidenced by a desire to follow all his teaching as your Lord and Master? If you do, then you have received the blessing. Just as the doe in this picture called to her fawn, knew that it was her fawn, would not accept a fawn that was not hers, and the fawn followed its mother gladly, God knows who are his children and calls them to himself, rejecting all who are not his, and his children hear his voice and follow him (John 10:26–28). What a wonderful loving Father! All praise and glory to Him! May you know Him now and forever. Confess your sin and trust in Jesus alone for your salvation.

111. You Must Repent

The times of ignorance God overlooked, but now he commands all people everywhere to repent Acts 17:30

The woods were awash in bright sunlight on this November morning. The rut should have been in full swing, but I had not seen any deer from the blind that morning. I was about a 150 yards into my half mile walk back to my vehicle when I spotted this buck to my right, moving into a stiff northwest wind. His path would cross mine about 25 yards ahead of me in a convenient open area. As he stepped into the opening, he looked towards me and was aghast to see an upright human form pointing an ominous looking object at him. Raising his tail, he turned east and beat a hasty retreat to its supposed safety.

The Greek words *metanoeō* (translated as "repent" or "repented," means to change one's mind or purpose) and *metanoia* (translated as "repentance," means a change of mind) occur a total of 56 times in the New Testament. Literally, this buck repented, that is he changed his mind or purpose about going northwest and headed east to get away from me.

Repentance is both a turning from and a turning to, because when unbelievers repent, they must turn from their life of sin to a life characterized by a desire to please God in all that they say and do. But, until unbelievers actually feel the full weight of their sin, they will see no need to change the way they are thinking or living. For example, as a new believer I quickly discovered I needed to repent, or in other words change my positions to align with biblical teaching on a number of issues since I had believed in evolution and affirmed abortion and gay rights.

Repentance is the result of regeneration (being "born again"). The only way to truly repent is to be born again to a new reality through faith in Jesus Christ. This does not mean that an unbeliever may not try to "clean up his act" if he perceives that he is headed for jail, or faces some other unpleasant consequence of his actions as imposed by society. But when we are born again we are motivated by a desire to please God and to spend eternity with Him. This desire springs out of a new understanding, through the power of the Holy Spirit, of the egregious nature of our sin, and the justice of being sentenced to hell for eternity. But even more, the believer's new nature delights in the mercy of God to all who put their trust in Jesus Christ, resulting in a desire to spend eternity with Jesus that is much greater than the desire to escape hell. Without fellowship with Jesus, heaven would just be an endless monotony of your concept of a perfect life on earth without any effects of the fall. Heaven is only a good deal if Jesus is there. Until you grasp this concept you do not truly understand regeneration.

According to Acts 17:30 repentance is not an option but God's command. Both John the Baptist and Jesus began their preaching ministry with, "Repent for the kingdom of heaven is near." (Matthew 3:1; 4:17) God does take into consideration what we know about Him. But ignorance is not bliss. Ignorance will not keep anyone from hell, because we are all without excuse since we know God exists by our observation of nature (Romans 1:18–23). Nor will it do to think, as many do today, that they can be born again but continue to live as the world lives. By reading this section, an unbeliever ignorant of the concept of repentance, will now be judged more severely if he does not come to faith. Unbelieving readers would of course still be destined for hell, but now their punishment will be greater unless they repent. Yes, repentance is commanded by God. Praise be to God that He does not leave us to our own resources, but graciously enables the elect to repent.

112. Seek First the Kingdom of God

seek and you will find... Matthew 7:7

About one week before breeding begins bucks start to eagerly patrol the woods searching for receptive does. The exact trigger for this behavior is unknown, but it may be that God has placed chemical signals in does' urine that informs bucks it is time to start locating does. As a doe approaches ovulation other chemical signals in her urine alert bucks that she should be pursued. Sometimes I have observed a doe urinate as she slowly browsed along a trail at first light and later seen a buck come to a dead stop and carefully smell the urine before resuming his search. This opening phase of the rut is called seeking. It is an exciting time to be out in the woods. Bucks generally move along established trails, walking at a steady pace with their nose to the ground. Occasionally, they utter a soft grunt as they walk along. The buck is extremely focused on finding receptive does and has thrown all caution to the wind. Nothing seems to deter them from their quest. I keep a supply of dry ¼ inch diameter sticks in the blind and break one to try to get bucks to stop to accommodate my camera's slow shutter speed mandated by the low light of early morning or late afternoon when they are most active. It is the only reliable way I have found to temporarily get their attention. The buck in this photo was very cooperative, passing by my blind about 8:00 in the morning in sufficient light to reasonably stop the action.

Oh, that any of us should seek after God with such fervor and single-mindedness as a buck seeks a doe! In the Sermon on the Mount, Jesus says: *But seek first the kingdom of God and his righteousness, and all these things will be added to you* (Matthew 6:33). Notice that Jesus gives both a command *("but seek first the kingdom of God and his righteousness")* and a promise (*"all these things will be added to you"*). Does this mean that if you passionately seek God you will get everything you want? In a way it does. However, the promise is for believers who, under the influence of the Holy Spirit, receive "all these things" that they need to fulfill God's call on their life. But "these things" are very different from what the carnal-minded person desires!

The carnal-minded person might suppose from this passage that by seeking God, they will get everything they want (a trophy buck, great sex, a new 4x4 truck, or a thousand other things a person may desire). The catch is that the carnal-minded person cannot seek God because:

None is righteous, no not one; no one understands; no one seeks for God (Romans 3:10–11). *For those who live according to the flesh set their minds on the things of the flesh, but those who live according to the Spirit set their minds on the things of the Spirit. To set the mind on the flesh is death, but to set the mind on the Spirit is life and peace. For the mind that is set on the flesh is hostile to God, for it does not submit to God's law; indeed, it cannot. Those who are in the flesh cannot please God* (Romans 8:5–8).

In this passage, "flesh" refers to the earthly nature apart from divine influence. So, we are left with a dilemma. On the one hand we are commanded to seek God, but we are told it is impossible for us to do so. To paraphrase St. Thomas Aquinas, unbelievers desperately desire the peace that only faith in Christ can deliver, but at the same time desperately flee from Him who provides it. We can only seek God after we become believers, but how can we become believers if we have no interest in God and are hostile to him? The answer is that God must seek us, but in a very different way than a buck seeks a doe.

113. God Seeks the Lost

For the Son of Man came to seek and to save the lost. Luke 19:10

The large diameter of his antlers combined with the relatively small and poorly formed, irregular rack bore witness to the advanced age of a buck well past his prime as he purposefully strode down the trail toward my blind. The doe he was pursuing had passed by me at a brisk walk less than a minute earlier. As the shutter snapped he was wetting his nostrils, which deer often do, to improve their sense of smell. It must have worked for this venerable patriarch since he proceeded to take the fork in the trail used earlier by the doe. I thought this buck would not live long, but two years later, I saw him again (see chapter 1).

The previous chapter ended with the observation that unless God seeks us we are without hope because in our fallen nature we are incapable of seeking God. So who does God seek and why does he seek them? Luke 19:10 quotes Jesus as saying he came to seek and to save the lost. The lost are all who do not believe in Jesus. In other words, everyone is lost, because we all start out as unbelievers. But at some point, some people come to believe in Jesus. Notice, however, that Jesus also says he came not only to seek the lost but to save them as well. Now we have another dilemma. We know that not everyone eventually believes in Jesus and is saved. However, if everyone is initially lost and only some are saved, what are we to make of Luke 19:10? Notice that since we know that not every person, eventually, believes in Jesus, then it is impossible that he could seek all the lost and save all the lost. So, we are left with only three possibilities. Either Jesus only seeks some of the lost and saves all of them or he seeks all of the lost but is only able to save some of them, or he seeks some of the lost and is able to save only some of them. But now there are two problems. If Jesus cannot save everyone he seeks, then he is impotent and not worthy of our belief. However, we know that this cannot be true since one of the attributes of the triune God is that he is omnipotent. Therefore, we are left with only the possibility that he seeks only some of the lost and saves all of them. But if he seeks only some of the lost what criteria does he use to determine whom he will seek?

Ordinarily, we seek things that we think will make us happy even though the cost may be high. For example, the buck is so desirous to procreate, that he exposes himself to incredible risk that often results in his death by colliding with a motor vehicle, or a projectile. But, this is not the way God works. Jesus did not seek us because he coveted some innate characteristic in us that he thought would make Him happy even though it risked His life. Jesus died on the cross for the joy of rescuing enemies of God from hell, who would in turn give glory to God. There was no risk in this. It had always been God's plan that He would do this, because it maximized His glory (Acts 2:22–24; Romans 5:6–10; Hebrews 12:2). The Bible's answer to the criteria question is that those whom God seeks (the elect or the called) were chosen freely by God (not because of any innate attribute) by grace (unmerited favor), before the world was made for the glory of his grace (Ephesians 1:3–10 and 2:1–10). In His divine providence, at His chosen time, He endows the elect with the Holy Spirit so that they desire Christ. When a person professes Christ as their savior it is the first evidence that God has effectively sought and saved them (see Acts 13:48 and 16:14, Romans 8:29–30). If you are not a believer may the Holy Spirit change your heart so that you may earnestly seek to know God better.

114. Fear of the Lord

The fear of the LORD is the beginning of wisdom; all those who practice it have a good understanding. Psalm 111:10

Anyone who has spent time around deer has encountered this scene. Whenever a deer is afraid it starts waving its "white flag." This is not a signal that it is ready to surrender to the threat, but, most likely, is a warning to other deer in the area that it has perceived a threat. Deer communicate different levels of alarm. In this case the deer is wisely walking briskly away from the danger indicating it is sure the threat is real, but that it is not so imminent that the deer should risk bounding away at full speed and blundering into an even more ominous danger.

A deer can only experience fear for its physical well being. We humans can and do experience all kinds of physical fears. However, it is not physical fear that the Bible commends to us. In fact, we are not to fear any physical harm because God is sovereign and loves Christians. *As a father shows compassion to his children, so the LORD shows compassion to those who fear him* (Psalm 103:13). But there is a fear that the Bible says we ought to have, the fear of the LORD.

To the modern secular mind, fear of the LORD is not even on the radar screen. The secular mind fears cancer, climate change, terrorist attacks, stock market crashes, pandemics, and many other things. But no thought is given to fearing a god the world merely gives lip service to and thinks does not really exist. The problem, of course, is that God does exist. True wisdom fears God because He is infinite in power. The worst harm that humans, "nature" or anything in the world can do to you is persecute or torture you for a lifetime, or kill you. But God can pour out his wrath against you for eternity. And since God is infinitely more powerful than the most powerful despot, or disease, or natural disaster, he cannot only afflict you forever but he can do it at unimaginable levels of intensity. Therefore, fearing God is the beginning of wisdom, showing that a person has understanding. The Bible calls people who do not fear God fools. *The fool says in his heart, "There is no God."* (Psalm 14:1)

There is another dimension to fearing God and that is to be in complete awe of his majesty and might. This comes through reflection on who God is. It is not mere intellectual belief in the existence of God. We live in a world that thinks information is everything, but lacks the wisdom to use the information wisely. You can possess all the necessary information (the Bible) but not understand it and therefore make foolish decisions (eat, drink and be merry). Take a lesson from the deer who waves its "white flag" to warn its colleagues of the danger it sees and then wisely walks away from it. Christianity is not a last ditch, desperate blind leap of faith into the unknown. Rather, it is a wise response to reality. Understand the Psalmist's warning. Let your stubborn rebellion and pride wisely wave the white flag of surrender by believing in the saving work of Jesus Christ on the cross and he will run to welcome you as the father ran to welcome home the prodigal son (Luke 15:11–32). *For this my son was dead, and is alive again; he was lost, and is found. And they began to celebrate.* (Luke 15:24)

May you have the proper fear of the LORD and know Him as your savior.

115. Two Natures

For I know that nothing good dwells in me, that is in my flesh. For I have the desire to do what is right, but not the ability to carry it out. Romans 7:18; see also Romans 7:19–8:17

   This unusual buck materialized, suddenly, out of some still green buckthorn about sunrise. His swollen neck testified of the coming rut and though I had seen several bucks previously in the pre-sunrise glow of the waning full moon, he was the first buck I had seen in 2008 in sufficient light to photograph. I had been praying that God would give me the pictures I needed for this book, but as I looked at this image, I wondered why had He given me this deer to photograph? But one day, as suddenly as the deer had appeared, I saw the message for this picture and praised God for His gracious answer to my prayer.

   It is obvious that this buck has a fairly normal left antler, but a very unusual right antler. Given his large size, the buck was probably quite old which might explain the "knobbiness" of his antlers, their small size and complete lack of symmetry. However, these antlers are a parable of sorts of the Christian life. We all come into this life hostile to God (by analogy the deformed antler). This hostile nature is what the Apostle Paul calls the "flesh" in Romans 7:18. We are not born morally pure, do some bad things and become corrupt. Our problem is ultimately not what we do but who we are. We are by nature sinners from the point of conception and as we mature from birth to adulthood our capability to sin increases. But when we receive the Holy Spirit and are born again we have a new nature (represented by the well-formed antler). Until we receive the Holy Spirit we are unable to please God and always choose to do what is displeasing to Him. This does not mean that unbelievers cannot be to some degree, kind, loving, charitable or merciful. But these works do not please God because they are tainted by sin. When we have received the Holy Spirit we become aware of a new reality and the desire to make choices that please God out of a heart of love and faith. Once again, the issue is not what we do but who we are. What we do arises from who we are! As Christians we live differently than we did before conversion and as true Christians we become more Christ-like (sanctified) with time.

However, when the new nature (Holy Spirit) comes to live in a person, it does not entirely drive out the old nature (flesh). So in the Christian, two natures are in conflict. The old nature can triumph in the short term, causing the believer to sin. Over time the ongoing process of sanctification results in progressively more Christ-like behavior, but the flesh is never completely conquered and even the godliest Christians commit sin. So Christians are, by way of analogy to the antlers in this picture, in possession of two natures: the new nature (analogous to the well-formed antler) and the flesh (analogous to the disfigured antler). Notice that this is very different from Jesus' two natures (chapter 104) because each of His natures is perfect, sinless and in harmony with each other. However, a Christian is still able to sin and the two natures are not in harmony but at war against one another (Romans 7).

Do you have the new nature? In retrospect can you see that you changed from a scoffer and a person hostile to God, to someone desiring to please God? Were you once participating in behaviors obviously contrary to the Ten Commandments, but now abhor such behavior even though you may still struggle against them? If not, earnestly ask God to give you this new nature through the indwelling of the Holy Spirit.

116. The Log and the Speck

Why do you see the speck that is in your brother's eye, but do not notice the log in your own eye? Or how can you say to your brother, 'Let me take the speck out of your eye,' when there is the log in your own eye? You hypocrite, first take the log out of your own eye, and then you will see clearly to take the speck out of your brother's eye.
Matthew 7:3–5

I affectionately named the yearling buck in this picture "Ernie" because he so earnestly sought after receptive does. For two weeks I saw him almost every day and several days I saw him two or three times as he frantically patrolled the area around my blind. But such enthusiasm eventually got him into trouble with a dominant buck and nearly resulted in an antler, not a log in his eye. At any rate Ernie's wound caused me to ponder anew the meaning of the familiar passage from Matthew. My "good" intentions inclined my heart to desire to treat Ernie's wound. After all from my perspective the solution was simple; a few dissolvable sutures and some antibiotics would quickly do the trick. But would Ernie welcome my "good" intentions?

It was easy to see Ernie's wound and judge it to be more serious than it really was. How similar this is to my ability to easily see where my brother falls short in his behavior. How tempting it is to deflect the attention from my sin to that of my brother's and smugly desire to fix my brother's eye. How good I might feel in providing such a "useful" service to my brother. However, even my best intended efforts to fix my brother might result in the same kind of response that Ernie would have displayed had I suddenly emerged from my blind with the required medical supplies! Ernie most likely would have either turned tail and headed for the next county, or aggressively resisted my efforts. Similarly, my brother may flee or resist as vigorously as Ernie would have if I was able to corner him and get close enough to suture the wound and administer the antibiotics.

Jesus tells us to fix ourselves first and consider our own sins as much greater than our brother's. By seeing our own sin as much more serious than our brother's, we may gain the attention of our brother in a much less offensive and threatening way and, hence, be able to lovingly, not judgmentally, minister to our believing brother or present the gospel to an unbelieving acquaintance in a more winsome manner by following the Apostle Peter's admonition: ...*always being prepared to make a defense to anyone who asks you for the reason for the hope that is in you; yet do it with gentleness and respect...* (1 Peter 3:15–16)

There is no such thing as a little sin. All sin, whether it is a speck or a log, is grievously offensive to God, and if unforgiven, results in death and hell. When it comes to sin, any manmade solution is inadequate even for the tiniest speck. The only antidote for sin is to trust in the blood of Jesus as the old hymn ***Nothing but the Blood of Jesus*** by Robert Lowry declares:

What can wash away my sin? Nothing but the blood of Jesus.
What can make me whole again? Nothing but the blood of Jesus.
O! Precious is the flow that makes me white as snow.
No other fount I know; Nothing but the blood of Jesus.

May you trust in the blood of Jesus to make you whole and wash away all your sins.

117. Do not be Anxious

Therefore do not be anxious, saying, 'What shall we eat?' or 'What shall we drink?' or 'What shall we wear?' For the Gentiles seek after all these things, and your heavenly Father knows that you need them all. But seek first the kingdom of God and his righteousness, and all these things will be added to you. Therefore do not be anxious about tomorrow, for tomorrow will be anxious for itself. Sufficient for the day is its own trouble. Matthew 6:31–34

As I sit down to write this chapter, the sun is just peeking over the eastern horizon as the temperature hovers at -24° F and 18 inches of snow blanket the ground. In about an hour, the school bus will stop across the street from my house to pick up the kindergarten children in their brightly colored snowsuits as we humans press on with our activities despite the cold. But somewhere in the woods behind my yard, a doe and her two fawns are hunkered down, preserving precious body heat. Ten days ago I watched though binoculars as two large bucks battled at dusk for breeding rights of the doe fawn. But today there is no such activity. The cold holds sway and to live is all that matters. Yesterday morning I saw them in the marsh behind my yard as they searched for food in a balmy -3° F. How will they endure the cold and find food today? Are they anxious about where their next meal will come from or when this cold will break? For now seven deer (Summer revealed the doe carried triplets and the recently impregnated doe fawn had a single fetus) tenaciously cling to life. The doe and her two fawns will know hunger today, but not cold in their snowy beds, for God has clothed them in a most amazing way.

A deer's normal summer coat has over 5,000 red-brown hairs per square inch, each being 0.003 inches in diameter (same as a human hair). Each of the hairs is about an inch long. At birth a fawn has a row of 30-40 white spots on either side of its spine and about 100 randomly positioned spots on each side of the body. These are not white hairs but are white tufts on a normal summer hair. These tufts wear off before the winter coat appears but initially camouflage the fawn as it lies curled up, giving the appearance of dappled sunlight and shadows on fallen leaves. As winter approaches the summer coat is replaced by a coat of two inch long, hollow guard hairs with a diameter of 0.007 inches. There are about 2,500 of these guard hairs per square inch. Under them is a layer of uncountable fine, kinky hairs like cashmere wool. Shielded from the wind and immersed part way in the snow, the deer are well insulated in their spectacular coats.

In the same way through God's providence the slow, but perceptible increase in January day length will eventually triumph over scarcity and cold to produce a cornucopia of summer abundance. But this abundance will in turn give way to shortening day length as cold regains the upper-hand in next winter's scarcity. The deer know nothing of this, nor are they anxious about finding food once the cold breaks. For now they patiently wait, instinctively knowing it is most prudent to conserve effort and heat as their dwindling summer fat reserves nourish and insulate them in their snowy beds.

If only we could trust God with the same peace as a deer. For just as God clothes and feeds the deer, so too He promises to clothe and feed you in His perfect timing. *Do not be anxious about anything, but in everything by prayer and supplication with thanksgiving let your requests be made known to God. And the peace of God, which surpasses all understanding, will guard your hearts and your minds in Christ Jesus.* (Philippians 4:6–7) *Fear not, little flock, for it is your Father's good pleasure to give you the kingdom.* (Luke 12:32)

118. What is God's will for my life?

In him we have obtained an inheritance, having been predestined according to the purpose of him who works all things according to the counsel of his will,... Ephesians 1:11

> *God, from all eternity, did, by the most wise and holy counsel of his own will, freely and unchangeably ordain whatsoever comes to pass: yet so, as thereby neither is God the author of sin, nor is violence offered to the will of the creatures; nor is the liberty or contingency of secondary causes taken away, but rather established.* Westminster Confession of Faith 3:1

A deer does not ponder God's will for them. They live in the moment simply focused on staying safe, fed and watered. Questions like should I chose one home range over another, or one mate over another never enter their minds. If circumstances force them to move to a new home range, they move. If a mate is available, they mate. They are content to be deer, doing what deer were created to do, and in essence are much better at living out God's will for them than we humans.

Perhaps the most common question Christians ponder is God's will for their lives. The Westminster Confession of Faith echoes Scriptures numerous passages that nothing happens apart from the will of God. But can a Christian specifically know God's will for their lives? To answer this we first need to distinguish between God's *necessary will* and *free will*. The *necessary will* of God is everything that God must will because of his nature. For example God cannot decide to sin, to not be omniscient or to cease to exist because these and many other things would be contrary to God's nature. God's *free will* includes all things that God decides to do but does not need to do because of his nature. For example, God did not need to create the universe or redeem a group of people by sending Jesus to die on their behalf.

Another important distinction is the difference between God's *secret will* and *revealed will*. God has determined everything that will happen but has not usually made it known to us. We have no idea what will happen in the next day, week, year and so on. All we can do is trust that God will do what is best in accordance with God's *necessary will*. On the other hand, God's *revealed will* contains his commands about Christian's moral conduct from the Old Testament moral law and its expansion and explanation in the New Testament.

The bottom line is that you usually cannot know God's specific will for you in many important aspects of life. For example, should you buy house A or B, be a doctor or a carpenter, or marry Amanda or Zelda? The best that you can do is to follow the instructions and comply with the restrictions imposed in God's *revealed will*. For example, Christians are called to be good stewards so they should not buy an extravagant house beyond their means. Christians must not choose an unlawful, God demeaning occupation like drug dealing or prostitution or marry an unbeliever. However, in Christ believers usually have much freedom to choose among a host of allowable options. As a result Christians should pray for God's wisdom to make the best possible choices, seeking the wise counsel of other Christians to correctly interpret and observe the revealed limits on the options. Christians can rejoice in full assurance that God's hand is upon them to sustain their faith until such time as it pleases Him to bring them home to heaven to be with Him forever. Until then Christians can be confident, nothing will happen to them apart from the sovereign will of God who guarantees that He is working every pain and pleasure they encounter for their eternal good (Romans 8:28).

119. The Book of Life

And if anyone's name was not found written in the book of life, he was thrown into the lake of fire. Revelation 20:15

Some whitetail hunters would be willing to sell their very soul in order to harvest a buck like the one in this picture if it would guarantee the inclusion of their name in the Boone and Crocket (firearms) or Pope and Young (archery) record books. For trophy hunters this is the holy grail of hunting; the highest honor that the world can bestow for deer hunting.

Revelation 20:12 also mentions two different books: *And I saw the dead, great and small, standing before the throne, and books were opened. Then another book was opened, which is the book of life. And the dead were judged by what was written in the books, according to what they had done.* The "books" contain a record of everything that every person has ever said, thought or done (Luke 12:2–3). This final judgment at the end of history is based upon what you did in life and determines the degree of reward (1 Corinthians 3:12–14 for believers) or punishment (Luke 12:47–48 for unbelievers). The final judgment does not determine who goes to heaven or who goes to hell. That is determined by whether or not one's name is in the *book of life*. My friend, let me assure you that this is the book you want your name in.

So what is the *book of life*? The *book of life* contains the names of all the people throughout history whom God has or will bring to saving faith in Jesus Christ. If your name is not in the *book of life*, your eternal destiny is the lake of fire (final state of eternal torment for unbelievers). Revelation 13:8 tells us that the names in the *book of life* were written in it before the universe was created. Ephesians 1:3–5 tells us God chose whom he would save before he created the universe. Did God in his omniscience look into a heavenly crystal ball and discern who would do good works and believe in Jesus and then choose those people? Did he choose arbitrarily who to save? Did he have some criteria? Is God a capricious tyrant? Is he unjust?

The biblical answer to these questions is that God is sovereign and acts out of mercy and compassion. As mere humans we have no right to question his choices (Romans 9:14–21). Salvation, inclusion in the *book of life*, has nothing to do with our merit. We who are saved are inherently no better than those who are not saved (Ephesians 2:1–10). The question to ask is not, why doesn't God save everyone? But, rather, why does he save anyone? God is not unjust. Believers receive forgiveness of their sins credited to them by faith in the sinless life of Christ and his atoning death while unbelievers receive justice for their sins because of their fatal sin in rejecting Christ. Furthermore, whether or not an unbeliever comes to saving faith is not governed by the effectiveness of the person presenting the gospel (John 1:12; Romans 9:16). Certainly the unbeliever has to understand the gospel to believe in it. However, even the impetuous Apostle Peter after the outpouring of the Holy Spirit at Pentecost (Acts 1) was more effective in his first sermon (Acts 2) than Jesus was in His ministry (John 12:37). For apart from the work of the Holy Spirit no one comes to faith (John 3; Titus 3:4–5). The believer's only proper response to all this is to join the Apostle Paul in grateful worship:

Oh, the depth of the riches and wisdom and knowledge of God! How unsearchable are his judgments and how inscrutable his ways! "For who has known the mind of the Lord, or who has been his counselor?" "Or who has given a gift to him that he might be repaid?" For from him and through him and to him are all things. To him be glory forever. Amen. (Romans 11:33–36)

120. I Only Believe Empirical Evidence

Claiming to be wise, they became fools Romans 1:22

We are near the end of this book. Yet, some readers are not persuaded. You may be one of them. If you are honest there is something missing in your life. Perhaps this is your last desperate stand. You say, "Give me tangible evidence and I will believe." I don't think so. Unless your hard heart is rescued from unbelief by a sovereign act of God you will die in your sin. Requiring empirical evidence before believing something is true sounds objective and intelligent, but this claim to wisdom has a foolish, fatal flaw.

Logical Positivism was a school of philosophy that taught a statement was only true and meaningful if it could be shown empirically to be true and meaningful. Of course their thesis was impossible to prove empirically and hence, the lofty sounding Logical Positivism succumbed to the same fallacious thinking as the statement that nothing is absolutely true which includes the statement that nothing is absolutely true! Sometimes the idea is arrogantly twisted to: "If I don't understand it, it can't be true." But there are many things that are empirically real that no one truly understands (for example, how gravity works or why light can appear to be both a particle and a wave), yet no one doubts their existence or effects. God did not give humans the ability to understand everything that is true, nor did He design the Creation so that humans could, by empirical data, conclusively prove that the Bible is true, that heaven and hell are real, or that salvation is only by faith in Jesus. At some point you must faithfully believe God. That is His design and His prerogative!

Empirically, it's obvious I photograph a lot of bucks. But I do not use elaborate stratagems deduced by pouring over reams of data. I've tried that and it didn't work nearly as well as employing a simple strategy and trusting God to give me the photos needed for this book, praying to the same ends. So if you want to see more bucks, find a trail junction heavily used by does. Watch it for two hours after sunrise and two hours before sunset during the first week of November (45° North latitude) and you will likely see bucks. The pictured buck delightfully confirmed and mimicked my strategy. At 7:32 AM on November 2, he plopped down a scant 40 feet from my blind. Eight minutes later a doe came down the trail *we* were watching. He jumped up and was off to the races. Nine days later, he laid down in almost the exact place at 8:36 AM. By 9:18, no deer had used the trail, so he got up and left. I gave him ten minutes to clear the area and went home, trusting he knew what he was doing!

There are some very difficult concepts in the Bible that the best theological minds have never completely understood nor are ever likely to fully understand on this side of heaven. But, that does not mean the Bible is untrue. Faith is required to see that the Bible is the word of God, not because the empirical evidence is insufficient, but because the unbelieving heart hates God and distorts the truth of scripture before conversion. I once was having lunch with a very intelligent, unbelieving, young man. We had discussed many thorny theological issues. Suddenly, he realized I always started with the assumption that the Bible was true and blurted out, "I never thought about assuming the Bible was true." If you resonate with this young man, I urge you to put away the haughty intellectualism of the fool that assumes itself capable of knowing everything, and tries to force everything into an empirical paradigm Assume the Bible is true and see if that answers more of life's vexing questions than assuming that only the empirical is true and the Bible is untrue.

121. Pascal's Wager

Not everyone who says to me "Lord, Lord," will enter the kingdom of heaven but the one who does the will of my Father who is in heaven. On that day many will say to me "Lord, Lord, did we not prophesy in your name, and cast out demons in your name, and do many mighty works in your name?" And then will I declare to them, "I never knew you; depart from me, you workers of lawlessness." Matthew 7:21–23

The temperature was about 0° F as I walked out of the woods having not seen a living creature until I spied this nine-pointer coolly taking the safe approach to let me pass as he trusted in his cover. Deer tend to play the odds, taking the safe approach when they encounter danger. Most of the time playing it safe will minimize one's losses but not always. Blaise Pascal (1623–62) is best known as a scientist and mathematician for his work in understanding pressure in fluids and pioneering work in the development of probability to understand games of chance. But when he had a profound religious experience, he turned from science and mathematics and became a Roman Catholic theologian. He was part of the Jansenism movement that attempted to align Roman Catholicism with the teachings of Augustine and the Doctrines of Grace. Eventually, Jansenism was condemned by the Pope. Pascal associated with intellectuals and scientists of his era who were very skeptical that there was any truth in the doctrine of heaven. His response to them has become known as Pascal's wager. The essence of Pascal's argument is that every person decides to live as though God exists or doesn't exist. If you live as though God exists, and He doesn't, you do not lose anything. But if you live as though God does not exist and He does exist, you lose everything by spending eternity in hell. So the wisest, safest course of action is to live as though God exists.

Pascal's deep faith caused him to reason it was best to live a life of delayed gratification, looking forward to eternity in heaven. Of course, this would mean that if God does not exist people would needlessly deny themselves many of the pleasures they could have had on earth. But this is not the problem with Pascal's wager. The real problem is that adherence to Pascal's wager is so rampant. Long before I knew what Pascal's wager was I had been exposed to it by my High School Spanish teacher who said, "You are a fool if you don't take one hour a week to go to church just in case there is a God." This cuts to the heart of the problem addressed by Matthew 7:21–23. Truly born again people do not just go through the motions and Pascal's seemingly safe approach will not save on Judgment Day. There is no safe way to heaven, apart from faith alone, by grace alone in Christ alone. Jesus demands fully committed disciples who are willing, if necessary, to give up their lives rather than deny faith in Christ (Matthew 10:32–33; 38–39). Churches are filled with people who think they are taking the safe approach by going to church every week, baptizing babies, taking communion and doing various acts of piety and charity. They hope Christianity is a works-oriented religion where a few simple acts will purchase fire insurance for eternity. The nine-pointer was betting his life I would not see him and pass by. But even a slightly imperfect strategy will eventually fail if you employ it often enough. If you take Pascal's wager you are not just gambling with your life, but with your eternal destiny. Worse yet, it isn't even a gamble because there is no chance of escaping hell with a cold, calculating heart void of true faith and affections for Christ as evidenced by thinking you can fool God with a play-it-safe strategy. Did playing it safe always work for the nine-pointer? Apparently not, for several weeks later, he was killed by a hunter.

122. Ask Not, Have Not

...You do not have, because you do not ask. You ask and do not receive, because you ask wrongly, to spend it on your passions. James 4:2–3

How should we pray and to whom should we pray? The Bible teaches we should pray privately (Matthew 6:5–8) and in groups of other Christians (Acts 4:24). Most of the New Testament teaching on prayer instructs us to pray to God the Father. But addressing prayer to Jesus (2 Corinthians 12:7–9) and to the Holy Spirit (Revelation 1:4) is sometimes appropriate. However, there is no Biblical warrant to pray to anyone else such as Mary. Petitions are the most common type of prayer in the Bible in which a person makes a request to God while expressing their faith and dependence on Him in all things.

James says that we have to ask, but when we ask we don't receive because we do not have the things of God in mind. In the famous passage from the Sermon on the Mount, Jesus says: *Ask, and it will be given to you; seek, and you will find; knock, and it will be opened to you* (Matthew 7:7).

Is this a contradiction with James? Does Jesus really mean that whatever we ask for we will receive? Is this the magic ticket to success in any human endeavor? Does a hunter merely have to say something like, "God, please let me shoot a world record buck," and lo and behold the biggest buck ever will conveniently present itself to be killed? Of course Jesus does not mean it is this simple, because in Matthew 7:11 he says: *If you then, who are evil, know how to give good things to your children, how much more will your Father who is in heaven give good things to those who ask him?* The point is you have to ask for good things and what is good in our sinful eyes is often not good in God's eyes.

For several days I had wrestled with this issue. I knew that despite all my years of experience with deer, one never really knows what a deer will do. Given all the things that can go wrong in trying to photograph a large buck, it is only by God's sovereign grace that I ever get a good photo. But James says, *you have not because you do not ask*, so I was praying specifically to be able to photograph a large buck that I had not previously seen or photographed. On the other hand, I did not want this to happen to make much of me but to make much of God. So, I prayed that photographing a large buck would give God more glory than if I still delighted in Him even though He didn't bring a big buck my way. Ordinarily, I was leaving the blind at 9:00 am, but on this particular day I felt compelled to stay 10 minutes longer. I had faithlessly just checked my watch at 9:05 to see if I had served my time when I noticed some horizontal motion in heavy cover about 70 yards away. Oftentimes, these flashes of motion are just a squirrel running along a horizontal branch, but then I saw part of an antler. The massive 11 pointer on the adjacent page slowly worked his way toward me passing within ten yards of the blind and, then, just to be sure I got good photos, circled around the blind, posing about 15 yards away before continuing on his way. Glancing at my watch, it read 9:10!

The Westminster Shorter Catechism says, "The chief end of man is to glorify God and enjoy him forever." My pastor, John Piper, says: "God is most glorified in us when we are most satisfied in Him." I left the woods that day praising God who gives so generously that He gave his only son to die in our place for our sins, that we may delightedly spend eternity with Him. If you do not know Him, ask for the best of all possible things – that God would give you eyes to see and ears to hear and a heart to believe the gospel!

123. Your Life is Like a Mist

Yet, you do not know what tomorrow will bring. What is your life?
For you are a mist that appears for a little time and then vanishes.
James 4:14

It was a cold sunny morning in early November. The woods were perfectly quiet except for the occasional scampering or chattering of a squirrel. In the thick brush to the west of my blind, I detected a slight motion that materialized into the shape of a deer. The sun glistened off his antlers as he methodically moved toward me. Clouds of mist erupted from his nostrils every time he exhaled. Finally, he stepped part way into a shooting lane and looked down the lane toward the blind exhaling two little clouds that quickly dissipated in the cold air. As the shutter opened and closed, I held my breath so as not to betray my position by exhaling. He perceived no danger, and stepped across the shooting lane continuing on his hopeful quest for a receptive doe.

Unbelievers are like this buck. They may feel strong and exude self confidence. But beneath that swagger, they are searching for some undefined peace or joy, randomly going through life on a quest for happiness, all the while denying or oblivious to the eternal danger their soul is in. Seeking pleasure will never make you happy. There is always more to be had and there is never enough. The peace you desire can only be found in Jesus. What is keeping you from becoming a Christian?

The Apostle James, the half brother of Jesus, penned the scripture reference in the context of a businessman arrogantly supposing he is in control of his destiny, rather than humbly realizing that *"...If the Lord wills, we will live and do this or that."* (James 4:15) James's point is that life is tenuous and under the sovereign control of God, not our control. As I write this I have no guarantee that I will live long enough to finish this book and you have no guarantee that you will live long enough to finish reading it. The fog that appears on a cool morning disappears quickly as the sun rises above the horizon. If you look closely at the picture, the cloud from the left nostril (present over his shoulder blade) has nearly vanished while the cloud from the right nostril is relatively large but endured only seconds. By grace, I was not armed and did not snuff out the buck's life. He had no idea of the danger he could have been in. We are the same. We do not know what danger awaits us today. Every breath we take is a gift from God and we do not know when the gift will be removed.

Prior to World War II, fledgling groups of what would be become the evangelistic organization known as the Navigators were actively witnessing and leading Bible studies within the U.S. military. One of these groups was active among the sailors of the USS West Virginia stationed at Pearl Harbor. Of the 1,541 men aboard, about 125 were meeting regularly for Bible studies. Early on the morning of December 7, 1941 one of these devout Christians was sent ashore on an errand. As he was returning from his errand, he looked across Pearl Harbor and saw a torpedo slam into the West Virginia in the exact place he would have been were it not for the errand. In the aftermath of the attack, he discovered that of the 130 men killed on his ship, he had presented the gospel to about 50, and about 30 had received Christ. Of the 20 that did not, every one said they would do it later! The mission statement of the Navigators is: *To know Christ and to make Him known.* If you know Jesus Christ as your Lord and Savior, what is keeping you from telling all those in your acquaintance about Him today? If you have not received Him, what are you waiting for?

For you are a mist that appears for a little time and then vanishes.

124. Seeing and Hearing

...Do you not yet perceive or understand? Are your hearts hardened? Having eyes do you not see, and having ears do you not hear? ...
Mark 8:17–18

A deer stays alive by using its nose, eyes and ears to detect danger. Ultimately, I have been able to take the pictures in this book because God has willed it to be so. But at a secondary level, these pictures have been possible because I have almost completely defeated a deer's ability to detect me via scent, sight and sound. I scrupulously wash my body and clothes before entering the blind as well as always entirely covering myself with two layers of scent control clothing. Lying on the ground in camouflage clothing disarms their eyes because they have no comprehension of a horizontal human. Finally, I can be almost totally silent except for the operation of the camera. Occasionally, a deer detects my slight movements in operating the camera or hears the camera and goes on alert, often approaching the blind for a better look and sniff. This leads to some exciting experiences and close-up pictures like the one in this chapter. Usually, they decide I am not a threat. They have eyes but cannot see me, ears but cannot hear me and a nose but cannot smell me. Simply put, I do not fit their sensory understanding of a dangerous human.

The context of Mark 8:17–18 is that the disciples are discussing the problem of not having any bread. Jesus speaks the referenced scripture and reminds them of the feeding of the 5,000 (Mark 6:30–44) and the feeding of the 4,000 (Mark 8:1-9). Finally, in Mark 8:21 Jesus rebukes them: *"Do you not yet understand?"* This passage seems incomprehensible since the disciples have been with Jesus and seen his miracles and, yet, they can think only in a secular, man-centered, faithless way. They still do not know how to get bread! How can this be so? The answer is that in Acts 1:8 we learn that they had not yet received the Holy Spirit. *The natural person does not accept the things of the Spirit of God, for they are folly to him, and he is not able to understand them because they are spiritually discerned.* (1 Corinthians 2:14) The disciples have eyes but cannot see who Jesus is, and ears but cannot hear who Jesus is. So, the parable is simply this: just as deer cannot discern my presence and would be in grave danger if I were armed, so people without the indwelling Holy Spirit cannot discern the things of God to their eternal peril. There is an ironic twist to this parable. Deer expect people to be vertical and are fooled by a horizontal human. Unbelievers can perceive only in the horizontal or earthly plane, and cannot perceive the vertical plane leading spiritually upward to God. Eventually, everyone will acknowledge that Jesus is Lord; some in willing, joyful, adoration in heaven and some as a vanquished enemy in chains in hell. In either case God is glorified (Philippians 2:9–11).

I wrote this book so that *those who have never been told of him will see, and those who have never heard will understand.* (Romans 15:21) I have come full circle to the book's Preface. If you have only seen some pretty good pictures and read a few interesting vignettes, but do not yet understand your need for the gospel, I pray Ezekiel 36:26–27 for you: *And I will give you a new heart, and a new spirit I will put within you. And I will remove the heart of stone from your flesh and give you a heart of flesh. And I will put my Spirit within you, and cause you to walk in my statutes and be careful to obey my rules.*

May God grant my readers eyes to see and ears to hear that they may believe in the gospel of Jesus Christ and be saved. To God alone be all the glory.

Appendix A: My Testimony

And you were dead in the trespasses and sins in which you once walked, following the course of this world, following the prince of the power of the air, the spirit that is now at work in the sons of disobedience – among whom we all once lived in the passions of our flesh, carrying out the desires of the body and the mind, and were by nature children of wrath like the rest of mankind... For by grace you have been saved through faith. And this is not your own doing; it is the gift of God, not a result of works, so that no one may boast. Ephesians 2:1–3 and 2:8–9

It was the second day of the 1960 Wisconsin gun season. My dad and cousin Clifford were supposed to noisily walk through the "ash swamp," in hopes of causing deer to flee toward my Uncle Johnny and me as we waited at two strategic locations. But when we arrived where I was supposed to stand, someone was already there, even though it was on our property! We proceeded to Uncle Johnny's stand and then I cut back to a point about 100 yards in front of the trespasser, shielded by very thick woods. I didn't know then why I decided to stand under that particular balsam tree. In retrospect, it was God's providence. My dad and Clifford had barely begun their march through the "ash" swamp when I glimpsed a deer heading for Uncle Johnny. The deer must have scented him, since it cut back toward me, stopping broadside at 15 yards. A single shot from my brand new 32 Winchester Special ended the life of my first buck. But in the picture, I was as spiritually dead as the buck was physically dead. I had no idea that 26 years later I would become a child of God.

I grew up in a loving, but unbelieving family. Generally, I was a "good boy," never in trouble with the law, respectful to my parents, hard-working and a good student. But such admirable character traits could not save my soul. I persisted in unbelief as a perfectly happy pagan, believing the big bang and evolution accounted for the creation rather than the Creator. My atheism started to unravel a bit when my wife was suddenly converted in the fall of 1984. About a year later, after a lively discussion, she quoted Herbert Spencer, "There is one thing that will keep a man in everlasting ignorance; rejection prior to investigation." I got her point, reading the "Living Bible" in about three months. I was not impressed. The Old Testament fulfilled my expectations of a bunch of mean and nasty characters in all kinds of sin. I looked forward to the New Testament, expecting to like Jesus. Instead, I saw Jesus as very unattractive and rude, because of the way he would criticise the Jewish religious leaders. I remained a pagan!

It was about 12:15 pm June 18, 1986. I had just finished my last training run before my third marathon. Inexplicably, I looked up at the sky and said, "Thank you, God, for seeing me through my training." Astonished by this spontaneous statement, I entered it in my running log book and went back to work. The next morning at breakfast I asked my wife, "How did you become a Christian?" She spoke of confessing her sin and believing in Jesus by faith, trusting in Him alone for her salvation (see chapters 55 and 56). I left for work saying, "Don't get your hopes up!" She got right on the phone and called a number of people to pray. About 10:00 AM, the clearest thought I have ever had popped into my mind. It was: *You have rebelled long enough. At noon you are to go to a certain place along Rice Creek, and there you are to receive Christ as your Savior.* This I did and came back a changed man. As I write these words, tears come to my eyes, so powerful was the conversion experience. I had not considered any pros or cons of becoming a Christian. I had been gloriously and graciously called from death to life. To God alone be all the glory!

Appendix B. Especially for Deer Hunters

The voice of the LORD makes the deer give birth and strips the forests bare, and in his temple all cry, "Glory!" Psalm 29:9

This doe and fawns were poised to flee from a marauding fork-horn patrolling his beat at the onset of the rut. I have purposely avoided hunting tips in this book, but in this chapter I will share what I think I have learned about the rut in over 55 years of observing deer. Most published hunting strategies focus on bucks, but I concentrate on understanding does. Does are quite predictable, as they methodically live out their lives in home ranges of 100 acres or less. Bucks are much harder to figure out. They have home ranges of a square mile or more, but spend most of their time idly sequestered away in small pockets of heavy cover. Except for the rut, they rarely leave these safe havens during daylight hours. My experience is that if I am consistently seeing does traveling between feeding and bedding areas, I will see bucks traveling these same routes once the rut begins.

I believe God has designed the rut to produce fawns at exactly the right time each spring, so that they do not succumb to cold, wet weather following birth, but still have ample time to grow before winter begins. Therefore, rutting primarily is controlled by length of daylight which is constant from year to year so that fawns are born at about the same date each spring as is commonly observed. It is widely believed today that the lunar cycle is the dominant factor controlling the dates of the rut. But if this was true, fawn birth dates could vary by the 29.53 day lunar month from year to year resulting in higher fawn mortality than if birth dates are consistent from year to year.

The deer I photograph live near a large urban area (45° N latitude) and may be more nocturnal than their rural cousins. With that caveat, my experience is that bucks don't earnestly seek does until the last week of October. About November 1st the bucks have become very reckless and start encountering receptive does. By mid-November the vast majority of fertile does are bred. Barring abnormal weather, following the completion of breeding, the dominant bucks are at peak vulnerability for a few days. They are hungry, and tired, but possessed by a frantic urgency to assure no receptive does remain in their area. I often must break a stick to get a buck to stop his desperate search and pose for a picture under low light conditions. By the third week of November buck activity has declined dramatically. They are recuperating from the rigors of the rut, but occasionally are seen in the presence of does, giving the illusion that rutting is still in progress.

In a typical year I photograph ten different bucks (three or four are Pope and Young caliber). Between October 30 and November 12, I see at least twice as many bucks daily as I do the week before or after this two week sweet spot. Most of my pictures are taken within the hour after sunrise or the hour before sunset. Cloudy days and extreme rutting activity may extend the time of activity. I am in the blind an hour before sunrise until two hours after sunrise. For the slightly less productive afternoon watch, I am in the blind the last 2.5 hours before sunset. I usually skip the less productive hour of mid-day activity.

As a retired engineer who loves to figure out how things work, I have enjoyed writing this chapter. My observations apply only to relatively undisturbed deer populations as encountered during bow season. Once the army of gun hunters takes to the woods, deer become nocturnal and are primarily focused on escape strategies during daylight hours. Finally, keep in mind deer are unpredictable, I am fallible, and God is sovereign over the rut and everything else.

Index of Non-biblical Names

Note: The Table of Contents can be used as an index of theological subjects. Individual chapters include references to other chapters as appropriate.

Scripture Index

Need additional copies?

To order more copies of

Parables of the

contact NewBookPublishing.com

❐ Order online at:
   NewBookPublishing.com/Bookstore

❐ Call 877-311-5100 or

❐ Email Info@NewBookPublishing.com

Reliance Media